BETHLEHEM STEEL

MINE AND INDUSTRIAL TRACKWORK CATALOG

CATALOG **470**

BETHLEHEM STEEL COMPANY
GENERAL OFFICES: BETHLEHEM, PA.

This Book Has Been Digitally Watermarked to Prevent Illegal Duplication

©2008-2010 Periscope Film LLC
All Rights Reserved
ISBN #978-1-935700-19-7
www.PeriscopeFilm.com

Table of Contents

	Page
INTRODUCTION	4-11
Table: Suggested Rail Weights	7
Determining Frog Number	8, 9
FROGS	13-25
Riveted-Plate Frogs	14, 15
Bolted-Rigid Frogs	16-19
Solid Manganese Steel Frogs	20-24
Rail-Bound Manganese Steel Frogs	25
SWITCHES	27-42
Heavy-Duty Switches for Use with Wood Ties	30-34
Switch Design for Medium Duty	35
Switch for Use with Steel Switch Tie Set	36
Switches for Use with Wood Ties	37, 38
Switch Heel Joints	39, 40
Switch Heel Block Joint	41
Winter-King Switch Heaters	42
SWITCH STANDS	45-61
Parallel-Throw Switch Stands	47-58
Automatic Switch Stand, Model 22	59, 60
Target Stand, Model 1205	61
GUARD RAILS	63-71
One-Piece Guard Rail for Wood Ties	64
One-Piece Guard Rail for Steel Turnout Tie Sets	65
Other Bethlehem Guard Rail Models	66, 67
Hook-Flange Guard Rail	68, 69
Heat-Treated Switch-Point Guard Rail	70, 71
CROSSINGS	73-78
Riveted-Plate Crossing for 20-lb to 100-lb Rail, Angles 30° to 90°	74
Bolted-Plate Crossings for 40-lb to 100-lb Rail, Angles 40° to 90°	75, 76
Bolted-Rail Crossings for 70-lb Rail, and Heavier, Angles 50° to 90°	77, 78
TIE SETS (For Switches and Turnouts)	81-89
Switch Tie Sets	82-84
Turnout Tie Sets	85-87
Frog Ties	88, 89
TURNOUTS	91-108
Main-Haulage Turnouts	92
Butt-Entry Turnouts	93
Room-Entry Turnouts	94

TURNOUTS—continued	Page
Turnout Data and Tables	95-107
Table: A.R.E.A. Practical Leads for Turnouts for Heavy Rails, Standard Gage	108

PREFABRICATED TRACK LAYOUTS ... 111-113

BETHLEHEM STEEL RAILS and ACCESSORIES ... 115-137
Rail Sections, 20-AS to 100-AS	115-126
Properties and Principal Dimensions of T-Rails, 20-lb to 100-lb	127
Standard Drilling for Rails and Splice-Bar Punching	128
Crane Rail Sections	129-131
Track Spikes and Bolts	133-135
Rails and Accessories for One Mile of Track, and Accessories for 1000 Net Tons of Rails	136, 137

STEEL MINE TIES (for Heavy-Duty Track) ... 139-168
Weights, Sizes and Properties of Ties	141, 142
Steel Tie Designs	143-160
Steel Ties with Depressed Ends	161
Riveted Clips	162, 163
Bolted Clips	164-167
Installing Steel Ties	168

MISCELLANEOUS TRACK EQUIPMENT ... 171-176
Gage Rods	172
Tie Plates	173
Hook-Twin Tie Plates	174
Rail Brace Design 806	175
Compromise Joint Design 976	176

YIELDABLE MINE ARCHES and ROOF ACCESSORIES ... 177-183
Yieldable Mine Arches	177, 178
Mine Roof Bolts	179, 180
Mine Roof Ties	181
Mine Roof Accessories	182, 183

OTHER BETHLEHEM PRODUCTS ... 184-186
Hollow Drill Steel	184
All-Steel Mine and Industrial Cars	185
List of Other Bethlehem Products for Mines and Industry	186

USEFUL INFORMATION ... 187-195
Types of Crossovers and Turnouts	187
Standard Wheel Contour	188
Recommendations for Laying Track in Mines	189, 190
Data for Curving Rails	190, 191
Lengths of Circular Arcs to Radius 1	194, 195
Fractions of Inches and Decimal Equivalents	194, 195

INDEX ... 196-204

INTRODUCTION

This is the fourth expanded catalog on Bethlehem trackwork. Earlier editions included Booklet 72 (1935), Booklet 72-A (1939), and Catalog 270 (1949).

The present Catalog 470 is not intended as a manual for heavy railroad trackwork, since most of these track items are covered by the A.R.E.A. Trackwork Plans, as published by the American Railway Engineering Association. By contrast, this catalog describes Bethlehem's complete line of track items for rails 20 lb to 100 lb per yd, made in accordance with American Mining Congress Standards for mine track. However, some manufacturer's standard and A.R.E.A. designs are included for use on sidings and in industrial plants. These items will be particularly applicable to tipple yards, and similar loading-point installations.

MODERN TRACK GREATLY IMPROVED

Within recent years there have been factors which severely tax the capacity of older track equipment — heavier locomotives, larger capacity mine and industrial cars, track-type mechanical coal-cutters and loading machines, and other mining machines, which handle heavy jobs more efficiently and safely.

Bethlehem Steel Company has redesigned and greatly improved its complete line of trackwork to meet these new demands, by making parts stronger and heavier, replacing castings with forgings, by using rolled-steel weldments, and the like. All trackwork components are produced from new billet steel.

DESIGNED FOR SAFETY

Bethlehem trackwork items are designed with *safety* as the keynote. Bethlehem Steel Company has had experience for almost 80 years in the manufacture of rail steel, and a wide diversity of other products for rail transportation systems. Over this long period, our engineers have worked closely with railroads, mines and industrial plants, to develop maximum safety, freedom from maintenance, and longer service life in trackwork components which sell at an economical price.

Safety always pays dividends. Apart from the humane aspects of reducing accidents, the facts show that mines, industrial plants and railroads are making substantial savings by reducing rolling-stock accidents, and creating much safer working conditions.

The backbone of this large mine — the track system — was completely built with Bethlehem heavy-rail track components.

The men themselves know from experience that trips can be run faster and much more safely over Bethlehem's rugged, durable and efficient trackwork. There is greater confidence in equipment, fewer lost-time accidents, and higher efficiency among working personnel.

FEATURES OF GOOD TRACK

From our experience we know that good trackage, substantially built of the highest-grade materials, has a very definite relationship to production.

When the several items which make up good track are planned and designed to be used together, there is a speeding up of haulage, both around curves and on straightaways. Time-outs for costly derailments are practically eliminated. The expense of track maintenance is reduced to a minimum. Production is increased, with added safety, efficiency and economy.

Good track depends on such factors as the correct weight of rail; good ties; a solid well-drained roadbed; easy curves and grades; proper alignment of track; and the use of the best types of switches and switch stands.

PREFABRICATED TRACK

Bethlehem prefabricated track for mines and industrial locations is planned in detail, precut and precurved in the Bethlehem shops to fit the transportation system.

Only Small Crew Needed. Rail lengths are such that only a small crew of men is needed to handle any piece, and all parts are numbered to simplify assembly with a minimum of labor.

Custom Built. Bethlehem men regularly work with mine operators and industrial engineers in producing track that is "custom built" to specifications. They visit the location with the customer, and after studying the conditions, design track best suited to that particular operation. All plans and specifications are approved by the customer before track fabrication begins.

Drawings Included. Maintenance of track is simplified further by giving a set of detailed drawings to the customer when the track is ready for installation. Then, in case a section of track has to be replaced later on, it is ordered by part and plan number, and will fit perfectly when received.

STEEL RAILS

Because of the wide variations in the types and weights of locomotives and cars, the rails used for main-haulage track range from 20 lb to 100 lb per yd, and follow ASCE designs. The following rule is often used to determine the weight of rail required to support a given weight of locomotive: Allow 10 lb per yd for each ton of weight on a wheel. Thus, a 10-ton locomotive with four wheels, would have 2.5 tons on each wheel. Following the rule and multiplying 2.5 by 10, we get 25 lb per yd.

This rule is intended only to find the *minimum weight* of rail. The minimum weight of rail is simply the lightest rail that reasonably good practice might justify. To this must be added a margin of safety to compensate for other factors, such as the condition of the roadbed, and the size and spacing of ties. Recommended weights are shown in the following table.

SUGGESTED RAIL WEIGHTS

Weight of Locomotive tons	Weight of rail, lb per yd	
	4-Wheel Locomotive	6-Wheel Locomotive
6	30	..
8	30	..
10	40	30
13	60	40
15	60	40
20	60	60
25	70	60
30	80	70
35	85	80
40	90	85
50	100	90

STEEL TIES

After the selection of proper rails, good ties come next in order of importance. Good track requires good ties. They should be of such size that, when properly ballasted, they will provide liberal bearing surface for the rail. They should be equipped with strong, secure rail fastenings, so as to insure stability to the track. Steel ties may be used for both underground and aboveground track.

Steel ties have many advantages. They are easy to attach, with either riveted or bolted clips. When riveted clips are used, a hammer is the only tool required. With bolted clips, only a wrench is needed. All ties can be furnished with bolted clips, when specified.

Steel ties hold rails securely, keeping them true to gage and in alignment. They possess unusually long life, even under severe conditions. Their scrap value is high. They are not a fire hazard. They cannot become spike-killed, or rotted.

Track is easily laid or removed when steel ties are used. Furthermore, steel ties make it a simple matter to advance the track as operations proceed. Steel ties add decidedly to the strength and efficiency of track, even when used in conjunction with wood ties.

Bethlehem steel ties are made for any weight or section of rail, and for any gage of track.

FROGS

(See pages 13 to 25 for a description of Bethlehem Frogs.)

In the average mine, and in industrial track systems, frogs of three or more different angles are likely to be required. These will be used in turning into rooms, partings or side-tracks on cross-entries, and in turning into cross-entries off the main haulageway. Under these conditions curves of different radii are usually required, and in order to have good track, the angle of the frog must be suitable for the radius of the curve.

Determining Frog Number. Frogs are designated by numbers which correspond to certain angles called frog angles. By referring to trigonometric tables the frog angle (A) may be found if the frog number (N) is known. The formulas expressing the relationship between A and N are:

$$N = \tfrac{1}{2} \cot \tfrac{1}{2} A$$

$$\cot \tfrac{1}{2} A = 2N$$

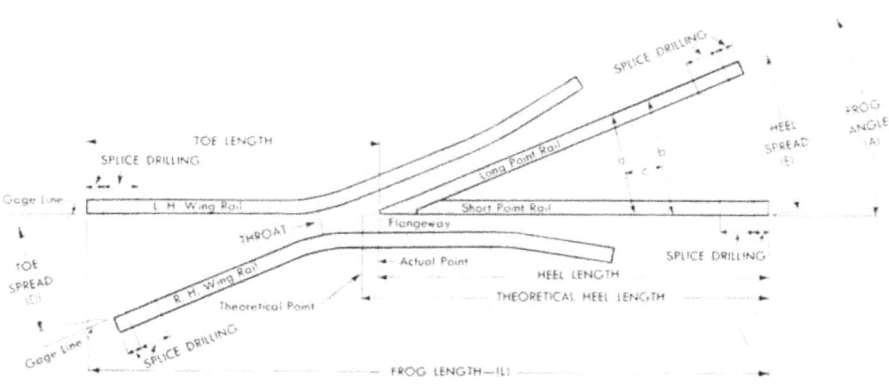

Various rules and simple formulas which do not involve trigonometry may be used to eliminate guesswork in selecting proper frogs for various curves. Two important ones are given here:

$$N = \sqrt{\frac{6R}{G}}$$

$$R = \frac{GN^2}{6}$$

Here N is the frog number, R the radius of curve in feet, and G the gage in inches. The first of these enables the frog number to be found when the radius and track gage are known; the second gives the radius of curve corresponding to a certain frog number and track gage.

For example: What number frog should be used for a curve of 36 feet radius and a track gage of 36 inches?

$$N = \sqrt{\frac{6 \times 36}{36}} = 2.5 \text{ (approx.)}$$

Therefore, a No. 2½ frog would be used.

What radius curve is proper with a No. 3 frog if the track gage is 42 inches?

$$R = \frac{42 \times 3^2}{6} = 63 \text{ feet}$$

The approximate frog number of any particular frog may be found by measuring the total length of the frog and dividing it by the sum of the spreads between gage lines at each end of the frog. Expressed as a formula,

$$N = \frac{L}{D+E}$$

where L, D and E are the measurements shown in the drawing on page 8. These measurements should be made in the same units — either all in inches, or all in feet.

A Fast Method. The following method is also used to find the number of any frog. Measure across the frog point at a place (a) where the distance between the gage lines is an even number of inches; measure again where the distance (b) is an inch greater than at (a); the number of inches (c) between the two measured sections (a and b) is the number of the frog. See drawing page 8.

Modern trackwork components are produced at two Bethlehem Steel Company plants at Johnstown, Pa., and Steelton, Pa. This view shows the Frog and Switch Shop at Johnstown.

MANUFACTURING FACILITIES

Manufacturing operations in Bethlehem's Frog and Switch Division are conducted at two large modern plants at Johnstown, Pa., and Steelton, Pa. At these plants, highly skilled workmen and the latest machinery and methods are used to produce the best modern track equipment at economical cost.

TRACK SERVICE FOR CUSTOMERS

When you are ready to plan new track, or to replace existing trackage, a Bethlehem engineer will be glad to give you additional information about today's improved trackwork. This service is without charge.

The engineering and sales staffs of Bethlehem Steel Company are available at all times to offer help and suggestions on the track requirement of customers. Bethlehem manufactures a wide range of track products, and a great deal of experience has been gained in developing and applying these products to rail transportation systems. Backed by this experience and knowledge, Bethlehem engineers can analyze any track problem pertaining to mines and industry, and can recommend accurately the right equipment for a practical solution.

This service assures the purchaser that the equipment furnished will provide the safest trackwork and the most economical and longest service life possible under the existing conditions.

The Frog and Switch Shop at Bethlehem's Steelton, Pa., Plant.

Bethlehem Heavy-Duty Trackwork provides safe, dependable service at this important intersection undergrou[nd]

BETHLEHEM FROGS

For any type of service above or below ground there is a Bethlehem Frog suited for the job. For light traffic, riveted-plate and manganese steel frogs find wide application. For more severe duty, the bolted-rigid and manganese steel frogs are recommended.

Where both rolling stock and traffic are extremely heavy, railbound manganese or cast manganese frogs are most suitable. The manganese steel frog has long life even under very severe operating conditions.

ORDERING FROGS

When ordering standard frogs, please specify:
1. The design number.
2. The frog number.
3. The weight and section of rail.

When ordering special frogs, however, the following information should be given: (1) the design (riveted-plate or bolted-rigid construction), (2) frog number or angle, (3) the toe length, (4) the overall length, (5) the weight and section of rail, and (6) the drilling for joint connection.

RIVETED-PLATE FROGS FOR LIGHT RAILS

Design 97

Frog Numbers 2, 2½ and 3

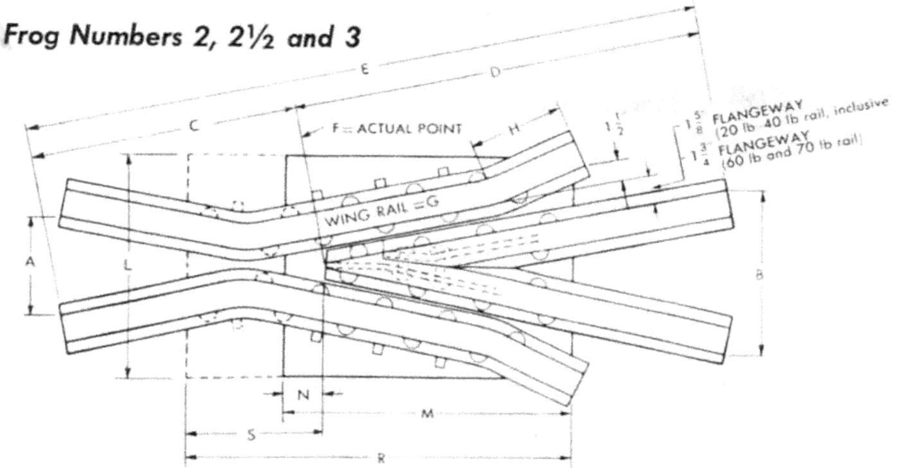

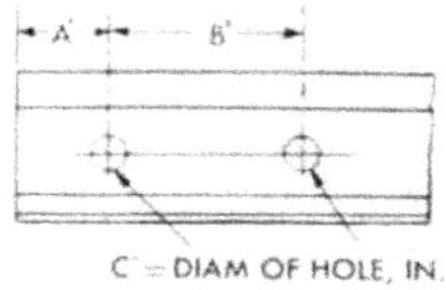

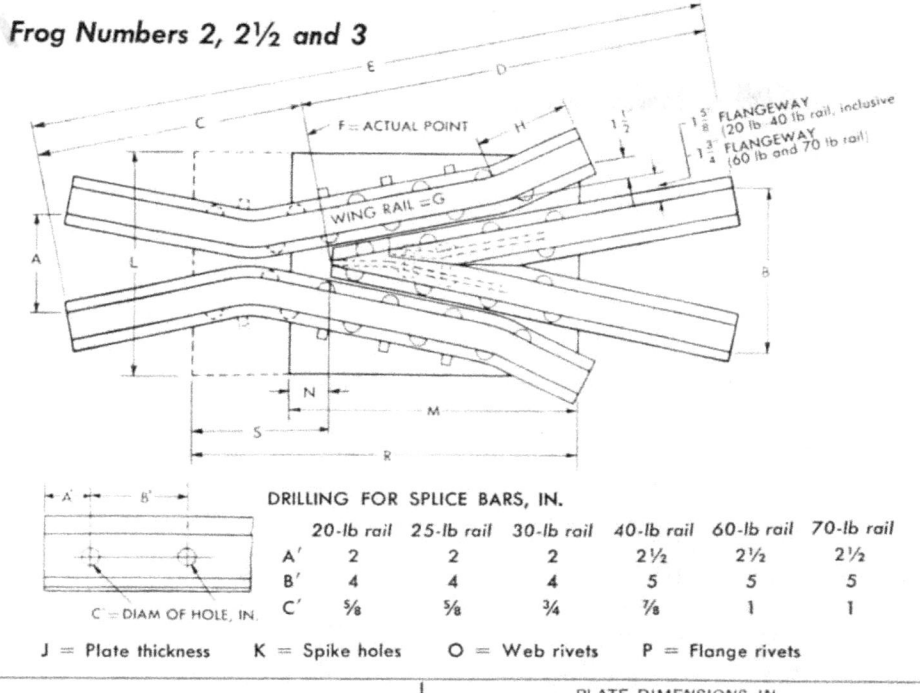

DRILLING FOR SPLICE BARS, IN.

	20-lb rail	25-lb rail	30-lb rail	40-lb rail	60-lb rail	70-lb rail
A'	2	2	2	2½	2½	2½
B'	4	4	4	5	5	5
C'	⅝	⅝	¾	⅞	1	1

J = Plate thickness K = Spike holes O = Web rivets P = Flange rivets

FROG DIMENSIONS, IN.											PLATE DIMENSIONS, IN.															
											STANDARD PLATE									ALTERNATE PLATE						
																O		P							P	
Frog No.	Rail Wt lb	Frog Angle	A	B	C	D	E	F	G	H	J	K	L	M	N	No.	Size	No.	Size	J	K	L	R	S	No.	Size
2	20	28° 04′ 21″	8	10 15/16	17	22	39	¼	30	6	⅜	⅝	12	20	7	1	⅝	24	½	⅜	⅝	12	—	—	—	—
2	25	28° 04′ 21″	8	10 15/16	17	22	39	¼	30	6	⅜	⅝	12	20	7	1	⅝	24	½	⅜	⅝	12	—	—	—	—
2	30	28° 04′ 21″	8	10 15/16	17	22	39	¼	30	6	⅜	⅝	12	20	7	1	¾	24	⅝	⅜	⅝	12	—	—	—	—
2	40	28° 04′ 21″	9 5/16	13 5/16	20	28	48	⅜	36	9	½	⅝	18	20	2½	1	¾	24	⅝	½	⅝	18	26½	9	30	⅝
2	60	28° 04′ 21″	9 5/16	13 5/16	20	28	48	⅜	36	9	½	⅝	18	20	2½	1	⅞	24	¾	½	⅝	18	26½	9	30	¾
2	70	28° 04′ 21″	9 5/16	13 5/16	20	28	48	⅜	36	9	½	⅝	18	20	2½	1	⅞	24	¾	½	⅝	18	26½	9	30	¾
2½	20	22° 37′ 12″	6¼	10¼	16½	25½	42	¼	33	6	⅜	⅝	14	18	2½	1	⅝	24	½	⅜	⅝	14	24	8½	30	½
2½	25	22° 37′ 12″	6¼	10¼	16½	25½	42	¼	33	6	⅜	⅝	14	18	2½	1	⅝	24	½	⅜	⅝	14	24	8½	30	½
2½	30	22° 37′ 12″	6¼	10¼	16½	25½	42	¼	33	6	⅜	⅝	14	18	2½	1	¾	24	⅝	⅜	⅝	14	24	8½	30	⅝
2½	40	22° 37′ 12″	7½	11⅜	20	28	48	⅜	41	9	½	⅝	17	22	3	2	¾	24	⅝	½	⅝	17	28	9	28	⅝
2½	60	22° 37′ 12″	7½	11⅜	20	28	48	⅜	41	9	½	⅝	17	22	3	2	⅞	24	¾	½	⅝	17	28	9	28	¾
2½	70	22° 37′ 12″	7½	11⅜	20	28	48	⅜	41	9	½	⅝	17	22	3	2	⅞	24	¾	½	⅝	17	28	9	28	¾
3	20	18° 55′ 29″	5 3/16	8⅝	16½	25½	42	¼	33	6	⅜	⅝	14	18	2½	1	⅝	24	½	⅜	⅝	14	24	8½	28	½
3	25	18° 55′ 29″	5 3/16	8⅝	16½	25½	42	¼	33	6	⅜	⅝	14	18	2½	1	⅝	24	½	⅜	⅝	14	24	8½	28	½
3	30	18° 55′ 29″	5 3/16	8⅝	16½	25½	42	¼	33	6	⅜	⅝	14	18	2½	1	¾	24	⅝	⅜	⅝	14	24	8½	28	⅝
3	40	18° 55′ 29″	7½	12 3/16	24	36	60	⅜	45	9	½	⅝	18	24	2½	2	¾	24	⅝	½	⅝	18	31	9½	28	⅝
3	60	18° 55′ 29″	7½	12 3/16	24	36	60	⅜	45	9	½	⅝	18	24	2½	2	⅞	24	¾	½	⅝	18	31	9½	28	¾
3	70	18° 55′ 29″	7½	12 3/16	24	36	60	⅜	45	9	½	⅝	18	24	2½	2	⅞	24	¾	½	⅝	18	31	9½	28	¾

Riveted Plate Frog Design 97 is recommended for use in mines, construction work and industrial plants where light rails are used.

Frog Numbers 4, 5 and 6

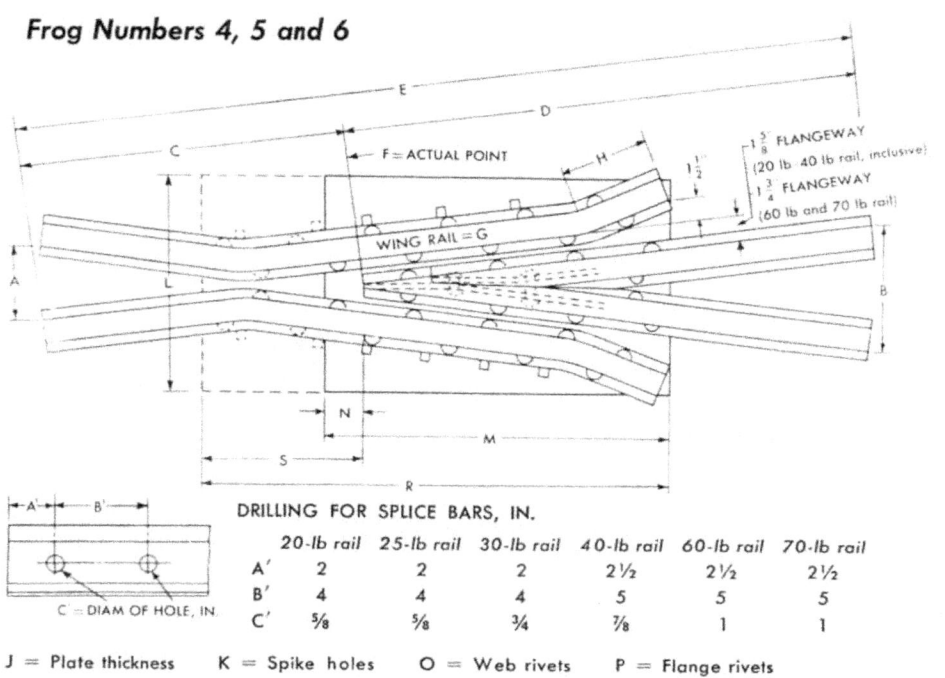

DRILLING FOR SPLICE BARS, IN.

	20-lb rail	25-lb rail	30-lb rail	40-lb rail	60-lb rail	70-lb rail
A'	2	2	2	2½	2½	2½
B'	4	4	4	5	5	5
C'	⅝	⅝	¾	⅞	1	1

J = Plate thickness   K = Spike holes   O = Web rivets   P = Flange rivets

		FROG DIMENSIONS, IN.													PLATE DIMENSIONS, IN.										
															STANDARD PLATE					ALTERNATE PLATE						
																	O		P							P
Frog No.	Rail Wt lb	Frog Angle	A	B	C	D	E	F	G	H	J	K	L	M	N	No.	Size	No.	Size	J	K	L	R	S	No.	Size
4	20	14° 15' 00"	4¹⁵⁄₁₆	8⁷⁄₁₆	21	33	54	¼	41	6	⅜	⅝	14	22½	2½	2	⅝	28	½	⅜	⅝	14	30½	10½	34	½
4	25	14° 15' 00"	4¹⁵⁄₁₆	8⁷⁄₁₆	21	33	54	¼	41	6	⅜	⅝	14	22½	2½	2	⅝	28	½	⅜	⅝	14	30½	10½	34	½
4	30	14° 15' 00"	4¹⁵⁄₁₆	8⁷⁄₁₆	21	33	54	¼	41	6	⅜	⅝	14	22½	2½	2	¾	28	⅝	⅜	⅝	14	30½	10½	34	⅝
4	40	14° 15' 00"	6⁵⁄₁₆	11⁹⁄₁₆	27	45	72	⅜	54	9	½	⅝	18	30	2½	2	¾	30	⅝	½	⅝	18	40	12½	36	⅝
4	60	14° 15' 00"	6⁵⁄₁₆	11⁹⁄₁₆	27	45	72	⅜	54	9	½	⅝	18	30	2½	2	⅞	30	¾	½	⅝	18	40	12½	36	¾
4	70	14° 15' 00"	6⁵⁄₁₆	11⁹⁄₁₆	27	45	72	⅜	54	9	½	⅝	18	30	2½	2	⅞	30	¾	½	⅝	18	40	12½	36	¾
5	20	11° 25' 16"	4¼	7¾	22½	37½	60	¼	42	6	⅜	⅝	13	26½	2½	2	⅝	29	½	⅜	⅝	13	36	12	35	½
5	25	11° 25' 16"	4¼	7¾	22½	37½	60	¼	42	6	⅜	⅝	13	26½	2½	2	⅝	29	½	⅜	⅝	13	36	12	35	½
5	30	11° 25' 16"	4¼	7¾	22½	37½	60	¼	42	6	⅜	⅝	13	26½	2½	2	¾	29	⅝	⅜	⅝	13	36	12	35	⅝
5	40	11° 25' 16"	5⅝	11⅛	30	54	84	⅜	58	9	½	⅝	16	36	2½	2	¾	32	⅝	½	⅝	16	46	12½	38	⅝
5	60	11° 25' 16"	5⅝	11⅛	30	54	84	⅜	58	9	½	⅝	16	36	2½	2	⅞	32	¾	½	⅝	16	46	12½	38	¾
5	70	11° 25' 16"	5⅝	11⅛	30	54	84	⅜	58	9	½	⅝	16	36	2½	2	⅞	32	¾	½	⅝	16	46	12½	38	¾
6	20	9° 31' 38"	4¼	7¾	27	45	72	¼	50	6	⅜	⅝	13	31½	2½	2	⅝	32	½	⅜	⅝	13	43	14	38	½
6	25	9° 31' 38"	4¼	7¾	27	45	72	¼	50	6	⅜	⅝	13	31½	2½	2	⅝	32	½	⅜	⅝	13	43	14	38	½
6	30	9° 31' 38"	4¼	7¾	27	45	72	¼	50	6	⅜	⅝	13	31½	2½	2	¾	32	⅝	⅜	⅝	13	43	14	38	⅝
6	40	9° 31' 38"	5⅝	10⅜	36	60	96	⅜	67	9	½	⅝	16	42½	2½	2	¾	36	⅝	½	⅝	16	54½	14½	42	⅝
6	60	9° 31' 38"	5⅝	10⅜	36	60	96	⅜	67	9	½	⅝	16	42½	2½	2	⅞	36	¾	½	⅝	16	54½	14½	42	¾
6	70	9° 31' 38"	5⅝	10⅜	36	60	96	⅜	67	9	½	⅝	16	42½	2½	2	⅞	36	¾	½	⅝	16	54½	14½	42	¾

BOLTED-RIGID FROGS
FOR LIGHT AND HEAVY RAILS

Design 15

This frog has gray cast-iron throat and flare filler blocks. The flare blocks provide foot-guard protection. All filler blocks are grooved sections with large bottom bearings.

Design 16

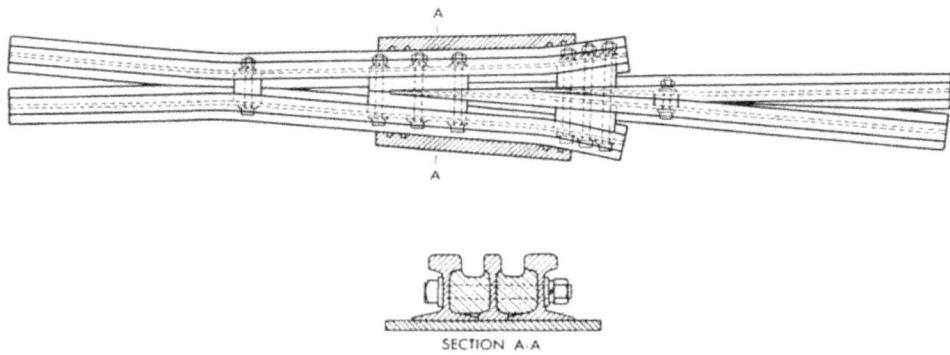

Design 16 is the same as Design 15, except that it is equipped with a base plate.

Design 72

A.R.E.A. Plan No. 320-55

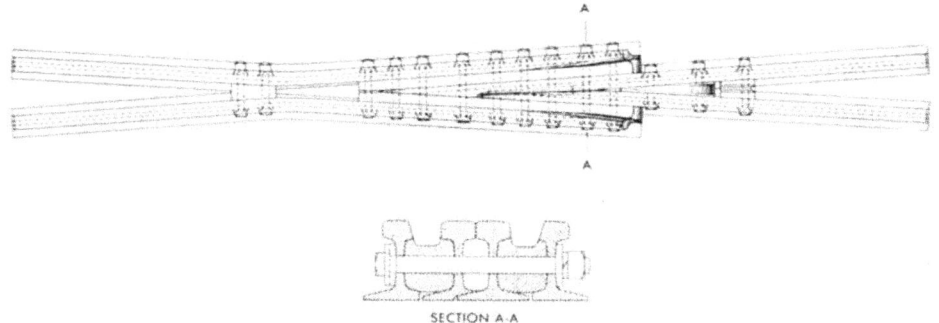

SECTION A-A

This frog is identical to the standard bolted rigid frog adopted by the American Railway Engineering Association, and follows the exact A.R.E.A. Specifications.

Frog No.	Rail Section	DESIGNS 15, 16 MINIMUM FROG LENGTHS			DESIGNS 15, 16 AND 72 A.R.E.A. STANDARD FROG LENGTH		
		Toe ft—in.	Heel ft—in.	Total ft—in.	Toe ft—in.	Heel ft—in.	Total ft—in.
3	40 AS to 70 AS	2-0	3-0	5-0	—	—	—
4	30 AS to 100 AS	2-3	3-9	6-0	3-4	4-8	8-0
5	30 AS to 100 AS	2-6	4-6	7-0	3-6½	5-5½	9-0
6	30 AS to 100 AS	3-0	5-0	8-0	3-9	6-3	10-0
7	30 AS to 80 AS	3-0	5-0	8-0			
	85 AS to 100 AS	3-0	6-0	9-0	4-8½	7-3½	12-0
8	30 AS to 60 AS	3-0	5-0	8-0			
	65 AS to 80 AS	3-6	5-6	9-0			
	85 AS to 100 AS	4-0	6-0	10-0	5-1	7-11	13-0
9	30 AS to 60 AS	3-4½	5-7½	9-0			
	65 AS to 100 AS	4-0	6-0	10-0	6-4½	9-7½	16-0
10	30 AS to 60 AS	4-0	6-0	10-0			
	65 AS to 80 AS	4-6	6-6	11-0			
	85 AS to 100 AS	4-6	7-6	12-0	6-5	10-1	16-6
11	30 AS to 100 AS	6-0	8-0	14-0	7-0	11-8½	18-8½
12	30 AS to 100 AS	7-0	8-0	15-0	7-9½	12-6½	20-4

RECOMMENDED LENGTHS FOR FROGS

All toe lengths measured from the ½-in. point.
Minimum lengths given above on stiff bolted frogs No. 6 and larger are based on the use of 24-in. joints. A.R.E.A. specifications apply to rails 90-lb. and over.

BOLTED-RIGID FROGS FOR LIGHT AND HEAVY RAILS

Design 83
A.M.C. Standard Bolted-Rigid Frog

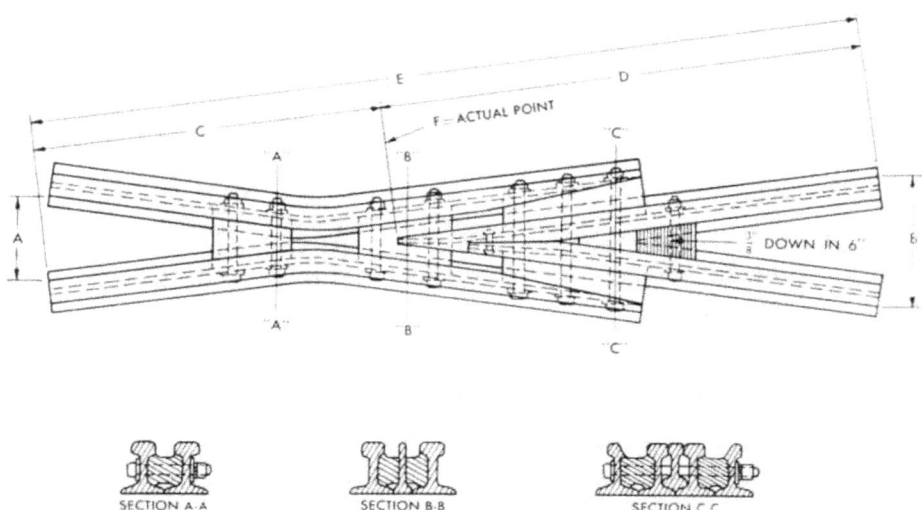

This frog is identical to the standard bolted rigid frog adopted by the American Mining Congress, for main haulage turnouts. Frogs No. 3, 4, 5, 6, 7 and 8 for 70-lb AS to 100-lb AS rail, inclusive.

Frog No.	Rail Weight lb	Frog Angle	DIMENSIONS						Number of Bolts
			A in.	B in.	C ft in.	D ft in.	E ft in.	F in.	
3	70-100	18° 55' 29"	9 11/16	14 5/8	2-7	3-7	6-2	½	7
4	70-100	14° 15' 00"	9 7/16	14 3/8	3-4	4-8	8-0	½	8
5	70-100	11° 25' 16"	7 15/16	13 9/16	3-6½	5-5½	9-0	½	9
6	70-100	9° 31' 38"	7	13	3-9	6-3	10-0	½	10
7	70-100	8° 10' 16"	7 9/16	13	4-8½	7-3½	12-0	½	11
8	70-100	7° 9' 10"	7 1/8	12 3/8	5-1	7-11	13-0	½	13

Fillers. Throat filler blocks are made of high quality gray cast iron. Body filler blocks are made of rolled steel in one continuous length, or of gray cast iron in two lengths, single or double-groove section. Heel risers are machined from short pieces of rail.

Bolts. The table on page 18 shows the minimum number of bolts that shall be used in the frog. Bolts 1¼-in. diam for rails of 3-in. fishing height and over, and 1⅛-in. diam for rails of less than 3-in. fishing height. All bolts have square heads and square nuts, and are equipped with head locks, lock-washers and bevel washers where necessary to afford square bearing. Suitable washers are placed under nuts to bring them out from under head of rail, so that they may be tightened with a standard wrench.

Rivets. Rivets through point rails are ⅞-in. diam and may be countersunk. If either button-head or cone-head rivets are used, filler blocks are cut out to clear rivets.

Bethlehem Heavy-Duty Cross-Over near shaft bottom.

SOLID MANGANESE STEEL FROGS FOR LIGHT RAILS

Design 289

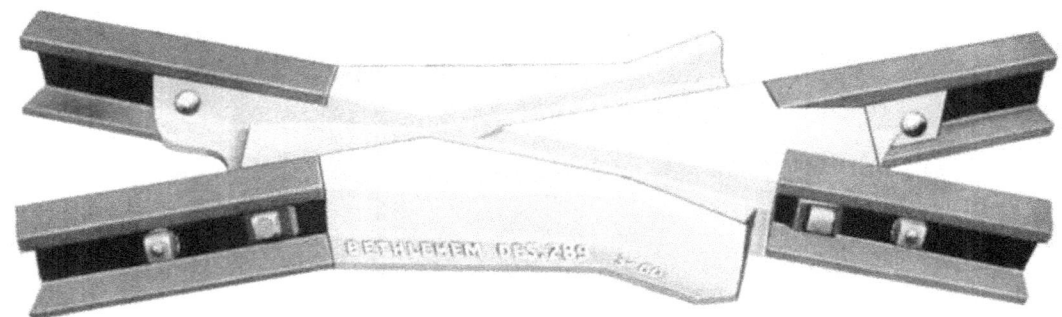

Design 289 is of one-piece construction, made of cast manganese steel. Being of one piece, there are no rivets or plates to work loose. It may be quickly installed, and will outwear several riveted plate frogs. No splice bars are required, the rails being bolted directly to the frog arms, and special long heat-treated bolts with beveled washers are furnished where necessary. Frogs are made with ½-in. points.

LENGTHS OF SOLID MANGANESE STEEL FROGS DESIGN 289

NOTE: Toe and heel lengths are measured to the ½-in. point.

Frog No.	Rail Weight lb	Length Toe ft in.	Length Heel ft in.	Total Length ft in.
2	20	0-7³⁄₁₆	0-7¾	1-2¹⁵⁄₁₆
	25	See Design 289-A, page 22		
	30	See Design 289-A, page 22		
	40	See Design 289-A, page 22		
	50	0-7³⁄₁₆	0-11⅞	1-7¹⁄₁₆
	60	0-7³⁄₁₆	1-0¹⁵⁄₁₆	1-8⅛
	70	0-7³⁄₁₆	1-1¹⁵⁄₁₆	1-9⅛
	80	0-7³⁄₁₆	1-2¾	1-9¹⁵⁄₁₆
	85	0-7½	1-3³⁄₁₆	1-10¹¹⁄₁₆

Frog No.	Rail Weight lb	LENGTH Toe ft in.	LENGTH Heel ft in.	Total Length ft in.
2 1/2	20	0-8 7/8	0-9 9/16	1-6 7/16
	25	See Design 289-A, page 22		
	30	See Design 289-A, page 22		
	40	See Design 289-A, page 22		
	50	0-8 7/8	1-2 11/16	1-11 9/16
	60	0-8 7/8	1-3 15/16	2-0 13/16
	70	0-8 7/8	1-5 1/4	2-2 1/8

Frog No.	Rail Weight lb	LENGTH Toe ft in.	LENGTH Heel ft in.	Total Length ft in.
3	20	0-9 1/8	0-11 7/16	1-8 9/16
	25	See Design 289-A, page 22		
	30	See Design 289-A, page 22		
	40	See Design 289-A, page 22		
	50	0-9 1/8	1-5 1/2	2-2 5/8
	60	0-9 1/8	1-7	2-4 1/8
	70	0-9 1/8	1-8 9/16	2-5 11/16
	80	0-9 1/2	1-9 11/16	2-7 3/16
	85	0-10	1-10 1/2	2-8 1/2
	90	0-10 5/8	1-11 5/8	2-10 1/4
	100	0-11	2-0 3/4	2-11 3/4

Frog No.	Rail Weight lb	LENGTH Toe ft in.	LENGTH Heel ft in.	Total Length ft in.
3 1/2	30	0-10 9/16	1-3 15/16	2-2 1/2
	40	0-10 9/16	1-5 11/16	2-4 1/4
	50	0-10 9/16	1-8 3/8	2-6 15/16
	60	0-10 9/16	1-10 1/8	2-8 11/16
	70	0-10 9/16	1-11 7/8	2-10 7/16
	80	0-11 1/16	2-1 1/4	3-0 5/16

Frog No.	Rail Weight lb	LENGTH Toe ft in.	LENGTH Heel ft in.	Total Length ft in.
4	20	1-0 1/16	1-3 1/8	2-3 3/16
	25	1-0 1/16	1-4 1/8	2-4 3/16
	30	1-0 1/16	1-6 1/8	2-6 3/16
	40	1-0 1/16	1-8 1/8	2-8 3/16
	50	1-0 1/16	1-11 3/16	2-11 1/4
	60	1-0 1/16	2-1 3/16	3-1 1/4
	70	1-0 1/16	2-3 1/4	3-3 5/16
	80	1-0 1/2	2-4 3/4	3-5 1/4
	85	1-1 1/2	2-6	3-7 1/2
	90	1-2	2-7	3-9
	100	1-2 5/8	2-8 3/4	3-11 3/8

Frog No.	Rail Weight lb	LENGTH Toe ft in.	LENGTH Heel ft in.	Total Length ft in.
5	20	1-3 1/16	1-6 7/8	2-9 15/16
	25	1-3 1/16	1-8 1/8	2-11 3/16
	30	1-3 1/16	1-10 5/8	3-1 11/16
	40	1-3 1/16	2-1 1/8	3-4 3/16
	50	1-3 1/16	2-4 7/8	3-7 15/16
	60	1-3 1/16	2-7 7/16	3-10 1/2
	70	1-3 1/16	2-9 15/16	4-1
	80	1-3 11/16	2-11 13/16	4-3 1/2
	85	1-5	3-1 1/2	4-6 1/2
	90	1-6 3/16	3-2 5/16	4-8 1/2
	100	1-6 3/16	3-4 13/16	4-11

Frog No.	Rail Weight lb	LENGTH Toe ft in.	LENGTH Heel ft in.	Total Length ft in.
6	20	1-6 1/16	1-10 9/16	3-4 5/8
	25	1-6 1/16	2-0 1/16	3-6 1/8
	30	1-6 1/16	2-3 1/8	3-9 3/16
	40	1-6 1/16	2-6 1/8	4-0 3/16
	50	1-6 1/16	2-10 5/8	4-4 11/16
	60	1-6 1/16	3-1 5/8	4-7 11/16
	70	1-6 1/16	3-4 5/8	4-10 11/16
	80	1-6 13/16	3-6 15/16	5-1 3/4
	85	1-7 1/2	3-8 1/4	5-3 3/4
	90	1-9	3-10 5/16	5-7 5/16
	100	1-9 13/16	4-0 15/16	5-10 3/4

Frog No.	Rail Weight lb	LENGTH Toe ft in.	LENGTH Heel ft in.	Total Length ft in.
7	40	1-9 1/16	2-11 1/8	4-8 3/16
	50	1-9	3-4 1/4	5-1 1/4
	60	1-9 1/16	3-7 7/8	5-4 15/16
	70	1-9 1/16	3-11 3/8	5-8 7/16
	80	1-9 15/16	4-2	5-11 15/16
	85	1-11 3/16	4-4 1/2	6-3 11/16
	90	2-1 7/16	4-5 9/16	6-7
	100	2-1 7/16	4-9 1/16	6-10 1/2

Frog No.	Rail Weight lb	LENGTH Toe ft in.	LENGTH Heel ft in.	Total Length ft in.
8	60	1-11	4-4	6-3
	70	2-0	4-6	6-6
	80	2-1 1/16	4-9 1/8	6-10 3/16
	85	2-5 1/16	4-11 1/8	7-4 3/16
	90	2-5 1/16	5-1 1/8	7-6 3/16
	100	2-5 1/16	5-5 1/8	7-10 3/16

NOTE: Toe and heel lengths are measured to the 1/2-in. point.

SOLID MANGANESE STEEL FROGS FOR LIGHT RAILS

Design 289-A

Modified to accommodate eight standard track bolts

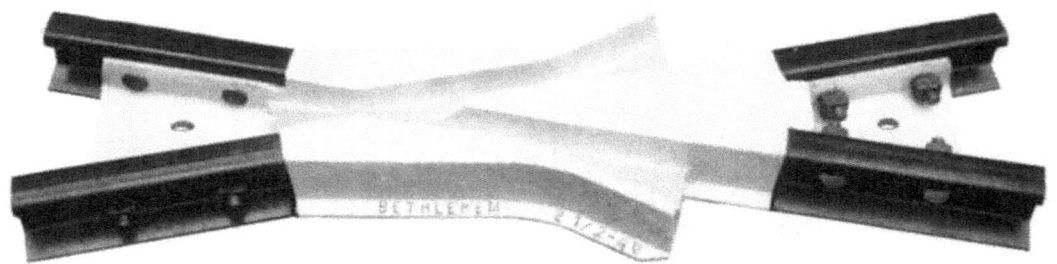

The popular sizes of room frogs are now available in the design shown above. The heel end of the frog has been extended so that eight standard track bolts may be used. This eliminates the long bolts and angle washers which were furnished with the same sizes of frogs formerly made strictly in accordance with AMC dimensions. Holes are cored in the toe and heel aprons to facilitate mounting on steel frog ties. Track bolts are not furnished with this type of frog. Frogs are made with ½-in. points.

Frogs will be furnished on all orders for solid manganese steel frogs in the following sizes in accordance with the dimensions listed.

LENGTHS OF SOLID MANGANESE STEEL FROGS DESIGN 289-A

Frog No.	Rail Weight lb	LENGTH, IN.		Total Length in.
		Toe	Heel	
2	25 AS	7³⁄₁₆	11¹⁄₁₆	18¼
2	30 AS	7³⁄₁₆	11¹⁄₁₆	18¼
2	40 AS	7³⁄₁₆	12¹³⁄₁₆	20
2½	25 AS	8⅞	13¼	22⅛
2½	30 AS	8⅞	13⅝	22½
2½	40 AS	8⅞	15¼	24⅛
3	25 AS	9⅛	16¾	25⅞
3	30 AS	9⅛	17¾	26⅞
3	40 AS	9⅛	18³⁄₁₆	27⁵⁄₁₆

Note: Toe and heel lengths are measured to the ½-inch point.

SOLID MANGANESE STEEL FROGS FOR HEAVY RAILS

Design 285

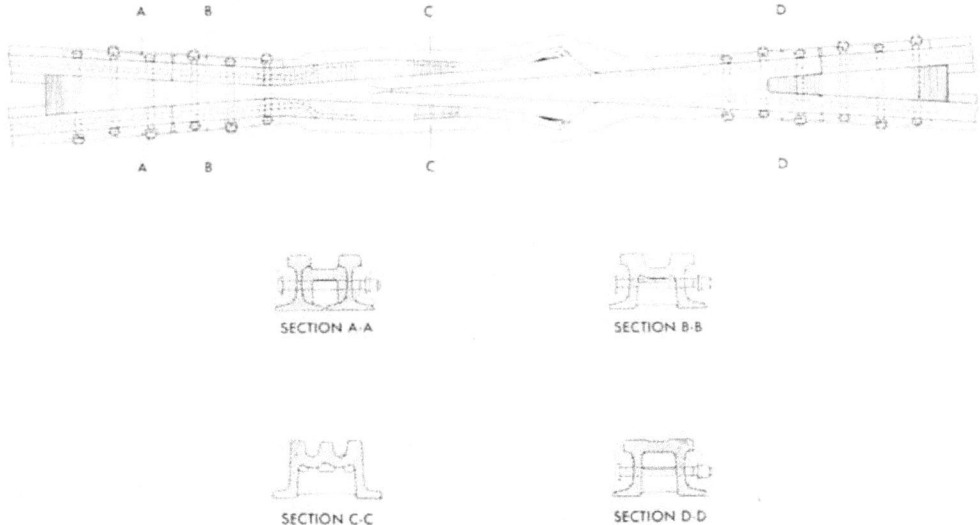

Bethlehem Design 285 is a solid manganese steel frog for heavy-rail use, and is identical to the frog designated by the American Railway Engineering Association as A.R.E.A. Plan No. 671-55 (see page 24).

Manganese steel frogs are recommended only for slow-speed locations. They will outwear several bolted-rigid frogs, and will show great economies when used at points of heavy traffic. The top of the frog is planer-ground to insure a smooth running surface. Wing wheel risers may be furnished when so desired.

Solid frogs are shorter than bolted-rigid, or rail-bound manganese types. To attempt to duplicate the long lengths of these frogs would render the cost prohibitive, and the manufacture more or less impractical.

The special length splice-bar bolts for connecting the rails are furnished with the frog and are of heat-treated steel. Splice bars are not furnished unless specified.

LENGTHS OF SOLID MANGANESE STEEL FROGS
DESIGN 285, A.R.E.A. Plan 671-55

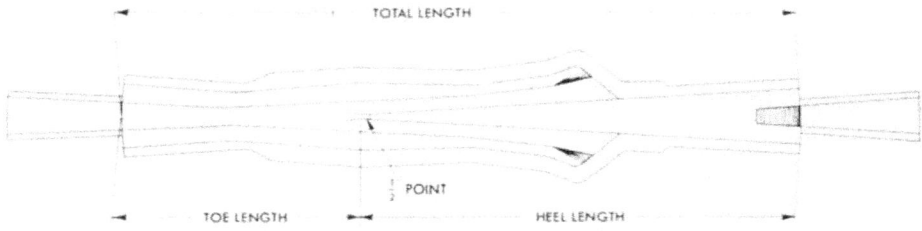

Frog No.	GROUP A RAILS			GROUP B RAILS			GROUP C RAILS		
	Total Length ft in.	Toe Length ft in.	Heel Length ft in.	Total Length ft in.	Toe Length ft in.	Heel Length ft in.	Total Length ft in.	Toe Length ft in.	Heel Length ft in.
4	5 – 8	0 – 22	3 – 10	5 – 8	0 – 22	3 – 10	5 – 8	0 – 22	3 – 10
5	6 – 0	2 – 0	4 – 0	6 – 0	2 – 0	4 – 0	6 – 0	2 – 0	4 – 0
6	6 – 5	2 – 3	4 – 2	6 – 5	2 – 3	4 – 2	6 – 5	2 – 3	4 – 2
7	7 – 2	2 – 5	4 – 9	7 – 0	2 – 5	4 – 7	6 – 9	2 – 5	4 – 4
8	8 – 0	2 – 7	5 – 5	7 – 10	2 – 7	5 – 3	7 – 7	2 – 7	5 – 0
9	8 – 10	2 – 9	6 – 1	8 – 7	2 – 9	5 – 10	8 – 4	2 – 9	5 – 7
10	9 – 9	3 – 0	6 – 9	9 – 6	3 – 0	6 – 6	9 – 2	3 – 0	6 – 2
11	10 – 9	3 – 4	7 – 5	10 – 4	3 – 2	7 – 2	10 – 0	3 – 2	6 – 10
12	11 – 10	3 – 8	8 – 2	11 – 3	3 – 5	7 – 10	10 – 9	3 – 4	7 – 5

Frog No.	GROUP D RAILS			RAILS 112 LB OR HEAVIER					
	Total Length ft in.	Toe Length ft in.	Heel Length ft in.	Total Length ft in.	Toe Length ft in.	Toe Spread in.	Heel Length ft in.	Heel Spread in.
4	5 – 8	0 – 22	3 – 10	5 – 11	2 – 1	$5^{11}/_{16}$	3 – 10	12
5	6 – 0	2 – 0	4 – 0	6 – 5	2 – 1	$4\frac{1}{2}$	4 – 4	$10\frac{1}{8}$
6	6 – 5	2 – 3	4 – 2	7 – 4	2 – 11	$5^{5}/_{16}$	4 – 5	$9^{5}/_{16}$
7	6 – 9	2 – 5	4 – 4	8 – 1½	2 – 11	$4\frac{1}{2}$	5 – 2½	$9^{13}/_{32}$
8	7 – 5	2 – 7	4 – 10	8 – 11	2 – 11	$3\frac{7}{8}$	6 – 0	$9\frac{1}{2}$
9	8 – 2	2 – 9	5 – 5	9 – 9	2 – 11	$3\frac{3}{8}$	6 – 10	$9^{19}/_{32}$
10	9 – 0	3 – 0	6 – 0	11 – 4½	3 – 9	4	7 – 7½	$9\frac{5}{8}$
11	9 – 9	3 – 2	6 – 7	12 – 2½	3 – 9	$3^{9}/_{16}$	8 – 5½	$9^{23}/_{32}$
12	10 – 6	3 – 4	7 – 2	13 – 0	3 – 9	$3\frac{1}{4}$	9 – 3	$9\frac{3}{4}$

GROUPING OF RAILS

RAILS 112 LB OR HEAVIER		GROUP A RAILS	GROUP B RAILS	GROUP C RAILS	GROUP D RAILS
Lengths shown will accommodate sections specified below. For other rails 112 lb or heavier see Note 5 (a).		Base 5¾ in. down to but not including 5½ in. Head 2⅞ in. to 2⅝ in. inclusive, or Head at or exceeding 2⅞ in. when Head + Base does not exceed 8⅜ in.	Base 5½ in. down to but not including 5¼ in. Head $2^{13}/_{16}$ in. to $2^{9}/_{16}$ in. inclusive, or Head at or exceeding $2^{13}/_{16}$ in. when Head + Base does not exceed $8^{5}/_{16}$ in.	Base 5¼ in. down to but not including 5 in. Head $2^{11}/_{16}$ in. to $2^{7}/_{16}$ in. inclusive, or Head at or exceeding $2^{11}/_{16}$ in. when Head + Base does not exceed $7^{15}/_{16}$ in.	Base 5 in. down to but not including 4½ in. Head $2^{11}/_{16}$ in. to $2^{7}/_{16}$ in. inclusive, or Head at or exceeding $2^{11}/_{16}$ in. when Head + Base does not exceed $7^{11}/_{16}$ in.
112 R.E. 112 T.R. 113 H.F.S.P. 115 R.E. 127 DUD. 129 T.R. 130 P.S.	131 R.E. 132 H.F.S.P. 132 R.E. 133 R.E. 136 L.V. 140 R.E.	100 A.S.C.E. 105 DUD.	90 A.S.C.E. 100 A.R.A.-A. 100 P. & R. 100 N.H. 100 R.E. 107 N.H. 110 R.E.	90 A.R.A.-A. 90 H.F.R.A. 90 C. & N.W. 90 I.R.T. 100 A.R.A.-B. 100 C. & N.W.	90 A.R.A.-B. 100 P.S.

NOTE 5 (A.R.E.A. PLAN 671-55) LENGTH OF FROGS

(a) Rails 112 lb and heavier. Lengths in table (except No. 4) have been designed for uniform tie spacing 19½ in. For rail sections with width of base plus head exceeding heel spread or base minus head exceeding toe spread, longer frogs shall be specified by increasing toe and/or heel lengths, or corner of rail base removed in field.

(b) Rails lighter than 112 lb. Lengths in table provide clearance for abutting rails; those below heavy lines were determined by this requirement, those above heavy lines are minimum and were fixed by other considerations.

RAIL-BOUND MANGANESE STEEL FROGS FOR HEAVY RAILS

A. R. E. A. Standard, Plan 600-55

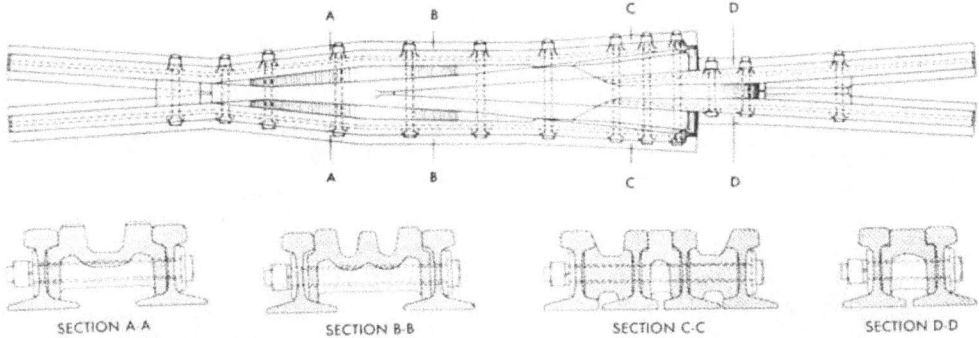

A rail-bound manganese steel frog combines safe construction and long wear. It is recommended for use at locations where traffic is heavy.

The manganese steel center is in one piece, ground to fit the rail section, and securely bound or reinforced for its entire length by the surrounding wing rails. All bolts are heat-treated and equipped with American Standard Heavy Nuts.

This rail-bound manganese steel frog is ideal for the heavy traffic encountered in steel plants and coal-tipple yards. Note that it is firmly supported and anchored by hook-twin tie plates.

A Bethlehem Heavy-Duty Switch in a main haulage track.

BETHLEHEM SWITCHES

A line of heavy-duty switches has been developed by Bethlehem to meet the severe demands of modern operating conditions. These switches are recommended for all locations in heavy-traffic lines where safety, long life, low maintenance and freedom from derailments are essential.

Several typical designs are shown here to illustrate the types of construction which will meet most mine and industrial requirements. Bethlehem switches are so designed that they may readily be modified by changing the number and location of slide plates, braces and other fittings.

COMPONENTS OF A SWITCH

A switch should not be confused with a complete turnout. (Turnouts are illustrated and described on pages 91 to 108.) A switch consists of a pair of switch points with side jaw clips attached, and one or more switch rods to connect the two points, and the necessary slide plates and rail braces required by a particular design number.

The hand (right-hand or left-hand) of individual switch points may be determined by standing between the switch points of a turnout and facing the frog.

It is necessary to keep the stock rail at the point of the switch and the heel of the switch firmly in position, because of the loose wheels on most mine and industrial cars. The loose wheels allow the cars to do considerable "nosing," or wobbling, which produces severe side thrusts on the switch.

For certain locations in and around industrial plants, or in places where paving is encountered, the use of tongue-and-mate construction is recommended instead of the ordinary split switch. Such an installation improves materially the roadway surface, and reduces upkeep. Complete information will be furnished upon request.

ORDERING SWITCHES

The switches described in this catalog are the ones commonly used, and are therefore generally carried in stock, ready for immediate shipment.

When ordering switches, please specify:

1. The Bethlehem switch design number.
2. The length of the switch.
3. Weight and section of rail.
4. Gage of track.
5. Drilling for joint connections.

HEAVY-DUTY SWITCHES

Heavy-duty switches have been developed for use primarily in mines where production requires the use of heavy locomotives and large-capacity cars, and where corrosion conditions exist. With the installation of heavy-duty switches, a large percentage of derailments can be eliminated, resulting in greater production and safety, at surprisingly lower cost.

Component Parts. Heavy-duty switches are equipped usually with Bethlehem parallel-throw switch stand Model 1201, or Model 1217, with screw-eye adjustment, and a connecting rod that is 2 ft, or 2 ft 6 in. long. The adjustment feature allows this stand to be used for any switch throw from 2½ in. to 5 in. at the switch head rod, and the points can be quickly adjusted for wear. The operating lever throws parallel to the track, occupies less space, and eliminates accidents. The parallel-throw switch stand is firmly spiked to two ties, and holds the switch points positively in position.

Bethlehem Switch Stand Model 1222 is a parallel-throw stand with 3 ft 10½ in. connecting rod, that is normally used with heavy-duty switches for heavy rails, 70-lb per yard and over.

(See the section, "Bethlehem Switch Stands," pages 45 to 61.)

Heavy Slide-Plates. Slide-plates used with Bethlehem heavy-duty switches have a thickness of ⅜ in., ½ in., or ⅝ in. Three sizes are furnished, as follows: ⅜ in. by 4 in. for 20-lb to 30-lb rails; ½ in. by 5 in. for 40-lb to 70-lb rails; and ⅝ in. by 6 in. for 80-lb to 100-lb rails.

Heavy Side-Jaw Clips. Heavy clips are used with heavy-duty switches, and are made from ⅜-in. stock for 20-lb to 40-lb rails; from ½-in. stock for 60-lb to 100-lb rails. These clips are forged to shape, and are usually riveted to the point. This eliminates the tendency of the wheel flange to shear off the bolt — a common occurrence where bolts are used to fasten clips on light switch points. Bolts are furnished to connect side-jaw clips to the switch rod. Switch points can be furnished equipped with transit clips.

Heavy Switch Braces. Switch braces for heavy-duty switches are made of ⅜-in. open-hearth steel, die-forged to make an accurate fit with the rail section.

Heavy Switch Rods. Switch rods, both head and back, have been made heavier. The rod is ⅝-in. thick for rails from 20-lb to 40-lb, inclusive; and ¾-in. thick for rails from 60-lb to 100-lb, inclusive. As a result, rods have great strength and stiffness, and are not likely to bend and put the switch out of adjustment when a heavy lump of coal or stone falls upon it.

Longer Life Under Corrosive Conditions. Corrosive elements in mines and many industrial installations, particularly where water is acid, cause rapid deterioration of equipment, requiring frequent renewals. Bethlehem heavy-duty switches and parallel-throw switch stands, with their heavy parts, will give far longer service under corrosive conditions.

Recommended Practice. Bethlehem heavy-duty switches are manufactured in standard lengths, and the following practice is suggested:

Design 393: Use this 3 ft 6 in. heavy-duty switch with turnouts No. 1½ to 2, inclusive.

Design 395: Use this 5 ft heavy-duty switch with turnouts No. 2½ to 3, inclusive.

Design 397: Use this 7 ft 6 in. heavy-duty switch with turnouts No. 4 to 6, inclusive.

Design 399: Use this 10 ft heavy-duty switch with turnouts No. 4 to 8.

Design 415: Use this 15 ft heavy-duty switch with turnouts No. 6 to 8.

Particular attention is called also to Bethlehem solid manganese steel frog, Design 289. This frog is recommended for use with heavy-duty switches.

Maximum Safety. Bethlehem heavy-duty switches and parallel-throw switch stands have numerous safety features which contribute toward a reduction in accidents and lower liability costs in mines and industrial plants.

While this heavy equipment weighs about 50 pct more than other types of equipment, it is only slightly more expensive. The moderate difference in cost is a decidedly profitable investment, because it assures maximum safety, longer life, increased output, continuous operation of equipment, lower maintenance, and reduced haulage costs.

HEAVY-DUTY SWITCHES FOR USE WITH WOOD TIES

Design 393   *3 ft 6 in. long*

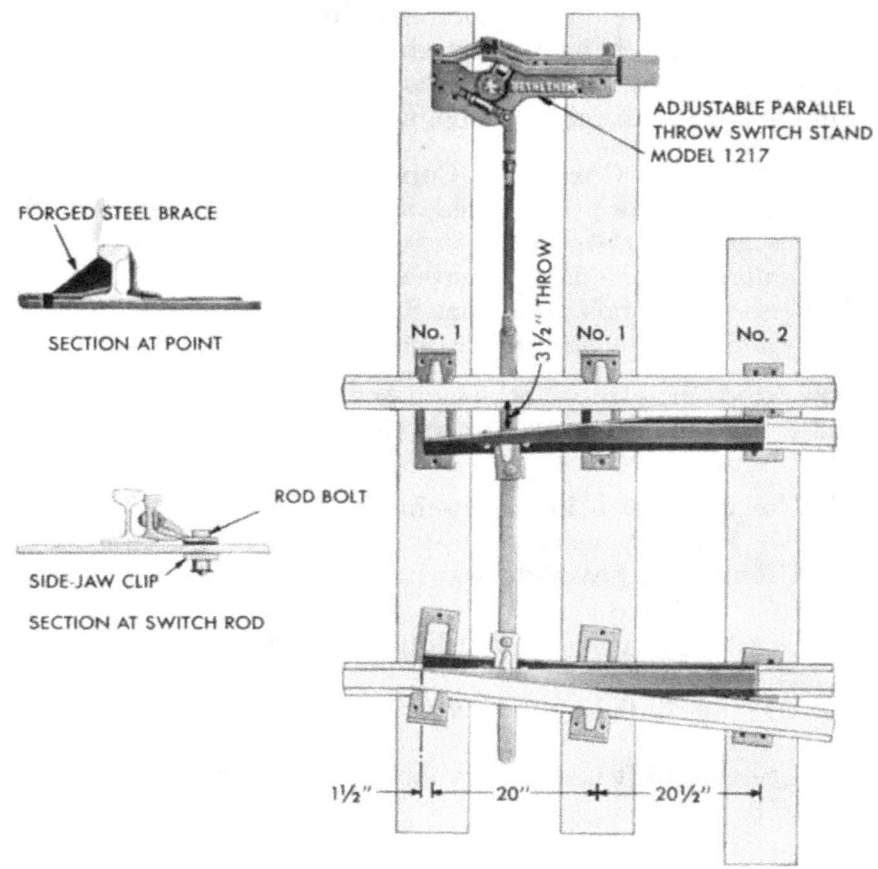

Heavy-duty Bethlehem Switch Design 393 is equipped with the following extra-heavy attachments:

    4 slide plates   4 switch braces
    2 heel plates   1 switch rod
          2 side-jaw clips

These heavy attachments fully protect the switch timbers and insure proper and safe operating conditions at all times.

When ordering switches, specify length and design number, weight and section of rail, gage of track, and drilling for joint connections.

Design 395 5 ft long

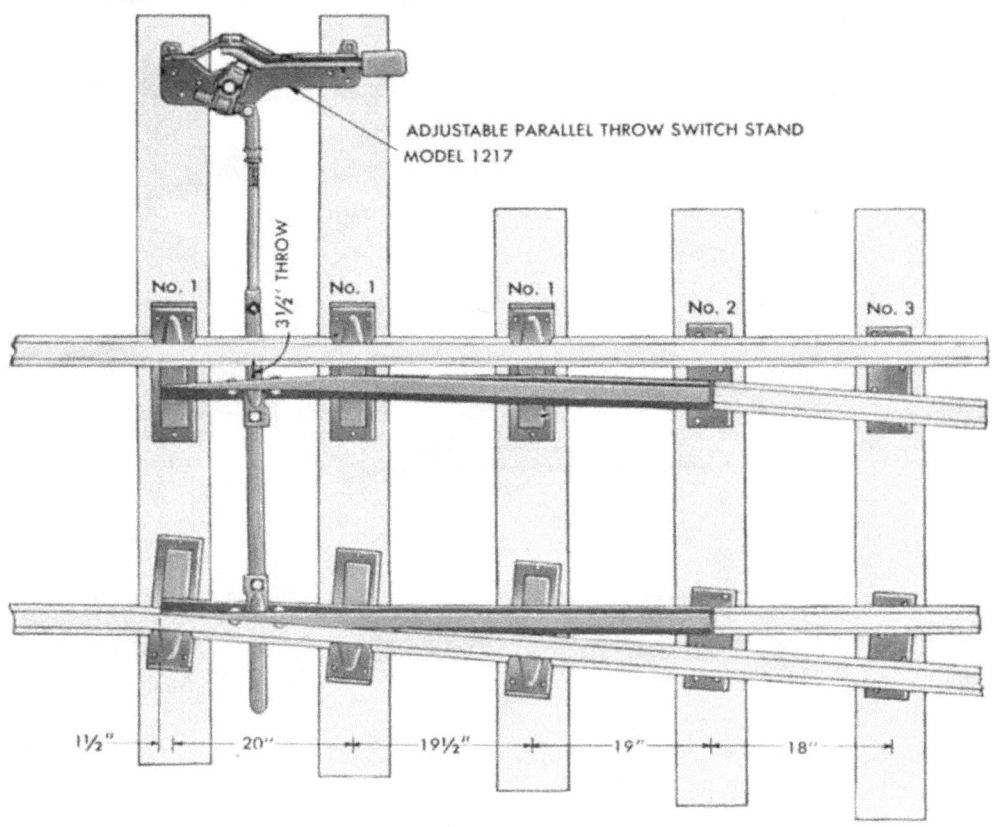

Heavy-duty Bethlehem Switch Design 395 is equipped with the following extra-heavy attachments:

        6 slide plates   6 switch braces
        4 heel plates   1 switch rod
                2 side-jaw clips

In addition to the customary plates and braces at the toe of the switch, intermediate slide plates, heel plates, and braces have been added to fully protect the switch timbers.

When ordering switches, specify length and design number, weight and section of rail, gage of track, and drilling for joint connections.

HEAVY-DUTY SWITCHES FOR USE WITH WOOD TIES

Design 397 *7 ft 6 in. long*

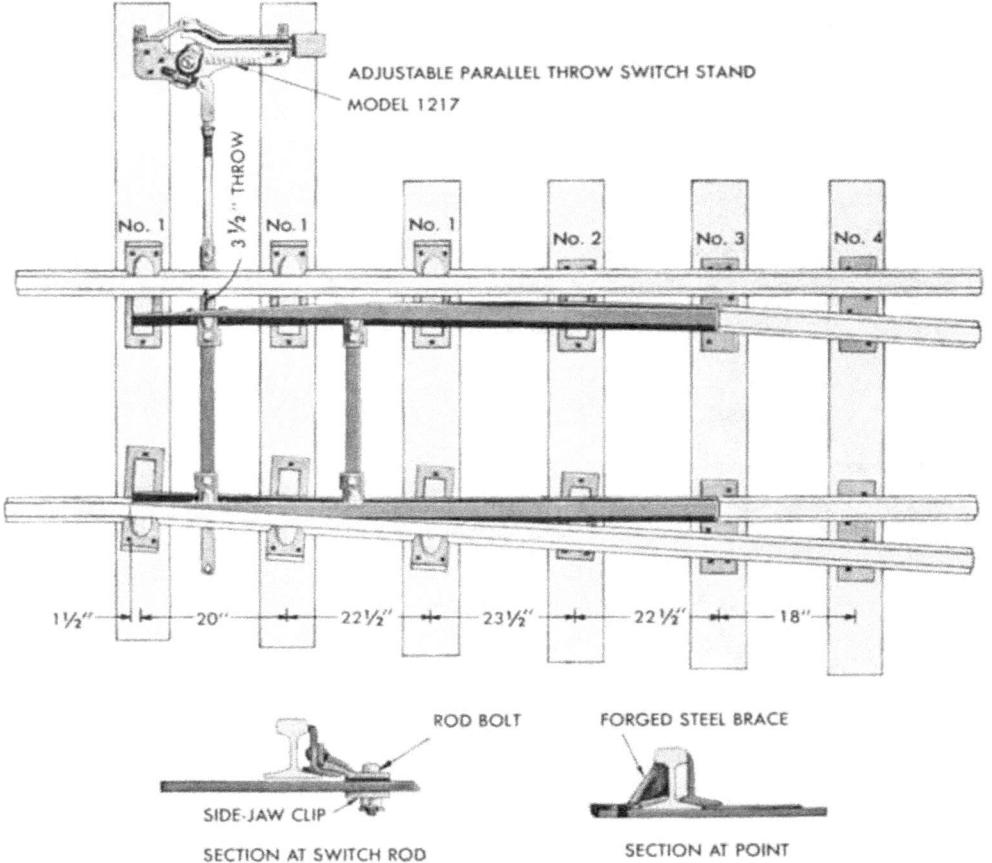

Heavy-duty Bethlehem Switch Design 397 is equipped with the following extra-heavy attachments:

    8 slide plates   6 switch braces
    4 heel plates   2 switch rods
            4 side-jaw clips

In addition to the customary plates and braces at the toe of the switch, intermediate slide plates, heel plates, and braces have been added to fully protect the switch timbers, and to insure proper and safe operating conditions.

When ordering switches, specify length and design number, weight and section of rail, gage of track, and drilling for joint connections.

Design 399   *10 ft long*

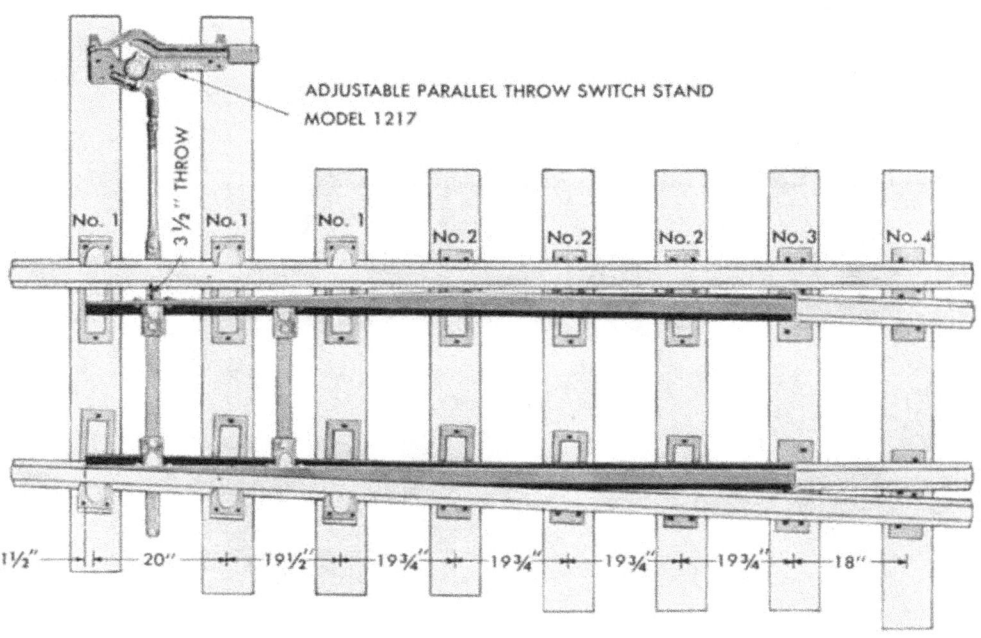

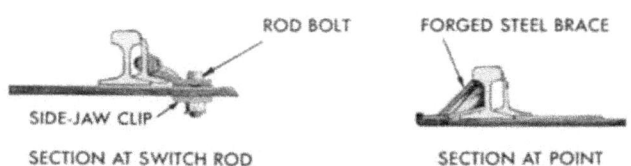

Heavy-duty Bethlehem Switch Design 399 is equipped with the following extra-heavy attachments:

>12 slide plates 6 switch braces
>4 heel plates 2 switch rods
>4 side-jaw clips

Intermediate slide plates, heel plates, and braces have been added, in addition to the customary plates and braces at the toe of the switch, fully protecting the switch timbers and insuring safe operating conditions at all times.

When ordering switches, specify length and design number, weight and section of rail, gage of track, and drilling for joint connections.

HEAVY-DUTY SWITCH FOR USE WITH WOOD TIES

Design 415

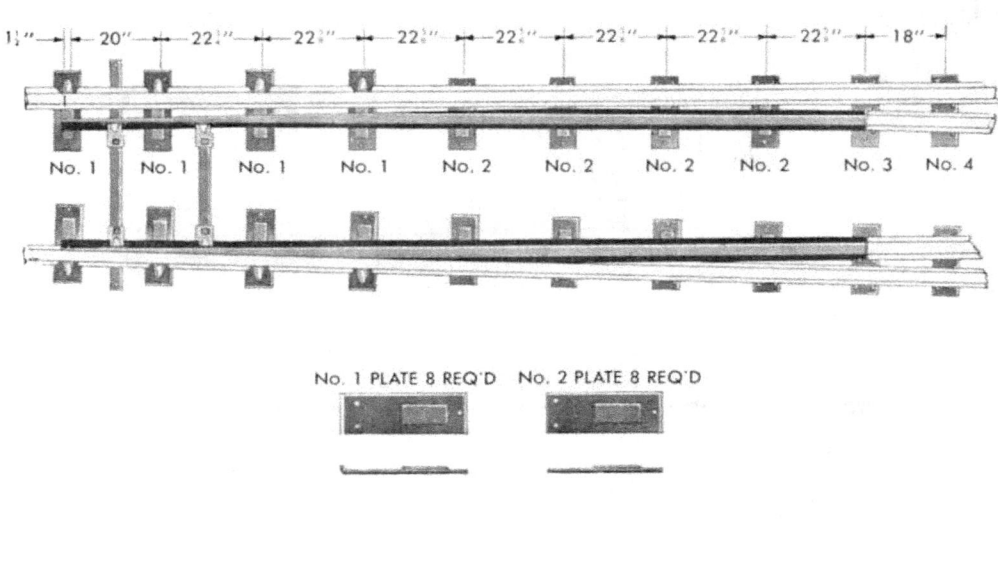

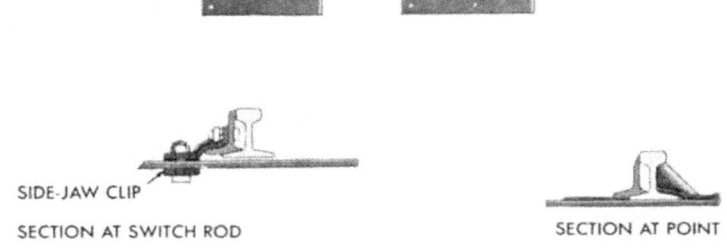

The switch shown here is a heavy-duty design complete with two switch rods, eight forged steel rail braces, and switch tie plates clear back beyond the heel of the switch. It is intended for railroad sidings for tipple tracks and industrial plants where severe service is encountered.

This switch is normally furnished 15 ft 0 in. long, as shown above, but it can be made 16 ft 6 in. long, for any heavy rail section.

When ordering switches, specify the length, design number, weight and section of rail, gage of track, and drilling for joint connections.

SWITCH DESIGN FOR MEDIUM DUTY

Design 365

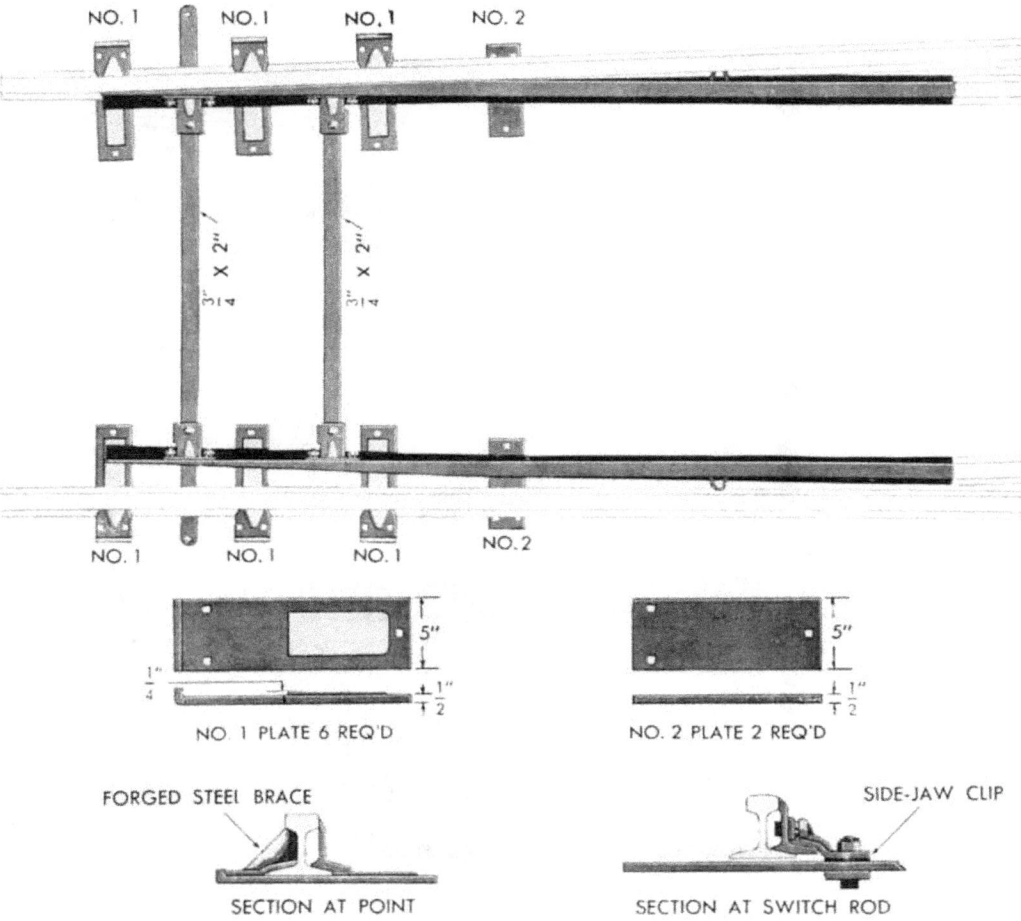

Bethlehem Switch Design 365 is constantly increasing in popularity because of its balanced design and moderate cost. Slide plates are heavy, being ½-in. thick and 5-in. wide. Rail braces are made of forged steel, ⅜-in. thick. Two switch rods are furnished, ¾-in. by 2 in. Side-jaw clips are of forged steel, ½-in. thick.

This switch can be made of rails of any weight up to 100 lb, and in lengths of 10 ft and 15 ft.

When ordering switches, specify length and design number, weight and section of rail, gage of track, and drilling for joint connections.

SWITCH FOR USE
WITH STEEL SWITCH TIE SETS

Design 388

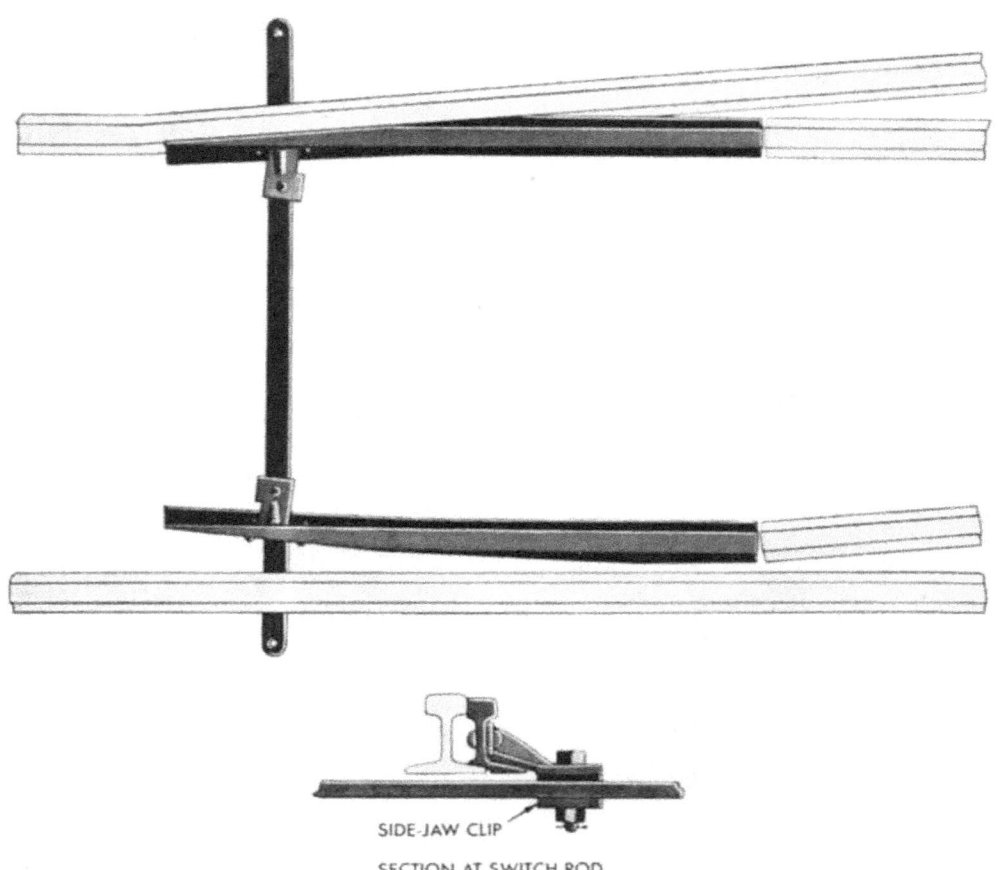

Bethlehem Switch Design 388 is especially adapted for use with steel switch tie sets. It consists of a pair of switch points with forged steel side-jaw clips attached, and a switch rod of the rigid type. No rail braces or switch slide plates are needed.

This switch is made in lengths of 3 ft, 3 ft 6 in., 4 ft, 5 ft, 6 ft, and 7 ft 6 in., for rails 20 lb to 80 lb.

When ordering switches, specify length and design number, weight and section of rail, gage of track, and drilling for joint connections.

SWITCHES FOR USE WITH WOOD TIES

Design 392 *(With Rail Braces)*

Design 389 *(Without Rail Braces)*

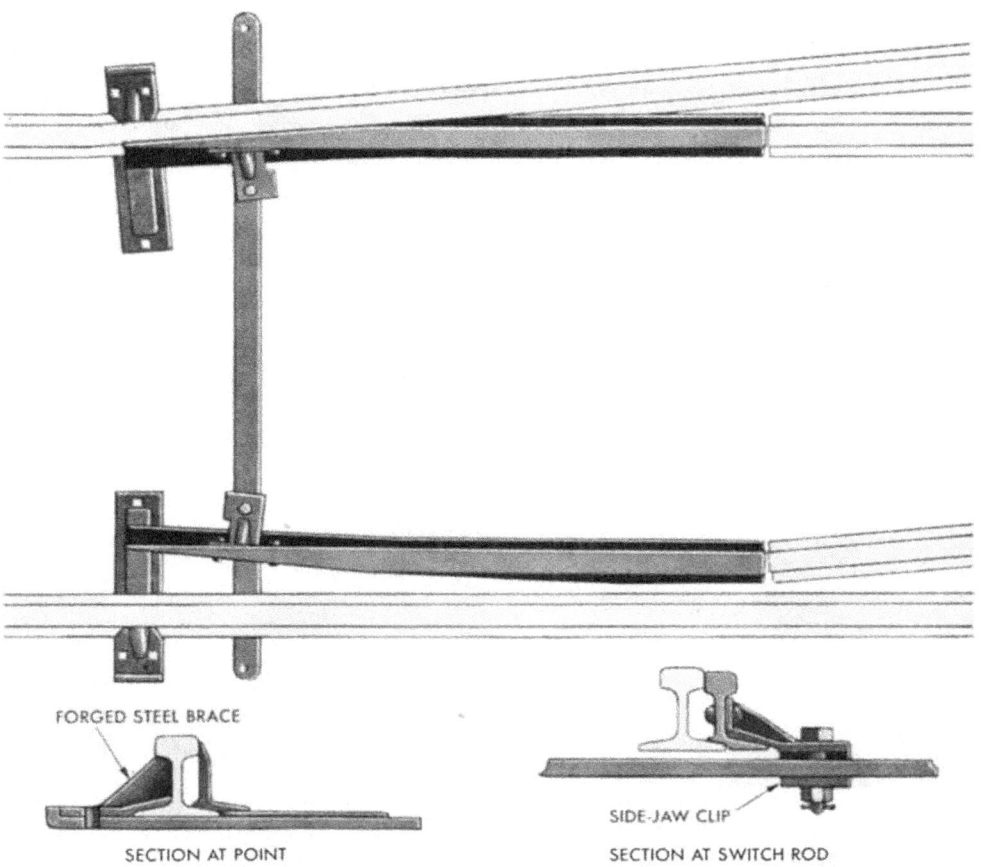

Bethlehem Switch Design 392 is a simple switch equipped with two slide plates, two forged steel rail braces, two side-jaw clips of forged steel, and a switch rod of the rigid type.

Bethlehem Switch Design 389 is of the same general type as Design 392, except that the two rail braces are omitted, and plain riser plates are furnished.

Switch Designs 392 and 389 are made in lengths of 3 ft, 3 ft 6 in., 4 ft, 5 ft, 6 ft, and 7 ft 6 in., and for rails 20 lb to 60 lb.

When ordering switches, specify length and design number, weight and section of rail, gage of track, and drilling for joint connections.

SWITCHES FOR USE WITH WOOD TIES

Design 390 *(With Rail Braces)*
Design 391 *(Without Rail Braces)*

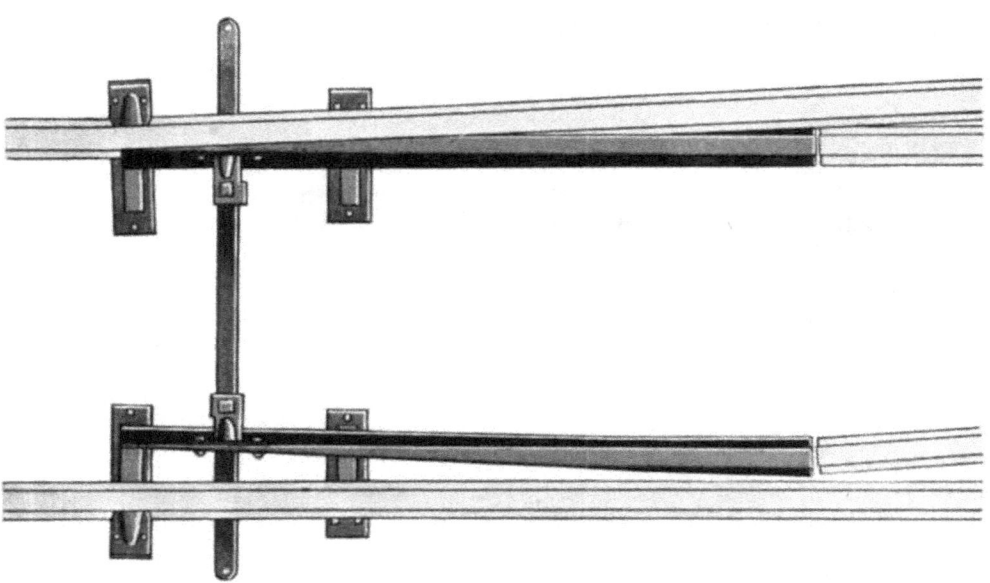

SECTION AT POINT

SECTION AT SWITCH ROD

Bethlehem Switch Design 390 is an inexpensive switch, equipped with four slide plates, two rail braces, two side-jaw clips of forged steel, and a switch rod of the rigid type.

Bethlehem Switch Design 391 is of the same general type as Design 390 except that the switch rail braces are omitted.

Switch Designs 390 and 391 are made in lengths of 3 ft, 3 ft 6 in., 4 ft, 5 ft, and 7 ft 6 in., and for rails 20 lb to 60 lb. For more important locations we recommend heavy-duty Bethlehem Switch Designs 393 to 399, inclusive.

When ordering switches, specify length and design number, weight and section of rail, gage of track, and drilling for joint connections.

SWITCH HEEL JOINTS

Switch heel joints are available to prevent unnecessary looseness at the heel of the switch points. The switch heel joint has either one or two pipe thimbles welded to one bar of the joint, which are inserted through holes in the switch point, and fastened with track bolts. This necessitates special holes in the switch point, through which both the thimble and the track bolt are inserted. The second joint bar is bent slightly. This construction allows the bolts to be drawn up tightly so the switch point is held firmly, and at the same time is allowed to move freely.

The switch heel joint is made of splice-bar sections. A joint consists of two joint bars, and the necessary track bolts.

Switch Length	Joints
6-ft long, and shorter	3-hole
Over 6-ft long	4-hole

Design 990

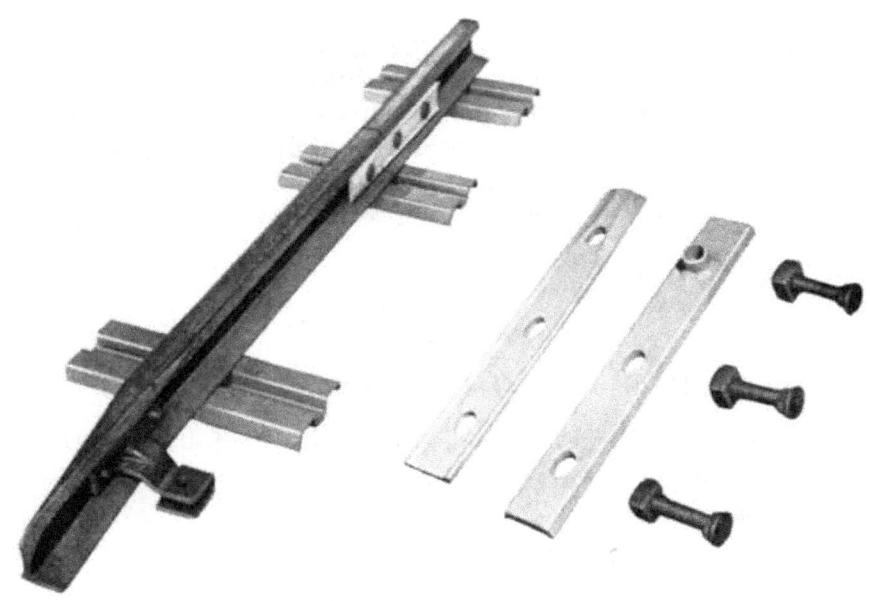

How to Install a Switch Heel Joint

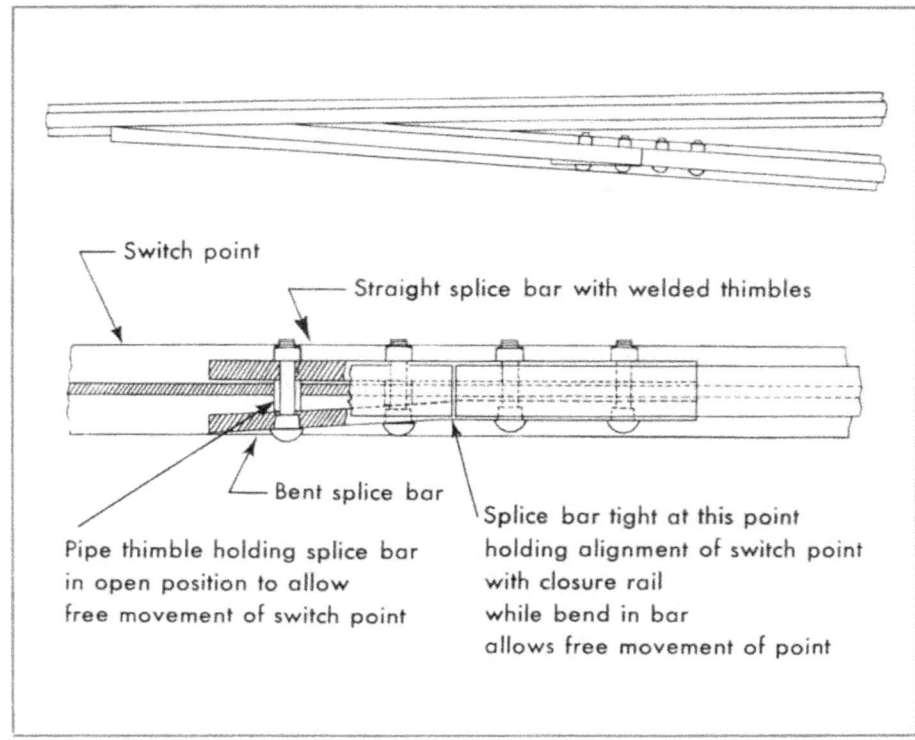

Recommended method of attaching a switch heel joint.

The recommended method of attaching a switch heel joint to a switch is illustrated in the drawing, above. Special holes to fit the thimbles are drilled in the switch point. This method permits the switch heel joint to be drawn up absolutely tight, so the switch point is held firmly and at the same time allowed to move freely. The switch heel joint is made of plain splice bars only.

Ordering Switch Heel Joint, Design 990

When ordering switch heel joints, please specify the following:
1. Number of joints (half RH, and half LH).
2. Length of switch.
3. Weight and section of rail.
4. Rail drilling (unless standard drilling is desired).

SWITCH HEEL BLOCK JOINT

Design 992

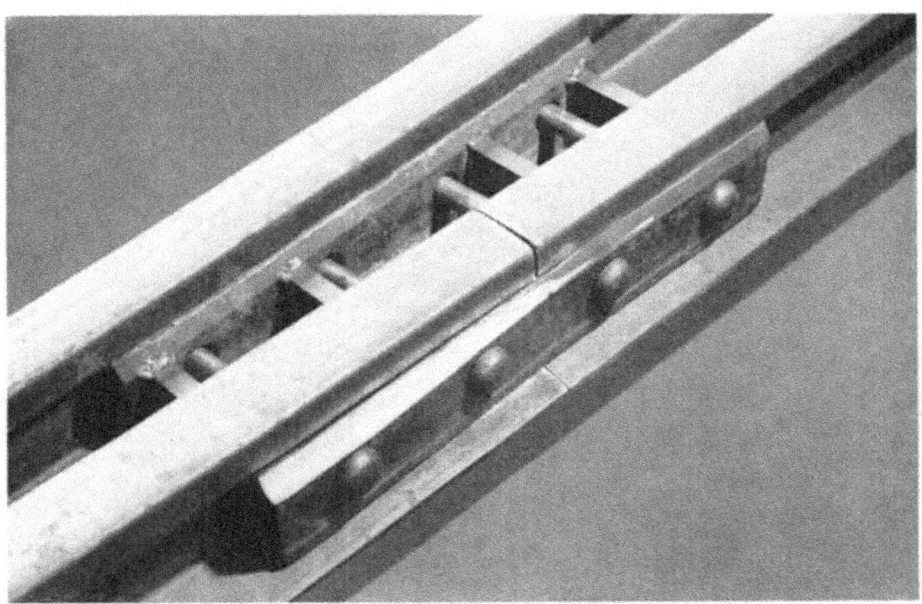

Close-up of Bethlehem Switch Heel Block Joint shows block in place between closure rail (right) and stock rail. Switch point is at lower left.

An important adjunct to any dependable, high-speed turnout is Bethlehem's new Switch Heel Block Joint. The heel block, welded together from tough rolled-steel components, can be made to fit switches of any length, and rail of any weight. A joint consists of the heel block and two splice plates and necessary long bolts.

This switch heel block joint does two things: (1) it adds safety to the switch; and (2) maintains gage at the heel end of a switch, keeping closure rail and switch point in correct alignment, both vertically and horizontally.

All bolts can be tightened without interfering with lateral movement of switch points.

When ordering switches, just specify "Equipped with Bethlehem Switch Heel Block Joints, Design 992," advising:

1. Number of joints (half RH, and half LH).
2. Length of switch.
3. Weight and section of rail.
4. Rail drilling (unless standard drilling is desired).

BETHLEHEM Winter King SWITCH HEATERS

Kerosene-burning Bethlehem *Winter King* Switch Heaters fit between the ties under the stock rails and switch points. They furnish constant heat and melt the snow as it falls. The shielded flame keeps burning, even in gusty winds.

Features. The heater itself consists of a box made of welded copper-bearing rust-resisting steel, 18-in. long, 4½-in. wide, and 5½-in. high. The two flanges at the burner end, which throw the heat against the rails and maintain the proper distance between wick and rail, increase the overall height to 7½ in. The wick is of rock-wool material, and is always in place when the heater is shipped. Groups of heaters can be stacked in a small amount of space for storage.

These heaters require virtually no attention except refilling. The fuel chamber has a capacity of 1½ gallons of kerosene, which is usually sufficient for from nine to fifteen hours of burning.

Write the nearest Bethlehem Steel Company office for Folder 602, which describes the installation and use of Bethlehem *Winter King* Switch Heaters.

Bethlehem Trackwork has served this haulageway well for many years.

This is the Bethlehem Model 1222 Switch Stand installed in a brand-new track layout. The stand is especially designed for use with heavy rails weighing 70-lb and over.

BETHLEHEM SWITCH STANDS

For nearly 80 years Bethlehem Steel Company has been manufacturing switch stands. During this long period Bethlehem engineers have designed and built all types, sizes and designs of stands for standard and narrow-gage service.

All the switch stands described in this catalog are of the parallel-throw type — a design of definite superiority for safe use in mine and industrial trackage. Both positive and automatic types are shown, each having its particular advantages.

POSITIVE-ACTION SWITCH STANDS

A positive-action switch stand is one that locks the points into position when it is fully thrown, and cannot be used for trailing movements. They are recommended for main-track locations, and the more important switches on a property. In this group are Bethlehem Models 1201, 1217, 1222, and 51-A New Century (when equipped with latches for positive action.)

AUTOMATIC SWITCH STANDS

An automatic switch stand is one that combines the features of a rigid stand with a spring mechanism to permit run-through movements without damage to either the stand or component parts of the switch. Automatic switch stands are recommended for yard, siding and ladder tracks, for use with standard tee rails, 60 lb per yd and over, where normal operations require provisions for trailing movements. Bethlehem Model 22 is a fully-automatic type.

Any of the positive-action stands shown may be furnished with spring rods, and when so equipped can be trailed through without injury to any part of the switch or switch stand mechanism.

INTERCHANGEABLE PARTS ON ALL MODELS

One of the outstanding features of Bethlehem switch stand design is the interchangeability of parts on all models, regardless of age. New parts and old parts can be used together, increasing the useful life of Bethlehem switch stands. A complete inventory of switch stands and parts is maintained, insuring prompt shipments to customers.

ORDERING BETHLEHEM SWITCH STANDS

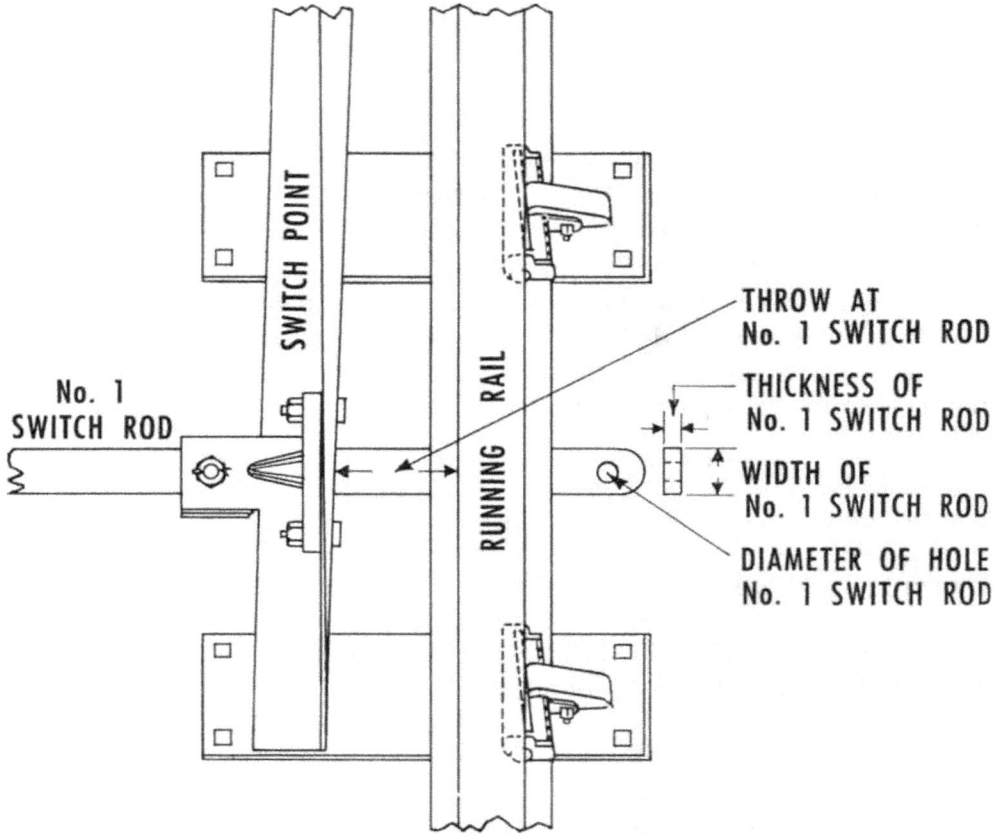

The following information should be given when ordering Bethlehem Switch Stands:

1. Model number of switch stand.
2. Throw of switch point at No. 1 switch rod.
3. Thickness and width of No. 1 switch rod.
4. Diameter of hole in No. 1 switch rod.
5. Design and color of targets, if any.
6. Type number of lamp tip.
7. Style and length of connecting rod (center to center of holes). If possible, standard lengths should be selected.
8. Model and type numbers of cranks wanted (when ordering Model 51-A).
9. Model and type numbers of switch stand accessories.

PARALLEL-THROW SWITCH STAND FOR LIGHT RAILS

Model 1201

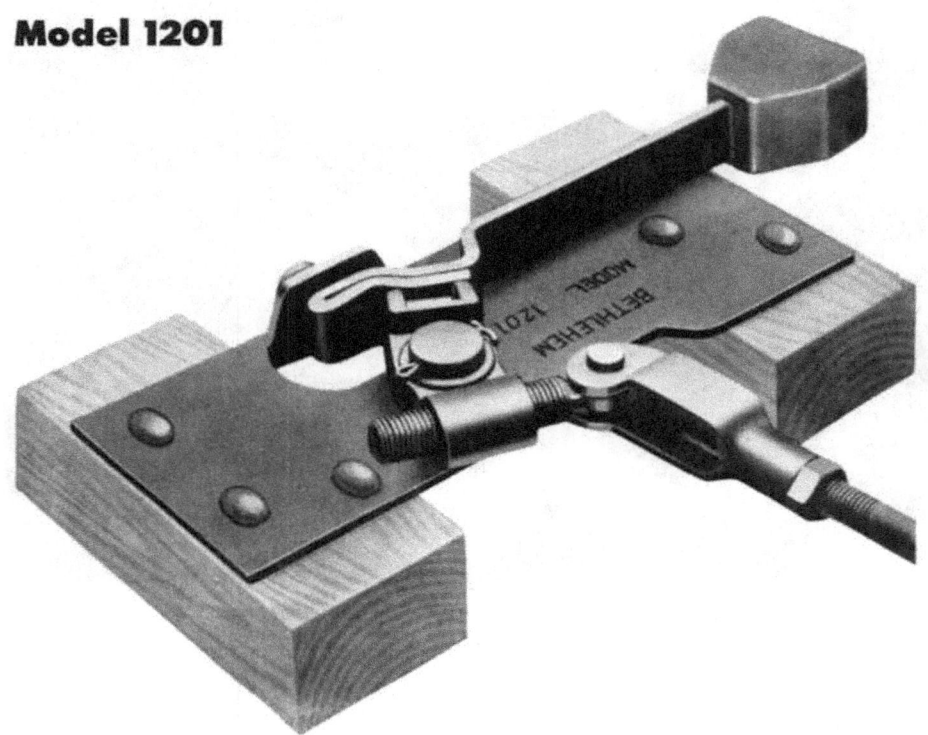

Bethlehem Switch Stand Model 1201 is a parallel-throw switch stand for use with rails up to 40 lb, inclusive. It has a height of only 3 in. measured from the top of the ties. All moving parts are above the ties, where they are readily accessible and free from dirt.

Self-Cleaning. Model 1201 is self-cleaning. A slot in the base beneath the sliding block allows dirt to pass through the space between the ties. The crank is slotted to prevent clogging.

Adjustable Throw. Easy and quick adjustment of the throw of the switch is provided by an adjustable screw-eye. Range of adjustment is from 2½ to 5 in.

Positive Action. When in the down position, the weighted lever will not move unless thrown manually, and requires no latches. If desired, this stand can be made automatic by the use of a spring connecting rod, Design 832.

Connecting Rod. The standard connecting rod used with this stand is Rigid Rod No. 8-VMS. The length of the rod is 2 ft, center to center of holes.

Bethlehem Model 1201 Switch Stand is ideal for room turnouts.

Rugged Construction. With the exception of the weight on the throwing lever, Model 1201 is made of rolled or forged steel. The weighted throwing lever (operated parallel to the track), insures safety to the operator, makes throwing easier, and provides positive closing of the switch points.

There are no bolts in the construction. The stand can be easily disassembled in the field, by simply removing one cotter pin. Model 1201 has only three moving parts: the throwing lever, the crank and the sliding block.

INSTALLING MODEL 1201 SWITCH STAND

Before spiking the stand, set the switch points at exactly one-half the throw. Raise the throwing lever until the screw-eye is parallel to the rail, and then fasten the connecting rod to the No. 1 switch rod, and spike down the stand.

If it is found, after spiking down the switch stand, that either switch point does not fit properly against the stock rail, this condition can be corrected by simply adjusting either the screw-eye on the stand, or the clevis on the rod, or both.

COMPONENT PARTS FOR MODEL 1201 SWITCH STAND

BASE No. 2305
Wide base of pressed rolled steel.

SLIDING BLOCK No. 1404
Made of rolled steel, machined. Can be used on all four sides for long life.

CRANK No. 2276
Made of forged steel, machined and threaded.

SCREW-EYE No. 1499
For use in Crank No. 2276. Six threads to the inch. Adjustment range: 2½ to 5 in.

LEVER No. 1952
Rolled steel lever, assembled with pinion shaft, 15-lb cast-iron handle.

Rigid Rod and Parts

CLEVIS No. 2273
Made of forged steel, machined, and threaded for Rigid Rod No. 8VMS.

RIGID ROD No. 8VMS (Complete)
Made of forged steel. Length, center to center of holes: 2 ft.

PIN No. 2274 **BOLT No. 425** **WASHER No. 1411** **COTTER PIN No. 1417**

Spring Rod and Parts

BOLT No. 2210

SPRING ROD No. 832 (Complete)
Springs are of heat-treated alloy steel. Length, center to center of holes: 2 ft.

THREADED ROD No. 2203 **PIN No. 1619** **WASHERS No. 2206**

CLEVIS No. 2205 **CAP No. 2212** **CASING No. 2204**

SPRING No. 0558 **FERRULES No. 1616** **JAM NUT No. 2211**

Please order all parts by name and number.

PARALLEL-THROW SWITCH STAND FOR LIGHT RAILS

Model 1217

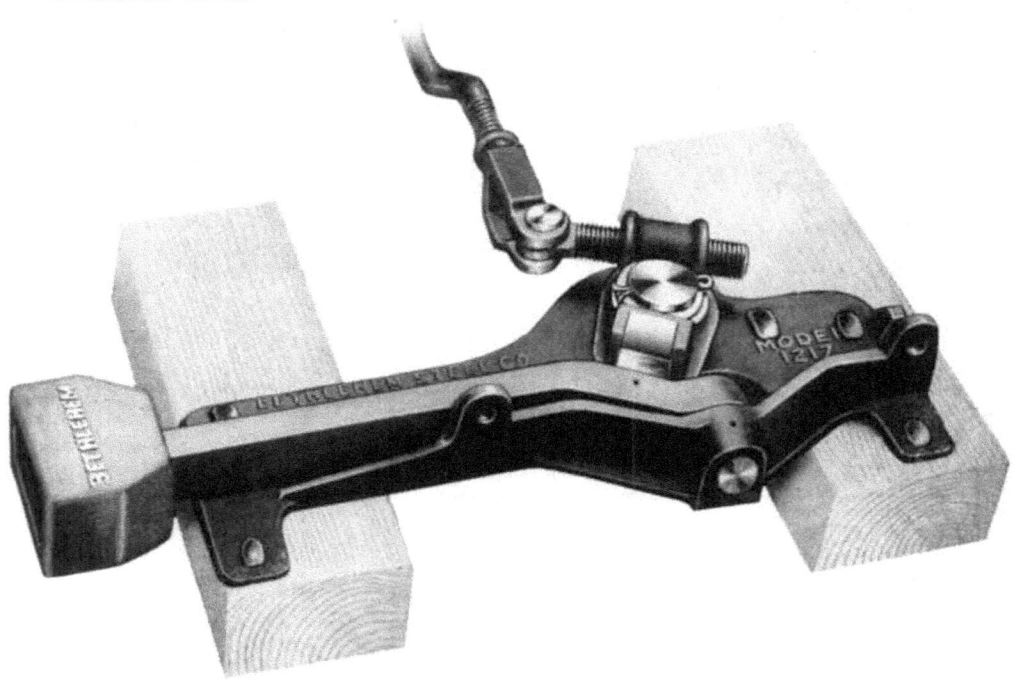

Bethlehem Parallel-Throw Model 1217 is a switch stand for use with rails up to 60 lb, inclusive, in mines, tunnels and surface industrial track. This stand is recommended for locations where low height and maximum safety are chief requirements.

Self-Cleaning. Model 1217 is self-cleaning. A slot in the base beneath the sliding block allows dirt to pass through the space between the ties. The crank is slotted to prevent clogging.

Adjustable Throw. Easy and quick adjustment of the throw of the switch is provided by an adjustable screw-eye. Range of adjustment is from 2½ to 5 in.

Positive Action. When in the down position the weighted lever will not move unless thrown manually, and requires no latches. If desired, this stand can be made automatic by the use of a spring connecting rod, Design 829.

Connecting Rod. The standard connecting rod used with this stand is Rigid Rod No. 8-VM. The rod is made of forged steel and is 2 ft 6 in. long, center to center of holes.

Three Inches High. The height from the top of the tie to the top of the stand is only 3 in. All working parts are above the ties. Made of forged steel or malleable iron for maximum strength. There are only three moving parts: the throwing lever, the crank and the sliding block. No rivets, bolts or set screws are used in the stand. Model 1217 can be quickly dismantled by removing one cotter pin.

INSTALLING MODEL 1217 SWITCH STAND

Model 1217 is easy to install, and is fully adjustable. Before spiking the stand, set the switch points at exactly one-half the throw. Raise the throwing lever until the screw-eye is parallel to the rail. Then fasten the connecting rod to the No. 1 switch rod, and spike down the stand.

If it is found, after spiking down the switch stand, that either switch point does not fit properly against the stock rail, this condition can be corrected by simply adjusting either the screw-eye on the stand, or the clevis on the rod, or both.

Bethlehem Switch Stands are standard equipment at this well-managed mine.

COMPONENT PARTS FOR MODEL 1217 SWITCH STAND

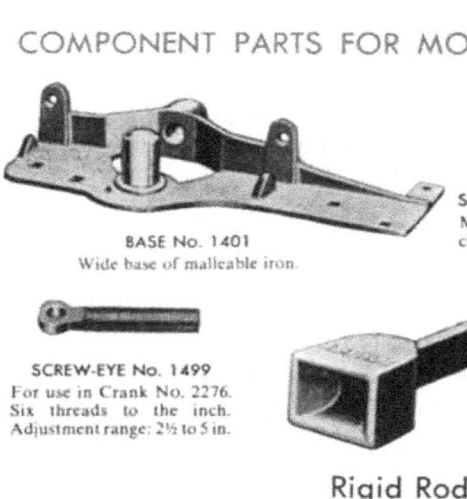

BASE No. 1401
Wide base of malleable iron.

SLIDING BLOCK No. 1404
Made of rolled steel, machined. Can be used on all four sides for long life.

CRANK No. 2276
Made of forged steel, machined and threaded.

SCREW-EYE No. 1499
For use in Crank No. 2276. Six threads to the inch. Adjustment range: 2½ to 5 in.

LEVER No. 1459
Rolled steel lever, assembled with pinion shaft, 15-lb cast-iron handle.

Rigid Rod and Parts

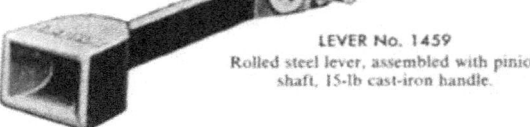

CLEVIS No. 2273
Made of forged steel, machined, and threaded for Rigid Rod No. 8VM

RIGID ROD No. 8VM (Complete)
Made of forged steel. Length, center to center of holes: 2 ft. 6 in.

PIN No. 2274 **BOLT No. 425** **WASHER No. 1411** **COTTER PIN No. 1417**

Spring Rod and Parts

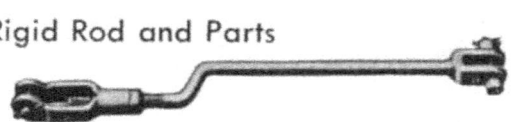

BOLT No. 2210

SPRING ROD DESIGN No. 829 (Complete)
Springs are of heat-treated alloy steel. Length, center to center of holes: 2 ft. 6 in.

THREADED ROD No. 2271 **PIN No. 1619** **WASHERS No. 2206**

CLEVIS No. 2205 **CAP No. 2212** **CASING No. 2270**

SPRING No. 0554 **FERRULES No. 1616** **JAM NUT No. 2211**

PARTS REQUIRED FOR MODEL 1217-T

PLUG LAMP TIP No. 1645 **TARGET CRANK No. 1498** **TARGET OPERATING ROD No. 1440**

Please order all parts by name and number.

PARALLEL-THROW SWITCH STAND WITH REFLECTOR TARGET

Model 1217-T

The switch stand shown here is the dependable Model 1217, with a built-on reflector target, and is designated as Model 1217-T. The target swings automatically through a 90-deg arc when the switch points are thrown. It is equipped with two red and two green 3-in. reflectors, which stand out brilliantly when a locomotive headlight is beamed on them. The motorman can see them so far away that he can control his trip with safety. The brakeman, too, is aided by the large, brilliant reflectors which pick up his cap-light and enable him to locate the stand quickly.

The reflector target is an integral part of Model 1217 stand. There are no extra connecting rods to install, no extra holes to drill in switch rods, no tie extensions. The position of the red and green reflectors can easily be reversed by removing two bolts and inverting the target-blade assembly.

The top of the target is a bare 12 in. above the ties, and being an integral part of the switch stand, it presents no installation problems.

PARALLEL-THROW SWITCH STAND FOR HEAVY RAILS

Model 1222

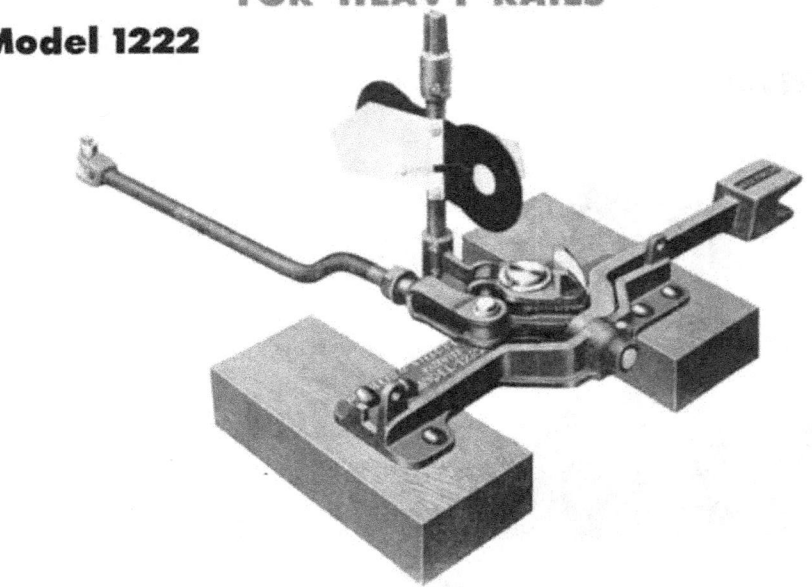

Bethlehem Switch Stand Model 1222 is a positive-type stand with great strength, maximum safety and easy operation. Model 1222 is for use with heavy rails 70 lb and over.

Positive Action. This stand is of the gearless type. It operates on the sliding block-and-crank principle, so it has a great leverage advantage which makes it easy to throw the heaviest type of switches.

When in the down position, the weighted lever will not move unless thrown manually, and requires no latches. However, locking holes are provided in the base to padlock the lever in either position. There are only three moving parts; no bolts, set screws, or rivets are used in the construction. All working parts are above the ties.

Adjustable Throw. An adjustable crank of the screw-eye type is provided, allowing easy and quick adjustment for length of throw. Range of switch throw is from 3½ to 6 in.

Extra Low. An unusual feature of Model 1222 is the low overall height of 3¾ in. from the top of the tie to the bearing flange of the lamp tip, making the stand especially useful for confined locations. Spring rods can be furnished when specified. The stand can also be equipped with a special crank to carry a standard target lamp, or target only. Also, it can be furnished with a reflector target, similar to the one shown on Model 1217-T, page 53.

Connecting Rods. The following connecting rods can be used with Model 1222: 11-HU and 11-UA (Rigid, Single-Adjustable Rods), 11-UY (Lorenz Rod), 11-SFU (Spring Rod).

COMPONENT PARTS FOR MODEL 1222 SWITCH STAND

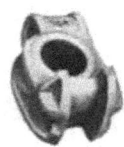

CRANK No. 1641
For use *without* target. Made of malleable iron, machined.

BASE No. 1902
Made of malleable iron.

CRANK No. 1640
For use with target. Made of malleable iron, machined.

ADJUSTABLE SCREW-EYE No. 1471
Made of forged special-analysis steel, heat-treated.
Range of adjustment from 3½ to 6 in.

THROWING LEVER No. 1643
Made of rolled steel, with 18 lb cast-iron handle.

11 UA STANDARD RIGID ROD — 3′ 6″ LONG

11 SFU SPRING ROD — 3′ 10½″ LONG

TARGET MAST 1644

PLUG LAMP TIP 1645

SLIDING BLOCK No. 1642
For use with either Crank No. 1640, or Crank No. 1641. Made of forged special-analysis steel, heat-treated, machined.

SOCKET LAMP TIP 127
For use with target mast

OIL CUP No. 1903

COTTER PIN No. 1677

WASHER No. 1438

Please order all parts by name and number.

PARALLEL-THROW SWITCH STAND FOR HEAVY RAILS

New Century Model 51-A *(Adjustable)*

New Century Model 51-A is recommended for use with heavy rails, 70 lb per yd and over, at all points of heavy traffic on main lines, branch lines, or in the yards. It is furnished in two styles: with plug lamp tip, for use with switch lamp having day target discs; and with socket lamp tip for use with a low target.

Construction. Model 51-A is a covered, low parallel-throw switch stand of unusually heavy construction. It is of gear-type construction, as distinguished from the sliding-block design of other types of Bethlehem switch stands. It can be made positive by the use of two Model 465 latches.

Adjustment. Model 51-A has an adjustment feature by which switch point clearances can be adjusted from inside the stand without disconnecting the stand from the rods. Adjustments are made by means of shims which adjust (but do not entirely remove) the free play on either side of the spindle lug. The shims are easy to reach in storage spaces under the adjustment cover at the top of the stand.

The adjustment is quickly and easily made. The only tool required is a hand wrench. If a switch point is not tight against the stock rail, the clearance is adjusted by transferring a sufficient number of shims from the storage space to slots on either side of the spindle lug. This increases the throw of the points by taking up some of the play between spindle lug and segment gear.

During adjustment, the points and stand are constantly in service. The range of switch point throw is about ⅛ in. per shim. The maximum adjustment of either of the switch points is approximately ¾ in.

Safe and Easy to Operate. Model 51-A is safe and easy to throw. The throwing lever swings through an arc of 30 deg before the mechanism begins to move the switch points. When the switch points begin to move, the momentum of the 30-lb weight helps the operator carry the lever through.

Connecting Rods. The following connecting rods can be used with New Century Model 51-A: 11-AN (Rigid, Non-Adjustable Rod), 11-TN (Rigid, Single-Adjustable Rod), 10-SFN (Spring Rod), 10-NY (Lorenz Rod).

The cover of Bethlehem Model 51-A Switch Stand provides access to adjustment shims.

COMPONENT PARTS FOR MODEL 51-A SWITCH STAND

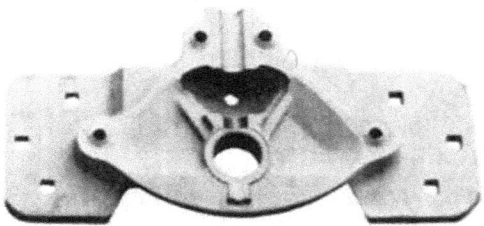

BOTTOM No. 43
Wide, heavy base of cast iron.

SPINDLE No. 63
Made of forged steel.

TOP No. 41
Made of cast iron.

THROWING LEVER No. 18
A rolled steel lever, assembled with pinion shaft and pinion gear.
30-lb cast iron weighted handle.

DOUBLE CRANK No. 69
Made of malleable iron.
Breakable, for yard use.

DOUBLE CRANK No. 1216
Made of forged steel for
main line use.

SINGLE CRANK No. 67
Made of forged steel for
main line use.

**ADJUSTABLE
GEAR SEGMENT No. 49**
Made of malleable iron.

THROWING LEVER REST No. 463

COVER No. 39
Made of malleable iron.

ADJUSTMENT BOLT No. 54

CROSS PIN No. 2228
Special shear-resistant steel.
RING No. 1611
This ring serves as a lock for cross
pin No. 2228.

**ADJUSTMENT SHIM
SET No. 1824**

Please order all parts by name and number.

BETHLEHEM AUTOMATIC SWITCH STAND

Model 22

Bethlehem Model 22 is an *automatic* switch stand sturdily built to stand up under the heavy abuse of continuous "run-through" operations. It is recommended for use with heavy rails, 70 lb and over, for all yard, siding and ladder tracks where frequent movements of trains require spring action, or for any switch location where there is a likelihood that the switch will be "run through."

Model 22 switch stand has been designed to eliminate the damage and delays that are caused when a rigid stand is subjected to "run-through" movements. When a Model 22 is used to replace a rigid stand and is "run through" in a trailing movement, the switch points are moved to the new position *automatically*. Another feature of Model 22 is that the hand lever can be used to set the switch points in either position for train movements.

Safe, Dependable Operation. In a "run-through" movement using the Model 22 switch stand, the first set of wheels moves the switch points to the new position. The movement is completed by a powerful spring mechanism. The points remain in the new position until reset by the switch being again "run through," or changed by throwing the switch-stand lever. The target changes with the points to show the new routing, but the lever remains unchanged until thrown by hand.

Strong, Sturdy Construction. The number of working parts has been kept to a minimum. Vital parts such as the swivel link, link and pins, and screw-eye are heat-treated for extra strength and durability. The base is of malleable iron, and has an extra-large bearing area on the ties for added rigidity. Model 22 uses a screw-eye crank, providing easy adjustment for the throw of the switch points. The height of the stand from the tie to the top of the lamp tip is 1 ft 5 in.

SAFETY FEATURES

Special safety features have been built into Model 22. For example, in automatic operation there is no reflex movement of the throwing lever, and therefore no latches are required to hold the arm in either position. All working parts are enclosed in a housing, shielding the mechanism from the elements.

There is a recoil of the spring-bolt when the switch is thrown automatically. This recoil takes place inside the housing. The bolt is in correct adjustment when the stand is assembled, and no further adjustment is necessary during the life of the automatic switch stand.

COMPONENT PARTS FOR MODEL 22

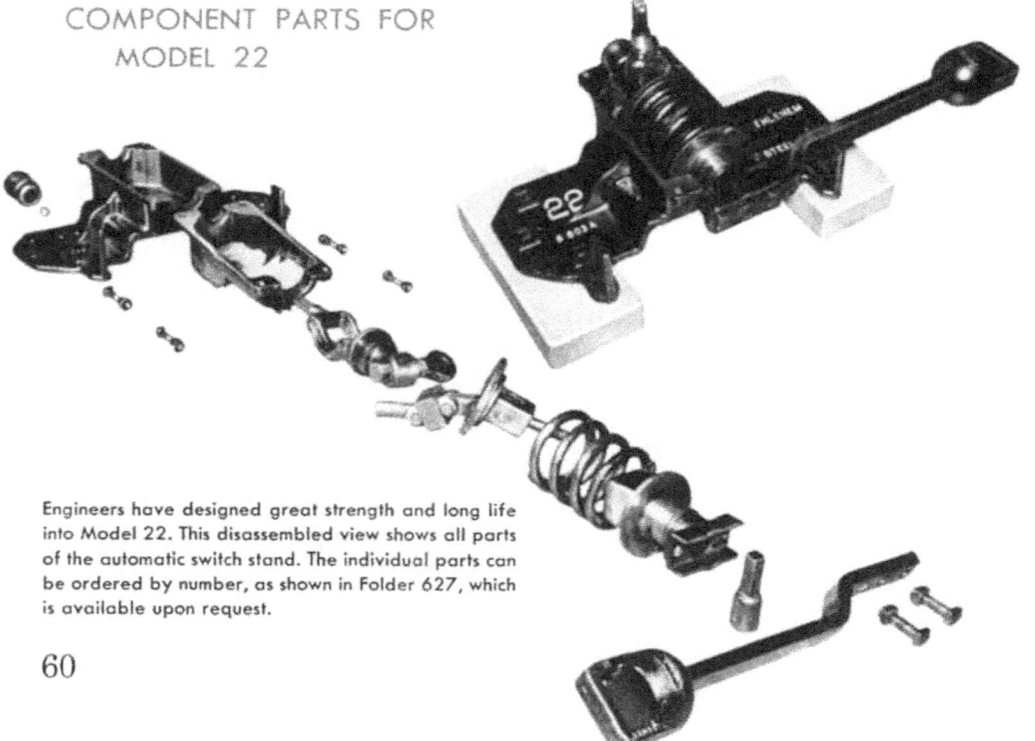

Engineers have designed great strength and long life into Model 22. This disassembled view shows all parts of the automatic switch stand. The individual parts can be ordered by number, as shown in Folder 627, which is available upon request.

BETHLEHEM TARGET STAND
Model 1205

Whenever trips approach turnouts or crossovers at high speed, safety considerations demand that the motorman be warned of the switch setting. This can be done economically with Bethlehem Target Stand Model 1205. The stand is a low-type, one-tie target stand of the reflector type, used with switch stands for track up to 85 lb per yd, inclusive. It is furnished complete with a connecting rod. No additional parts are needed to complete the assembly.

The target stand can be installed on either wood or steel ties, as shown above. The red and green reflectors have a 3-in. diameter which reflects a clear penetrating gleam from the headlight at 500 or more feet away. Model 1205 operates from the No. 1 switch rod, usually on the opposite side of the track from the switch stand. The minimum height to the top of the target is 12 in. The position of the red and green reflectors can be reversed by removing two bolts and turning around the target blade assembly.

Bethlehem Guard Rail Design 745 of the one-piece type for greatly reduced maintenance. It is not necessary to drill bolt holes in the running rail.

BETHLEHEM GUARD RAILS

Guard rails have been the subject of careful study and experiment by Bethlehem engineers. As a result, the several types illustrated here have been developed to meet the various conditions for mine and industrial trackage.

ONE-PIECE DESIGN

The older style is the bolted guard rail equipped with bolts and chock blocks for bolting the guard to the running rail. This type is fast giving way to the guard rail of one-piece design because of greatly reduced maintenance, and the ease with which the one-piece guard rail can be installed. No drilling of the running rail is necessary for bolt holes.

For ordinary use in mines and in many industrial locations, we strongly recommend Bethlehem Guard Rail Design 745. This guard rail embodies all of the advantages of one-piece construction, and is made entirely of rolled steel.

ROLLED-STEEL ONE-PIECE GUARD RAIL FOR WOOD TIES

Design 745

Bethlehem Guard Rail Design 745 is of the one-piece type with depressed ends, for use with wood ties. It is made entirely of rolled steel, complete with foot guards, ready for installation. No loose parts, such as clamps, bolts, braces, etc., are required. To install, simply slip the guard rail under the main rail, and spike into position.

Guard rails can be adjusted easily for wear by changing the position of the spikes in the graduated spike notching. Design 745 is recommended for mine and industrial track, preferably with rails 20 lb to 100 lb, inclusive. Standard lengths are 4 ft 3 in., 5 ft 3 in., 6 ft 9 in., and 8 ft 3 in.

ROLLED-STEEL ONE-PIECE GUARD RAIL FOR USE WITH STEEL TURNOUT TIE SETS

Design 745-M

Guard Rail Design 745-M is of the one-piece type with depressed ends, similar to Design 745, shown on page 64, but designed principally for use on steel ties rather than on wood ties. It can, however, be used on wood ties, when desired. It is made entirely of rolled steel and welded to two short pieces of steel mine ties, complete with clips for easy installation. There are no loose parts such as bolts and chocks.

To install, simply slip the guard rail under the stock rail, and knock the movable clips into holding position. No drilling of stock rails is necessary.

It is recommended for mine and industrial track, preferably with rails of from 20 to 90 lb, inclusive. Standard lengths of this guard rail are 3 ft 6 in., 4 ft 0 in., and 4 ft 6 in.

OTHER BETHLEHEM GUARD RAILS

Design 731

Bethlehem Guard Rail Design 731 has the flares bent. It is made for rails from 25 lb to 30 lb, inclusive, for which it is not necessary to plane off the flange. Standard lengths are 3 ft, and 4 ft.

Design 732

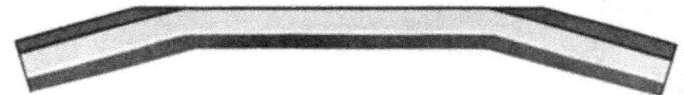

Bethlehem Guard Rail Design 732 has the flares bent and flange removed. It is made for rails of 30 lb and heavier. Standard lengths are 4 ft 6 in., and 6 ft.

Design 733

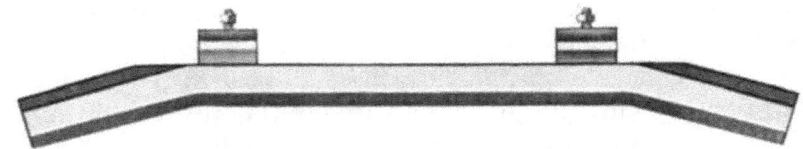

Bethlehem Guard Rail Design 733 has the flares bent and flange removed. It is equipped with two bolts and cast-iron chocks. Made for rails 30 lb, and heavier. Standard lengths are 4 ft 6 in., and 6 ft.

Design 734

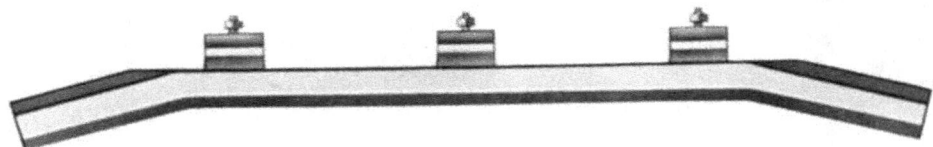

Bethlehem Guard Rail Design 734 has the flares bent and flange removed. It is equipped with three bolts and cast-iron chocks. It is made for rails 60 lb, and heavier. Standard lengths are 6 ft, and 7 ft 6 in.

Design 735

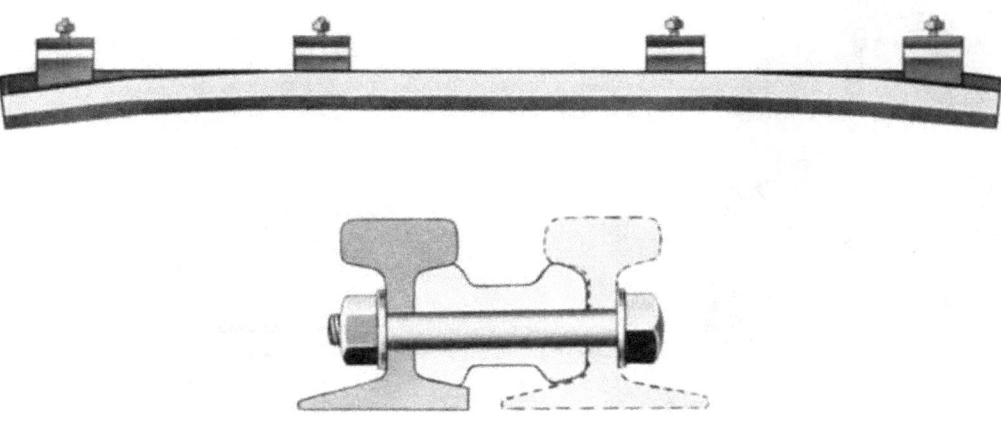

Bethlehem Guard Rail Design 735 has the flares bent and flange removed. It is equipped with four bolts and cast-iron chocks. It is made for rails 80 lb, and heavier. This design is usually furnished in lengths of 8 ft 3 in., 11 ft, and 16 ft 6 in.

BETHLEHEM HOOK-FLANGE GUARD RAIL

Design 750

Bottom view.

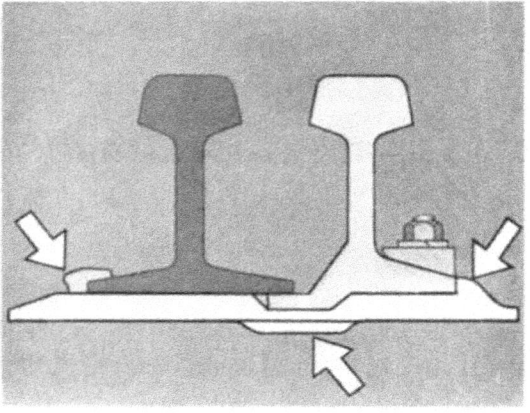

Cannot spread. Shoulder on tie plate on one side and spike through tie plate on the other, lock guard rail in position. The depressed base-plate between the ties affords greater stiffness.

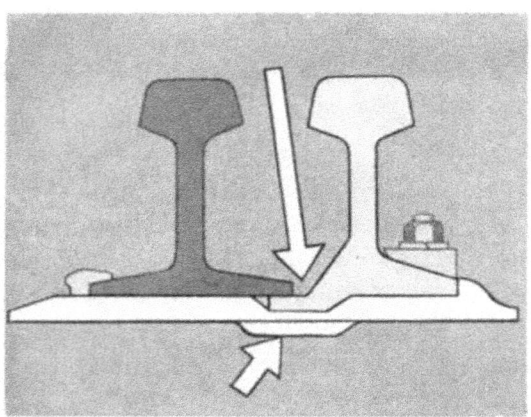

Cannot turn over. Weight of train on running rail anchors "hook" of guard rail regardless of side thrust against it. The depression of the plate is planed off for even bearing on the ties.

Bethlehem Hook-Flange Guard Rail Design 750 is recommended for yard and tipple tracks of standard railroad gage, and for use with rails 80 lb per yd and heavier. Its one-piece construction simplifies installation and maintenance. Its design insures greater safety and security, with more cushioning effect than any other type of guard rail. The assembly is extremely rugged with both guard rail and base-plates made of rolled steel.

No Braces or C-Clamps. The hook-flange guard rail is made up of a rolled-steel rail bolted to special tie-plates. The guard rail proper is of special cross-section, with one flange lowered, forming a hook that fits under the base of the running rail. Each tie plate spans two ties, has a shoulder on the guard-rail side, and is depressed to take the hook-flange. No special adzing of ties is required. Notched spike holes on the running-rail side allow for adjustment of the flangeway width. Heat-treated, high-tensile steel bolts, fitted with lock nuts, hold the guard rail to the tie plates; foot guards are riveted into position.

No Holes To Drill. Bethlehem Hook-Flange Guard Rail design 750 is shipped in one piece ready for installation. No bolt holes are necessary through the running rail. Simply slip it under the running rail and spike it down.

ORDERING INFORMATION

Length. Standard Hook-Flange guard rail lengths are 6 ft 0 in. for No. 4 and No. 5 frogs, and 9 ft 0 in. for No. 4 to No. 15 frogs, inclusive.

Running Rail Section. The Bethlehem Hook-Flange Guard Rail can be furnished to fit any section and weight of running rail from 75 lb to 155 lb. Please specify details. It can be furnished higher, level with, or lower than the running rail. Tie plates are punched to accommodate any particular rail section.

Flangeway Width. Flangeway adjustment, in steps of ¼ in., can be provided. Normally, a stepped spike hole is punched so that three flangeway widths are possible with each guard rail. This permits adjustment for wear.

Tie Plates. Tie plates for the heavier standard running-rail sections are available for canted or vertical running rails. All tie plates are ¾-in. thick, and can be furnished in copper-bearing steel.

Curved Guard Rail. Since the Bethlehem Hook-Flange Guard Rail is similar to a standard T-rail with a depressed flange, it can be curved readily in the field to match a curved running rail.

Shipped Assembled. The Bethlehem Hook-Flange Guard Rail Design 750 is shipped from Steelton, Pa., complete in one piece. Tie plates are bolted to guard rail; foot guards at each end are permanently fastened to prevent injuries to personnel.

BETHLEHEM HEAT-TREATED SWITCH POINT GUARD RAIL

Model 755

Model 755 switch point guard rail assembly, showing 3 slide plates and 2 filler blocks. Guard rail, slide plates and filler blocks are shipped as an assembly, ready to install.

The raised head of Model 755 guard rail holds the flange of the car wheel away from the actual point of the switch where it meets the stock rail.

Bethlehem Steel Company has developed a rugged Heat-Treated Switch Point Guard Rail Model 755, that is just 4 ft 9 in. long, designed to prolong the life of switch points and stock rails, and to reduce the frequency of derailments at switches in yard operations.

Model 755 is securely bolted to the base plates, *but requires no bolts through the stock rail.* There are heavy side braces welded to the base plates to give great rigidity to the guard rail where it is most needed — opposite the switch point.

How It Works. As shown in the illustration, the head of the guard rail stands higher than that of the running rail. The principle of operation is that of the self-guarded frog. That is, by guiding the outside edge of the car-wheel rim, the flange of the wheel is held away from the actual point of the switch and the stock rail.

This eliminates flange-cutting, and also prevents wheels with a worn flange from climbing the switch point and derailing.

For most efficient use of Model 755, it is important that the wheels of rolling stock have uniform rim widths. When ordering Model 755, state the overall rim width and wheel-tread width.

Heat-Treated. Model 755 guard rail is heat-treated to give extra-long life in service. Bethlehem's heat-treating process is a carefully-controlled combination of operations involving the heating, oil-quenching, and tempering of guard rails within controlled, pre-determined limits. As a result, wear-resistance is greatly increased in the guard rail, which has a Brinell hardness within the A.R.E.A. specified range of 300-375. The heat-treatment makes it possible for the Model 755 guard rail to take more abuse and last far longer than a non-treated rail.

Reversible. Any individual Model 755 Guard Rail may be used for either a right-hand or left-hand turnout.

Accessories. The Model 755 is furnished with three slide plates or with one gage plate (either insulated or non-insulated) and two slide plates. The desired quantity of each type should be specified on your order. Only when gage plates are wanted, is it necessary to specify the "hand" (right-hand or left-hand) of the turnout.

One Length Only. The overall length of the guard rail is 4 ft 9 in., providing a 2 ft 3 in. straight guarded face. The beveled ends give the rail an easement feature which softens the shock to car and lading.

The switch point guard rail is securely bolted to the plates, but no bolts are required through the running rail. The plates have braces in the straight guarding area.

Bethlehem Crossings are accurately made in our well-equipped shops to fit any specification as to design, weight of rail, track gages, and angle or curvature.

BETHLEHEM CROSSINGS

Bethlehem's well-equipped shops are particularly well-adapted to the manufacture of railroad crossings. On the following pages some of the popular Bethlehem crossings are shown, designed for use in mines and industrial locations, for rail weights from 20 lb to 100 lb per yd.

COMPONENTS OF A CROSSING

A crossing is installed where two tracks intersect at grade to permit the locomotive and cars on one track to cross the other track with ease and safety.

The crossing types shown here are for light and medium weight rails, and are of the riveted-plate, bolted-plate, and bolted-rail construction, manufactured at angles from 30 deg to 90 deg, as specified. Four frogs are combined in a crossing, one frog for each set of intersecting rails.

CROSSING TYPES

Crossings are accurately made to suit any particular specification as to design, weight of rail, track gage, and angle or curvature. For light rail, 20 lb per yd and over, the riveted-plate type of construction is satisfactory for light traffic. On page 74 we have shown Design 233, a "guarded" 2-rail, riveted-plate crossing.

The average industrial track with medium traffic, however, requires a more substantial type of construction. For this class of service, the bolted-plate crossing, and the bolted-rail crossing are widely used. Several of these types are shown here, of both 2-rail and 3-rail design. The 3-rail type is built with an "easer" or third rail, which adds materially to the strength and life of the crossing.

For heavy-duty service, solid manganese, or manganese-insert crossings are recommended. These crossings last several times longer than riveted or bolted types. For heavy-duty railroad use we recommend Bethlehem Heat-Treated Bolted-Rail Crossings.

BETHLEHEM RIVETED-PLATE CROSSING
FOR 20-LB TO 100-LB RAIL
ANGLES 30° TO 90°

Design 233

Bethlehem Riveted-Plate Crossing Design 233 is of the 2-rail "guarded" type. This crossing is suitable for use with light rail, 20 lb to 100 lb per yd, and at locations where the traffic does not necessitate a heavier type of crossing.

BETHLEHEM BOLTED-PLATE CROSSINGS FOR 40-LB TO 100-LB RAIL ANGLES 40° TO 90°

Design 400 *2-Rail Type*

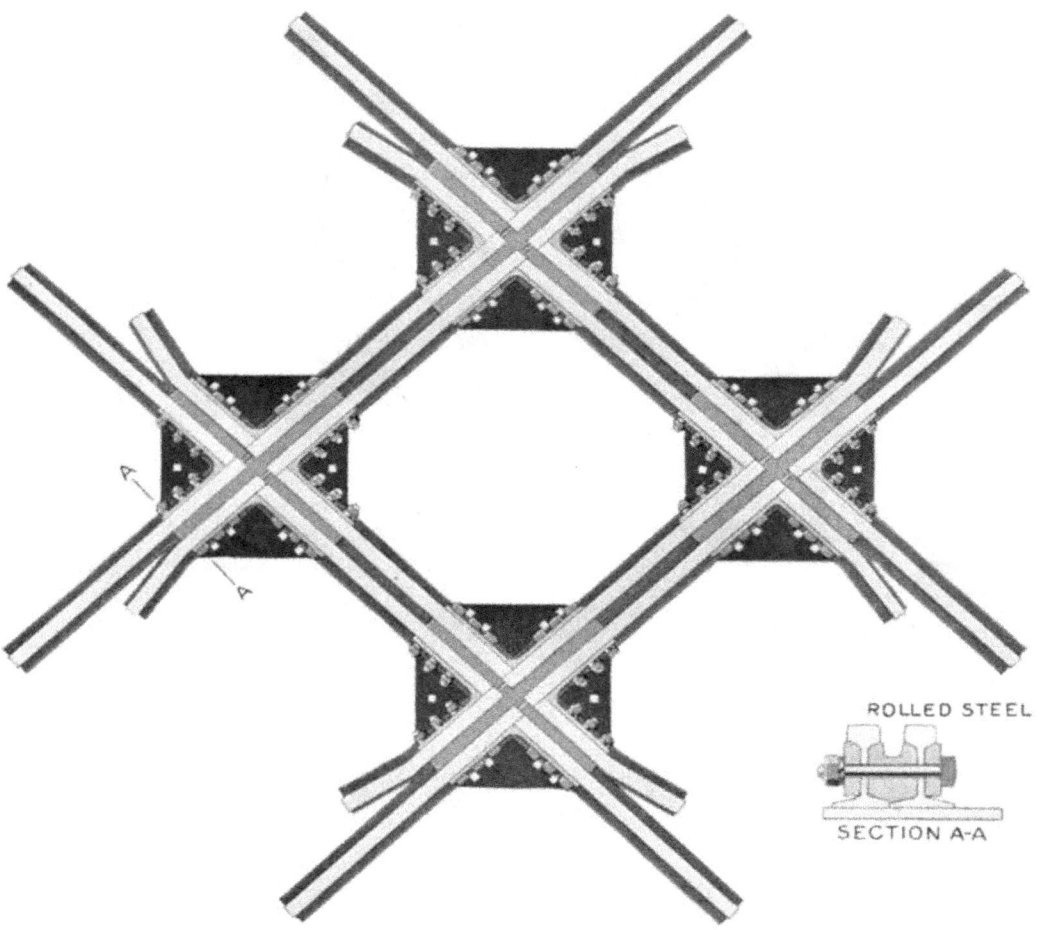

Bethlehem Bolted-Plate Crossing Design 400 is a 2-rail type crossing of bolted design. Fillers and braces are of rolled steel, and corners are supported on heavy base plates. All bolts are heat-treated steel, and the crossing is built exceptionally strong to stand up under heavy-duty service.

BETHLEHEM BOLTED-PLATE CROSSINGS FOR 40-LB TO 100-LB RAIL ANGLES 40° TO 90°

Design 229 *3-Rail Type*

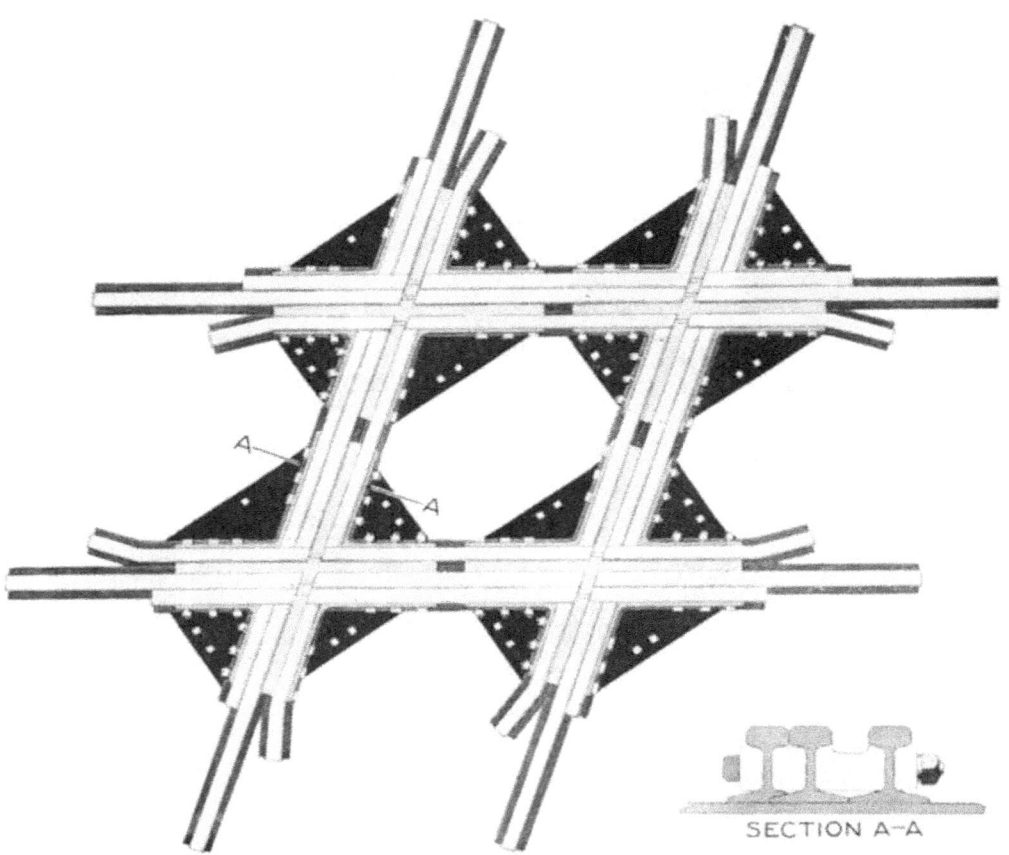

Bethlehem Bolted-Plate Crossing Design 229 is a 3-rail type crossing for heavy duty. The three rails consist of guard rail, main running rail, and easer rail. The easer rail acts as a support for badly worn wheels. Fillers and braces are of rolled steel. All bolts are heat-treated. Corners are supported on heavy base plates.

BETHLEHEM BOLTED-RAIL CROSSINGS FOR RAILS 70 LB AND HEAVIER ANGLES 50° TO 90°

A.R.E.A. PLAN 702-55 2-Rail Type

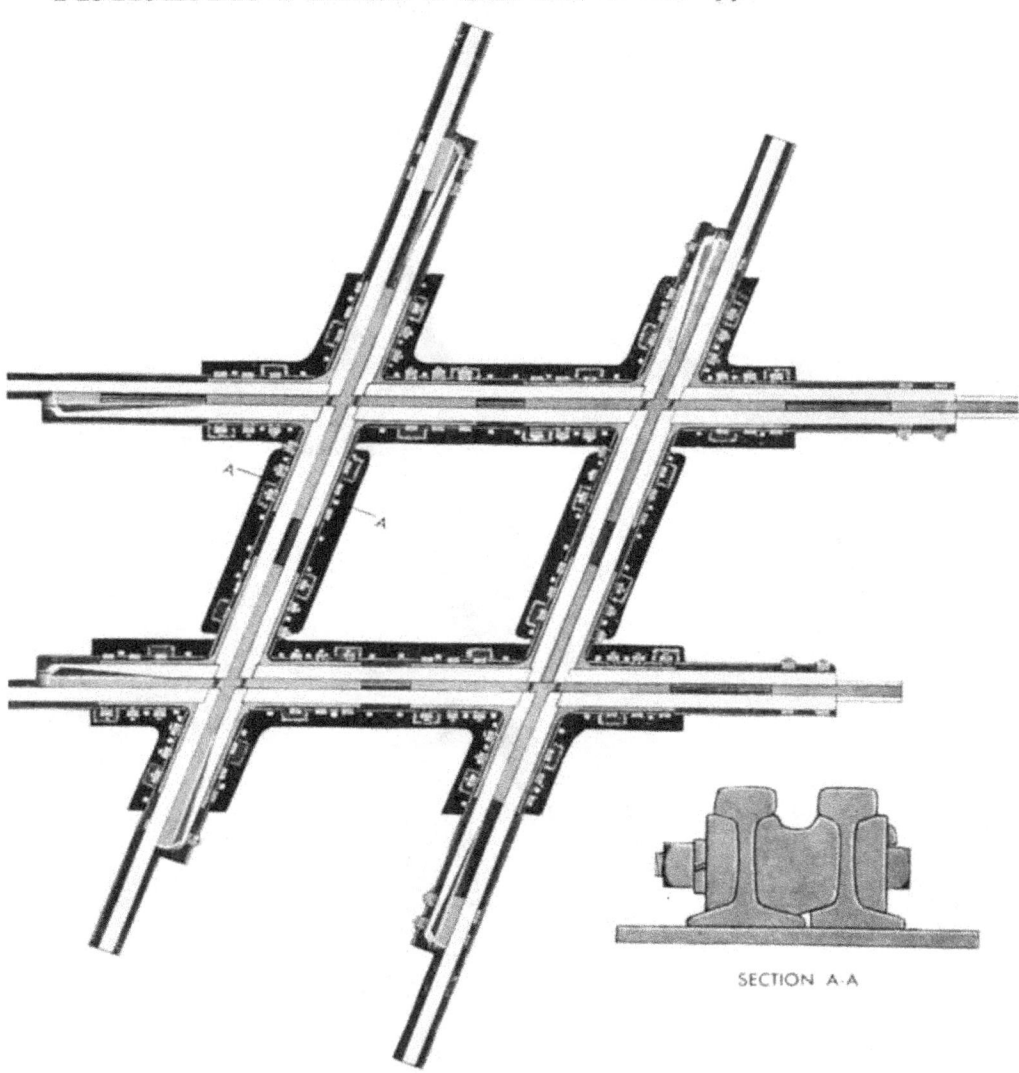

SECTION A-A

This is a Bethlehem Bolted-Rail Crossing that is identical to A.R.E.A. Plan 702-55. It is a 2-rail bolted-type crossing. Fillers and braces are of rolled steel, and the crossing is supported throughout by heavy integral base plates. All bolts are of heat-treated steel. The crossing is built exceptionally strong to stand up under heavy-duty service. This crossing may be furnished heat-treated.

BETHLEHEM BOLTED-RAIL CROSSINGS FOR RAILS 70 LB AND HEAVIER ANGLES 50° TO 90°

A.R.E.A. Plan 701-55 3-Rail Type

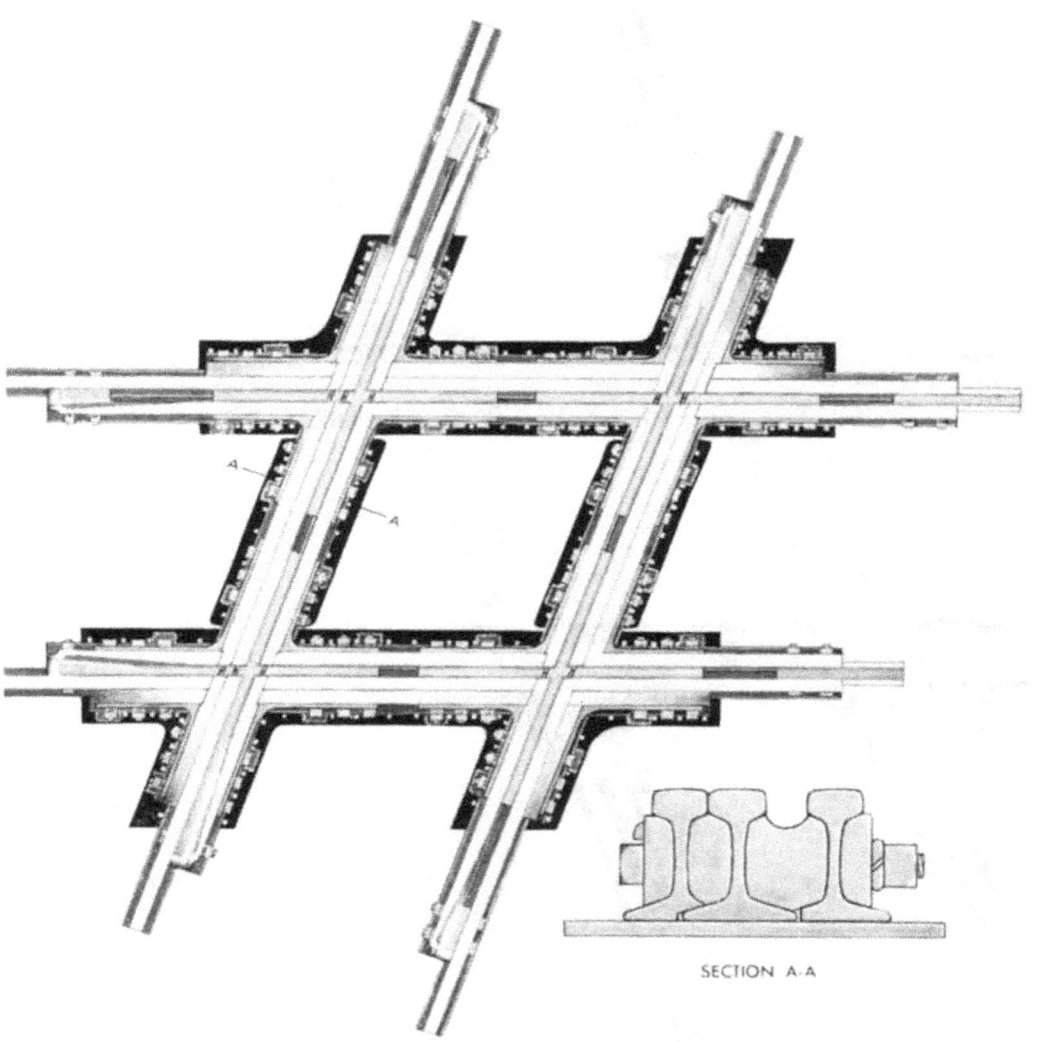

A Bethlehem Bolted-Rail Crossing that is identical to A.R.E.A. Plan 701-55. It is a 3-rail bolted-type crossing. The three rails consist of guard rail, main running rail, and easer rail. The easer rail acts as a support for badly worn wheels. Fillers and braces are of rolled steel, all bolts are heat-treated, and corners are supported on heavy base plates. This crossing may be furnished heat-treated.

Bethlehem specializes in prefabricated trackwork, such as this heavy-duty double crossover.

Bethlehem Tie Sets are made to support the switch and switchstand. Frog ties are added to support the frog and to hold the track to gage.

BETHLEHEM TIE SETS—for Switches and Turnouts

Bethlehem Switch and Turnout Tie Sets are becoming increasingly popular because of economies in track laying, and ease of installation. Bethlehem Switch Tie Sets are designed to support the switch and switch stand. Bethlehem Turnout Tie Sets are comprised of switch tie sets and two frog ties to support the frog and hold the track to gage.

TIE SET CONSTRUCTION

All tie sets are of riveted-and-welded construction. They are designed to be used for right-hand or left-hand turnouts, with the switch stand on either side of the track.

The first two ties are made long enough to accommodate a parallel-throw switch stand. These ties have heavy forged-steel braces welded to riser tie-plates, which in turn are riveted to the steel ties. All ties are of one-piece construction, the only loose parts being the standard track bolts for mounting the switch stand on the ties. Movable clips are fastened to the ties with heavy rivets.

USE OF FROG TIES

It is common practice to intersperse conventional steel ties between the switch and frog, and to use two easily-installed frog ties to support the frog and hold the tracks positively to gage at this critical location. Two designs of frog ties, bolted and riveted types, are available.

TRACK-LAYING ECONOMY

By using steel tie sets, mine operators are realizing great economies in track laying. For instance, when laying room switches on steel ties, the necessity for many rail braces and slide plates is eliminated. Miners can lay complete room turnouts in one-fourth the time required to lay the same turnout on wood ties. In many mines, two men regularly lay a complete room turnout in less than one hour.

ORDERING TIE SETS

To facilitate ordering tie sets, we are showing eight popular sets of switch and turnout ties in the following pages. You may select the set that is applicable to your requirements, and specify on your order to us the necessary data, as listed.

BETHLEHEM SWITCH TIE SETS

Switch Tie Set "A"

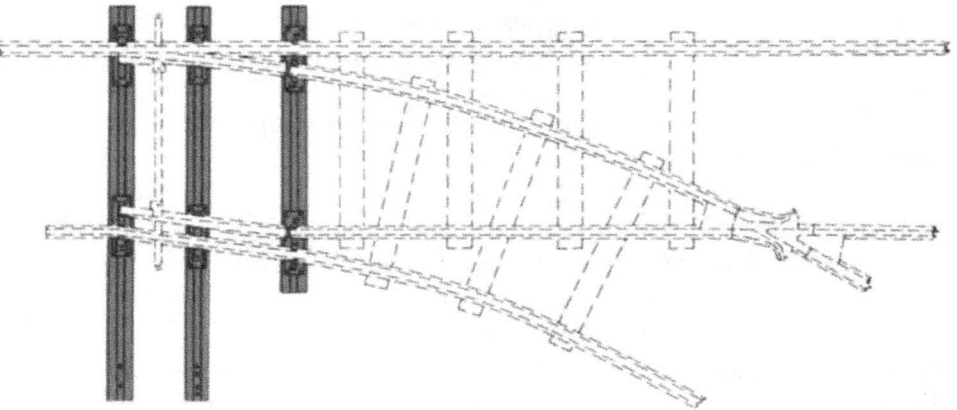

Switch Tie Set "A" may be used for 3 ft 6 in., and 4 ft switches. The tie set includes two long ties for the parallel-throw switch stand, and one tie under the switch heel.

Switch Tie Set "B"

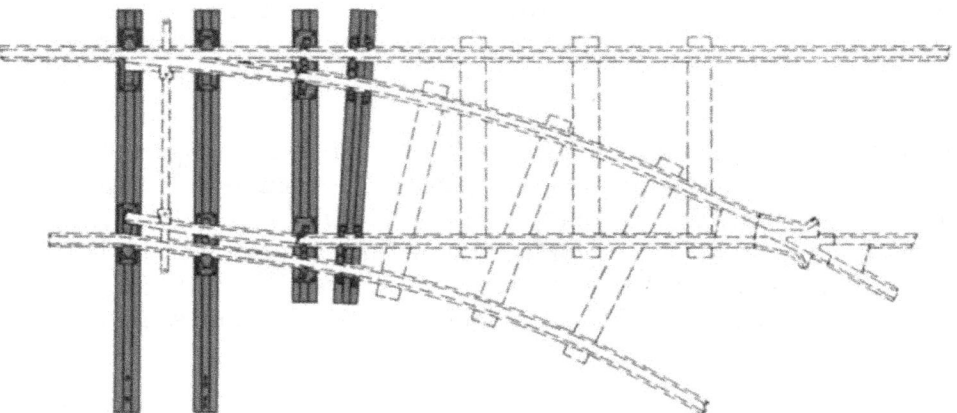

Switch Tie Set "B" is recommended for 3 ft 6 in., and 4 ft switches. The tie set includes two long ties for the parallel-throw switch stand, one tie under the switch heel, and one tie beyond the switch heel.

The throw ties are made long enough to accommodate a parallel-throw switch stand. Notice the safety clearance provided for the brakeman.

Switch Tie Set "C"

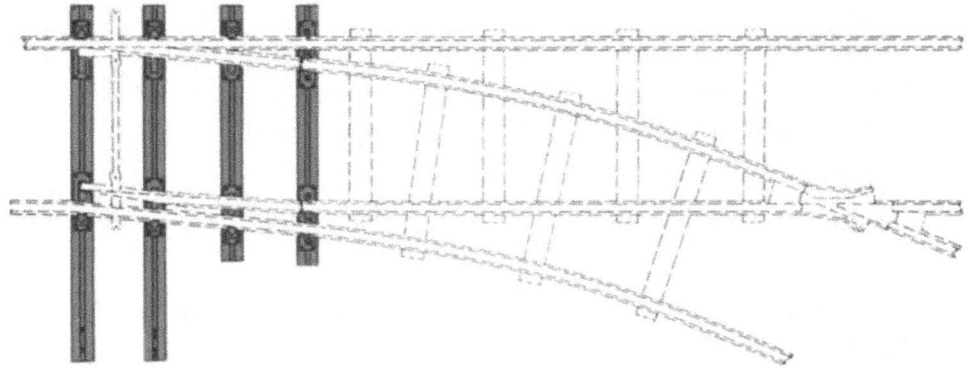

Switch Tie Set "C" may be used for 5 ft, or 6 ft switches. The tie set includes two long ties for the parallel-throw switch stand, one intermediate tie, and one tie under the switch heel.

83

Switch Tie Set "D"

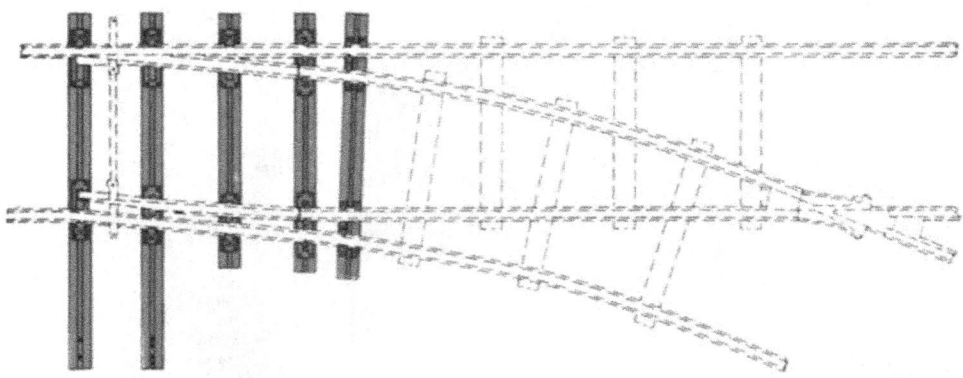

Switch Tie Set "D" is recommended for 5 ft, or 6 ft switches. The tie set includes two long ties for the parallel-throw switch stand, one intermediate tie, one tie under the switch heel, and one tie beyond the switch heel.

SUGGESTIONS FOR ORDERING BETHLEHEM SWITCH TIE SETS

Please include the following information when ordering Bethlehem Switch Tie Sets:

1. Quantity of tie sets required.
2. Specify the type of tie set ("A", "B", "C", or "D", shown on pages 82 to 84).
3. Give the Tie Section Number (No. 4, No. 5, or No. 6, as described on pages 143 and 144).
4. Weight of rail to be used.
5. Length of switch points.
6. Gage of track.
7. Specify whether straight ends, or depressed ends are desired.
8. Number and design of frog.
9. Indicate the model of switch stand that will be used, and the design of the connecting rod. See pages 45-52 (Model No. 1201 or 1217).

BETHLEHEM TURNOUT TIE SETS

Turnout Tie Set "E"

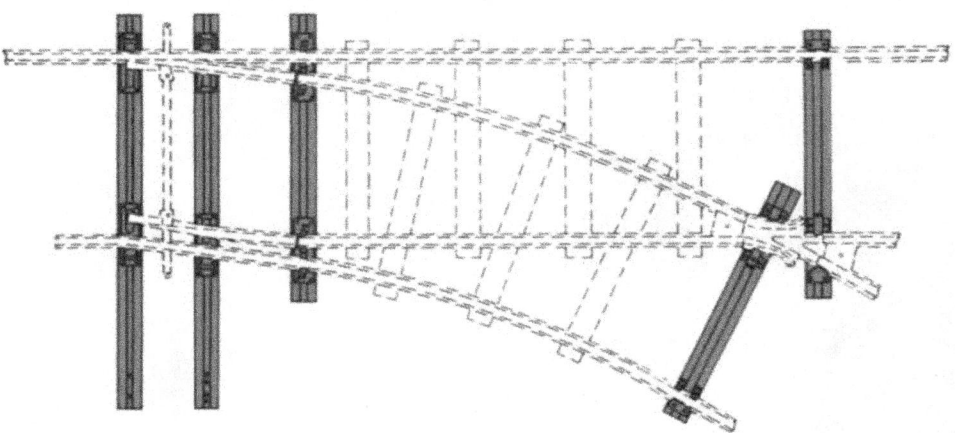

Turnout Tie Set "E" is shipped complete with riveted frog ties (shown above), and may be used for turnouts having 3 ft 6 in., or 4 ft switches. The complete tie set includes two long ties for the parallel-throw switch stand, one tie under the switch heel, and two frog ties. Bolted instead of riveted frog ties can be specified (see pages 88 and 89).

Turnout Tie Set "F"

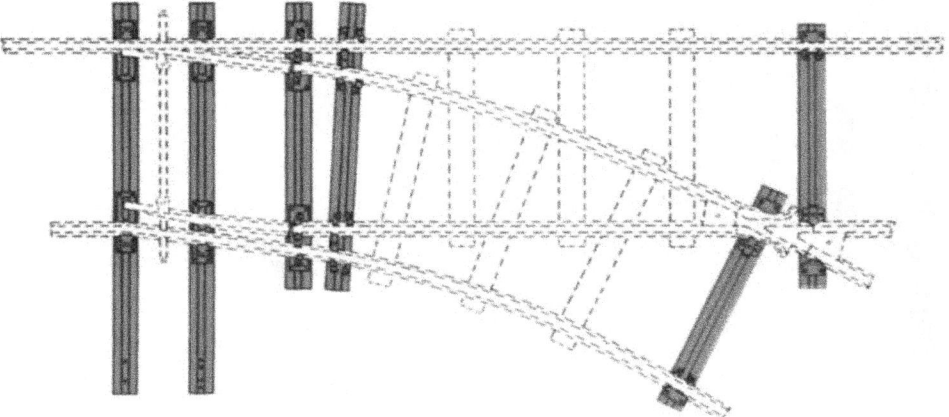

Turnout Tie Set "F" is shipped complete with riveted frog ties (shown above), and is recommended for turnouts having 3 ft 6 in., or 4 ft switches. The complete tie set includes two long ties for the parallel-throw switch stand, one tie under the switch heel, one tie beyond the switch heel, and two frog ties. Bolted instead of riveted frog ties can be specified (see pages 88 and 89).

Bethlehem Turnout Tie Sets are easily laid and dismantled. Furthermore, they save valuable headroom

Turnout Tie Set "G"

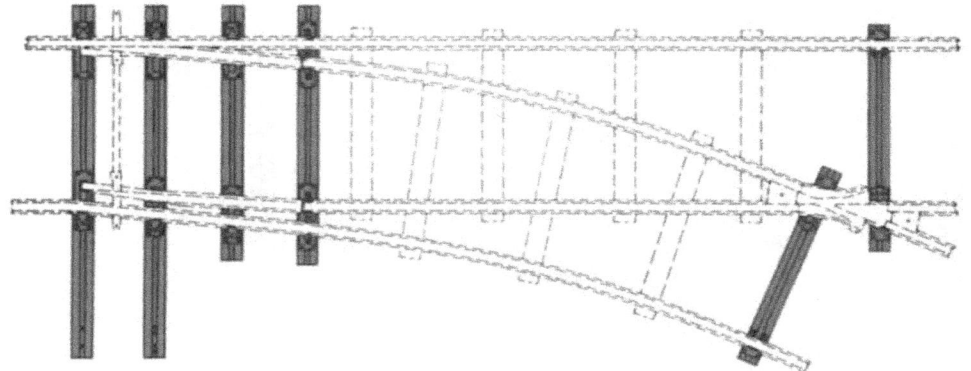

Turnout Tie Set "G" is shipped complete with riveted frog ties (see above), and may be used for turnouts having 5 ft, or 6 ft switches. The complete tie set includes two long ties for the parallel-throw switch stand, one intermediate tie, one tie under the switch heel, and two frog ties. Bolted instead of riveted frog ties can be specified (see pages 88 and 89).

Turnout Tie Set "H"

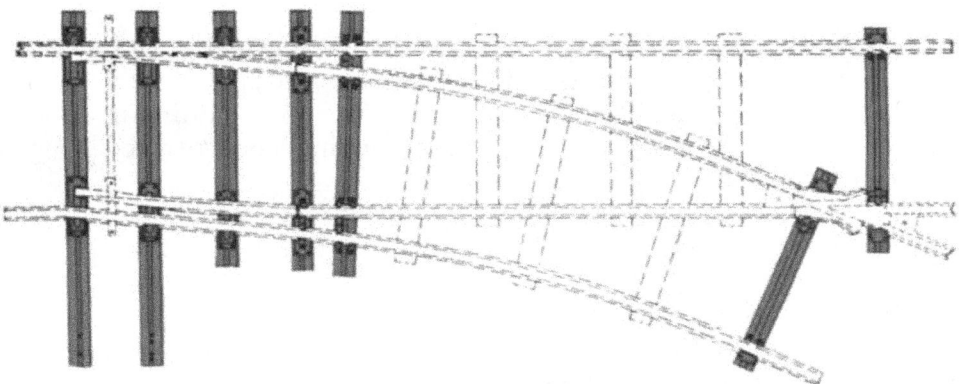

Turnout Tie Set "H" is shipped complete with riveted frog ties (see above), and is recommended for turnouts having 5 ft, or 6 ft switches. The complete tie set includes two long ties for the parallel-throw switch stand, one intermediate tie, one tie under the switch heel, one tie beyond the switch heel, and two frog ties. Bolted instead of riveted frog ties can be specified (see pages 88 and 89).

SUGGESTIONS FOR ORDERING BETHLEHEM TURNOUT TIE SETS

Please include the following information when ordering Bethlehem Turnout Tie Sets:

1. Quantity of tie sets required.
2. Specify the type of turnout tie sets ("E", "F", "G", or "H", shown on pages 85 to 87).
3. Give the Tie Section Number (No. 4, No. 5, or No. 6, as described on pages 143 and 144).
4. Weight of rail to be used.
5. Length of switch points.
6. Gage of track.
7. Specify whether straight ends, or depressed ends are desired.
8. Number and design of frog.
9. Indicate the model of switch stand that will be used, and the design of the connecting rod. See pages 45-52.
10. Give the construction of frog ties desired (bolted or riveted). See pages 88 and 89.
11. Specify whether or not the frog ties will be used with Bethlehem Guard Rail Design 745-M.

BETHLEHEM FROG TIES

Bethlehem Frog Ties are used in conjunction with steel switch tie sets to form turnout tie sets. Steel frog ties are particularly adaptable where it is desired to install turnouts in a minimum amount of time to keep pace with a fast-moving concentrated mining operation.

FROG TIE CONSTRUCTION

Two frog ties are required for each turnout. Frog ties in pairs may be purchased to be used with existing steel switch tie sets, to make up complete turnout tie sets. All frog ties are made from No. 4, No. 5, or No. 6 tie sections (see pages 143 and 144), and are available in either bolted or riveted types, depending on the method of fastening the ties to the frog. Both bolted and riveted types have conventional riveted fastenings at the end which support the stock rail.

BOLTED FROG TIES

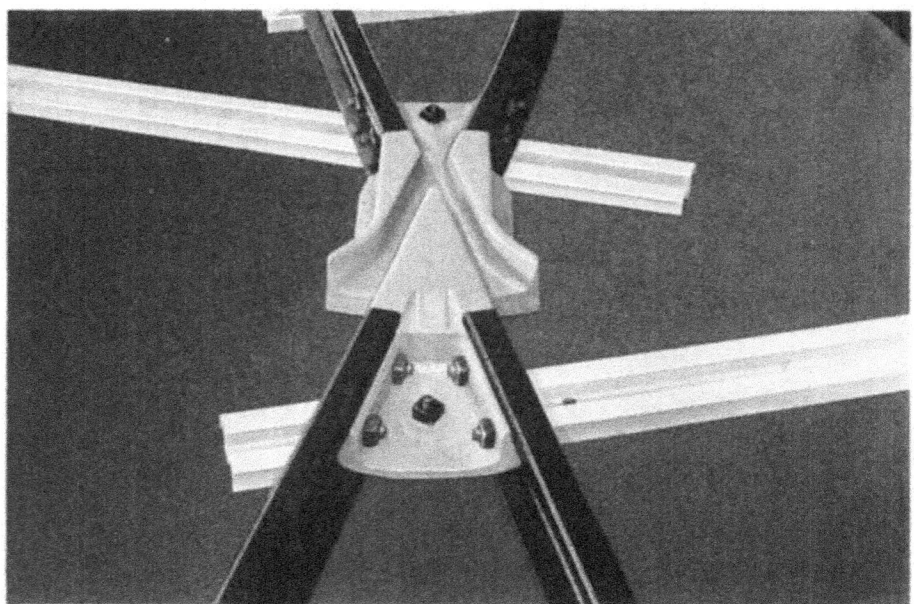

Bolted frog ties are fastened directly to the frogs by means of standard track bolts placed in holes through the toe or heel apron of the frog. Each tie is made with two oval holes in the central groove of the tie, to provide a head-lock for the oval neck of the track bolt. The track bolt is thus held in position, and prevented from turning while fastening the nut.

Bolted frog ties can be used interchangeably at the toe or heel of the frog. These ties can be supplied for cast manganese steel frogs No. 2, No. 2½, No. 3, Design 289-A, for 25-lb, 30-lb and 40-lb ASCE rails only. Each frog has holes cored in the toe and heel aprons to accommodate the track bolts.

Bolted frog ties are reversible so they may be used for right-hand, or left-hand turnouts.

RIVETED FROG TIES

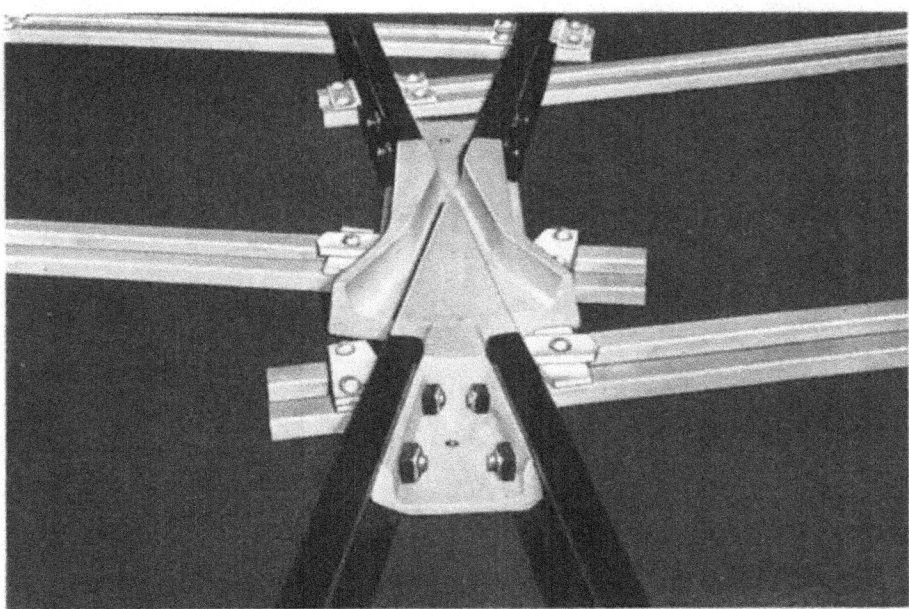

Riveted frog ties can be specified for either cast or riveted-plate frogs, in sets of two ties for each frog. Frogs are fastened to the ties by means of one heavy revolving clip, and one stationary riveted clip. Both clips are mounted on reinforcing plates which take the side thrust at the base of the frog. All parts are integral with the ties, so they will not be lost when transferring the ties from one location to another.

Riveted frog ties are reversible so they may be used for right-hand, or left-hand turnouts.

ORDER "BOLTED" OR "RIVETED"

When ordering frog ties, please specify the design required (bolted, or riveted), the tie section, the number and design of the frog, the weight of rail, and the track gage.

A typical underground intersection with crossing and turnouts. Bethlehem track equipment is used throughout.

BETHLEHEM TURNOUTS

Many users of track equipment have decided that it is far more economical to buy closure rails made to correct dimensions, than to depend upon their trackmen to cut and form the rails with the inadequate equipment at their disposal.

ORDER COMPLETE TURNOUTS

As a consequence, customers now order complete turnouts consisting of the frog, switch, switch stand, straight closure rail, curved closure rail, and guard rails. This results in greater initial economy, and greater overall efficiency of the transportation system, because of the standardization of turnouts with complete interchangeability of parts.

TYPICAL TURNOUT WITH NAMES OF PARTS

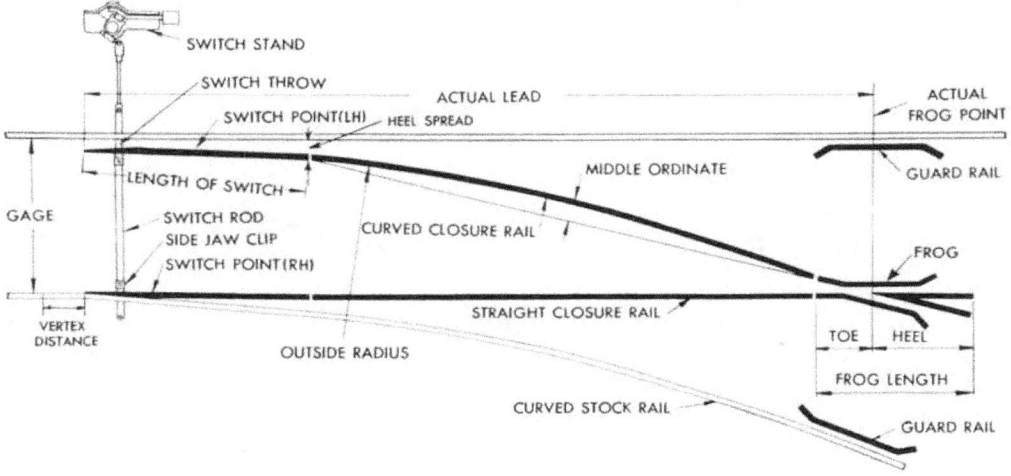

The above diagram shows a typical turnout, with the preferred names of the various parts. Bethlehem Turnouts are manufactured from the highest grade materials, and will stand up under long, severe service. Unless otherwise specified, closure rails are furnished in accordance with American Mining Congress standards.

MAIN-HAULAGE TURNOUTS

The main haulageways of a mine are the arterial routes of the transportation system. With the increased use of heavier locomotives and mine cars at faster speeds, these haulageways must be maintained in the best condition, to prevent delays which cripple mine production. One of the best ways to avoid derailments and other costly delays, is to install the best heavy-duty turnouts obtainable, and then to maintain them with good maintenance crews.

A typical main-line turnout is shown here with Bethlehem turnout parts indicated.

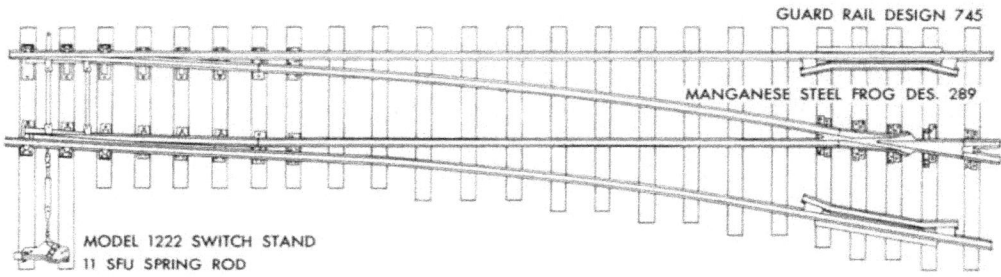

A TYPICAL ORDER

An example of an order for main-line haulage turnouts is as follows:

10 Bethlehem No. 6, 85-lb AS rail, 42-in. gage turnouts, each to consist of:

    1 Design 289 Cast Manganese Steel Frog

    10 Hook-Twin Frog Plates, 3 in. x 20 in. x ⅝ in.

    1 Heavy-Duty Switch, Design 399, 10 ft 0 in. long

    2 Switch Heel Block Joints, Design 992 (one RH, one LH)

    1 Straight Closure Rail

    1 Curved Closure Rail

    2 Guard Rails, Design 745, 6 ft 9 in. long

    1 Model 1222 Switch Stand, with Design 11-SFU Spring Rod.

BUTT-ENTRY TURNOUTS

Butt-entry turnouts are part of the intermediate or secondary haulageways which connect the main haulageways to the working sections.

Since these secondary tracks are essential to the continuous flow of coal from the working areas, heavy-rail and heavy-duty turnouts should be installed to insure safe, maintenance-free operation.

A typical butt-entry turnout is shown here with Bethlehem turnout parts indicated.

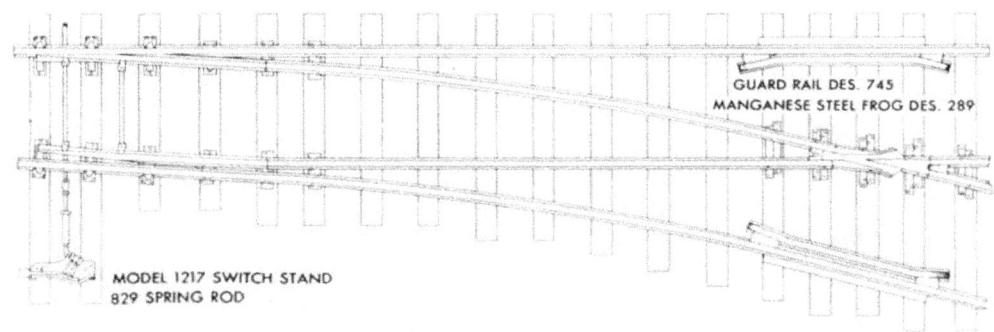

A TYPICAL ORDER

An example of an order for butt-entry turnouts is as follows:

15 Bethlehem No. 4, 60-lb ASCE rail, 42-in. gage turnouts, each to consist of:

- 1 Design 289 Manganese Steel Frog
- 10 Hook-Twin Frog Plates, 3 in. x 20 in. x ½ in.
- 1 Heavy-Duty Switch, Design 397, 7 ft 6 in. long
- 2 Switch Heel Block Joints, Design 992 (one RH, one LH)
- 1 Straight Closure Rail
- 1 Curved Closure Rail
- 2 Guard Rails, Design 745, 6 ft 9 in. long
- 1 Model 1217 Switch Stand with Design 829 Spring Rod.

ROOM-ENTRY TURNOUTS

For room-entry turnouts, most mine operators purchase completely-assembled units for use with steel ties, as shown in the drawing, below.

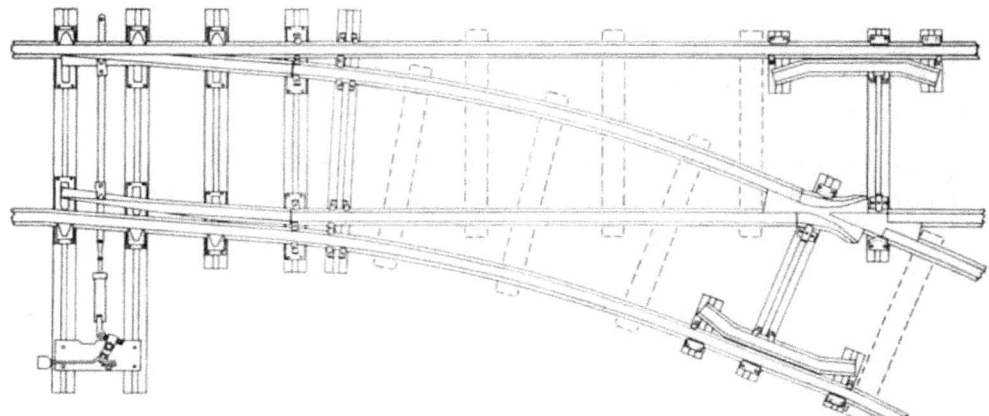

As a rule, room turnouts are continually being laid down and taken up. In a fast-moving, concentrated mining system, some turnouts are moved two to four times in a month. The turnout illustrated here may be used for turns to the right or left, with the switch stand on either side of the track. The component parts of the turnout are standardized, so that the parts of one may be used interchangeably with those of another turnout of the same specifications. Bethlehem Turnouts of this type may be quickly assembled or dismantled.

A TYPICAL ORDER

An example of a typical order for room-entry turnouts is as follows:

25 Bethlehem No. 2½, 40-lb ASCE rail, 42-in. gage turnouts, for use on steel ties each to consist of:
- 1 Design 289-A Manganese Steel Frog
- 1 Switch, Design 388, 5-ft long
- 2 Switch Heel Joints, Design 990 (one RH, one LH)
- 1 Straight Closure Rail
- 1 Curved Closure Rail
- 2 Guard Rails, Design 745-M, each 4-ft long
- 1 Model 1201 Parallel-Throw Switch Stand, with Design 832 Spring Rod
- 1 Set of Type "H" Turnout Ties of No. 6 section, with straight ends for use with above. Riveted frog ties.

TURNOUT DATA

The following pages cover the standard practice for various turnouts, as formulated for all rails up to and including 100 lb, as approved by the American Standards Association. These standards were submitted to the American Standards Association by the American Mining Congress. The recommended and approved practices are generally referred to as "American Mining Congress Standards."

TURNOUT FORMULAS (Theoretical Dimensions)

The American Mining Congress Standard, Drawing No. 500-31 (American Standards Association, M-7-1-1933), contains the formulas for computing the theoretically correct dimensions of turnouts. This drawing is reproduced below.

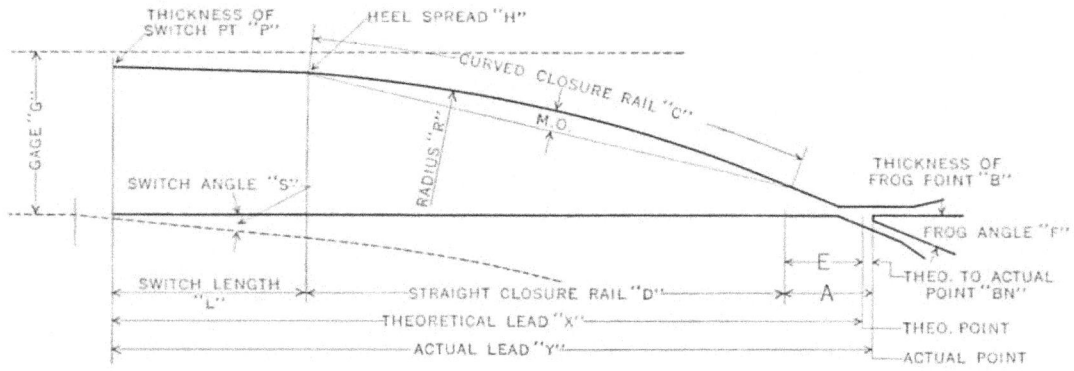

A = The distance from the actual point of a frog to its toe.
B = The thickness of the frog point.
C = The length of the curved closure rail.
D = The length of the straight closure rail.
E = The distance from the theoretical point of frog to its toe.
F = Frog angle.
G = Gage.
H = Heel spread of switch.
L = Length of switch.
MO = Middle ordinate.
N = Frog number.
P = Thickness of switch point.
R = Radius of curved closure rails.
S = Switch angle.
X = Theoretical lead.
Y = Actual lead.

Formula and Example

(Example based on No. 2 cast frog, 3' 6" switch, 42" gage, 30-lb rail)

B = ¼"   L = 3' 6"   F = 28° 04' 21"   N = 2   P = ⅜"   A = 6¹¹⁄₁₆"   H = 5"   G = 42"

(1) *Switch angle*

$$\sin S = \frac{H - P}{L}$$

$$= \frac{5'' - \tfrac{3}{8}''}{42''}$$

$$= 0.110119$$

$$S = 6° 19' 20''$$

$$L' = L \cos S$$

$$= 42'' \times \cos(6° 19' 20'')$$

$$= 41.745''$$

(2) *Theoretical toe distance*

$$E = A - B \times N \text{ (if cast frog, add 10'')}$$

$$= 6^{11}\!/_{16}'' - (¼'' \times 2) + 10''$$

$$= 16^{3}\!/_{16}''$$

(3) *Theoretical lead*

$$X = L' + \left\{ \frac{G-H-E \sin F}{\tan ½ (F+S)} \right\} + E \cos F$$

$$= 41.745'' + \frac{42'' - 5'' - 7.618''}{.309501} + 14.283''$$

$$= 150.9615'' \text{ or } 12' 6^{15}\!/_{16}''$$

(4) *Actual lead*

$$Y = X + BN = 12' 6^{15}\!/_{16}'' + ½''$$

(5) *Radius*

$$R = \frac{G-H-E \sin F}{2 \sin ½ (F+S) \sin ½ (F-S)}$$

$$= \frac{42'' - 5'' - 7.618''}{.111566}$$

$$= 263.360'' \text{ or } 21' 11^{3}\!/_{8}''$$

(6) *Length of straight closure rail*

$$D = X - L - E \text{ (if cast frog, add 10'')}$$

$$= 12' 6^{15}\!/_{16}'' - 3' 6'' - 16^{3}\!/_{16}'' + 10''$$

$$= 8' 6¾''$$

(7) *Length of curved closure rail*

$$C = R(F-S) \text{ in radians (if cast frog, add 10'')}$$

$$= 263.36'' \times .379614 + 10''$$

$$= 109.9751'' \text{ or } 9' 2''$$

(8) *Middle ordinate*

$$MO = R - R \cos ½ (F-S)$$

$$= 263.360'' - 263.360'' \times .9820406$$

$$= 4.730'' \text{ or } 4¾''$$

HELPFUL CALCULATIONS

For Determining A.M.C. Theoretical Turnout Dimensions

Some mines use track gages, lengths of switches, or angles of frogs which are not covered by American Mining Congress drawings. In such cases it is necessary to compute the theoretical turnout dimensions from the formulas given above.

Bethlehem engineers have computed values of certain trigonometric functions used in the A.M.C. formulas, and they are published here for your convenience. These values may be substituted in the formulas where called for, and will simplify the calculations and lessen chances for error.

All Bethlehem cast frogs are made with ½-in. points.

Frog Data

(N) Frog No.	(F) Angle	(E) Theoretical Point to Toe (includes 10-in. Tangent) in.	E sin F in.	E cos F in.
Cast Frogs (20-lb to 60-lb rail, inclusive)				
2	28° 04′ 21″	16 3/16	7.618	14.283
2½	22° 37′ 12″	17 5/8	6.779	16.269
3	18° 55′ 29″	17 5/8	5.716	16.672
4	14° 15′ 00″	20 1/16	4.938	19.445
5	11° 25′ 16″	22 9/16	4.468	22.116
6	9° 31′ 38″	25 1/16	4.148	24.717
Cast Frogs (70-lb to 80-lb rail)				
3	18° 55′ 29″	18	5.838	17.027
4	14° 15′ 00″	20 1/2	5.046	19.869
5	11° 25′ 16″	23 3/16	4.592	22.728
6	9° 31′ 38″	25 13/16	4.272	25.456
7	8° 10′ 16″	28 7/16	4.042	28.149
8	7° 9′ 10″	31 1/16	3.868	30.821
Cast Frogs (85-lb to 100-lb rail, inclusive)				
3	18° 55′ 29″	19 1/2	6.324	18.446
4	14° 15′ 00″	22 5/8	5.569	21.929
5	11° 25′ 16″	25 11/16	5.087	25.179
6	9° 31′ 38″	28 13/16	4.769	28.415
7	8° 10′ 16″	31 15/16	4.539	31.613
8	7° 9′ 10″	35 1/16	4.366	34.790
Riveted-Plate Frogs (20-lb and 30-lb rail)				
2	28° 04′ 21″	16 1/2	7.765	14.559
2½	22° 37′ 12″	15 7/8	6.106	14.654
3	18° 55′ 29″	15 3/4	5.108	14.899
Riveted-Plate Frogs (40-lb rail)				
2	28° 04′ 21″	19 1/4	9.059	16.985
2½	22° 37′ 12″	19 1/16	7.332	17.596
Riveted-Plate Frogs (40-lb and 60-lb rail)				
3	18° 55′ 29″	22 7/8	7.419	21.639
4	14° 15′ 00″	25 1/2	6.277	24.715
5	11° 25′ 16″	28 1/8	5.569	27.568
6	9° 31′ 38″	33 3/4	5.586	33.284

Switch Data

(L) Length ft—in.	(S) Angle	(L') L cos S in.
20-lb to 60-lb rail, inclusive; 5-in. heel spread		
3–6	6° 19' 20"	41.745
4–0	5° 31' 45"	47.777
5–0	4° 25' 15"	59.821
6–0	3° 40' 59"	71.851
7–6	2° 56' 44"	89.881
10–0	2° 12' 32"	119.911
70-lb and 80-lb rail; 6-in. heel spread		
5–0	5° 22' 46"	59.736
7–6	3° 35' 00"	89.824
10–0	2° 41' 12"	119.868
15–0	1° 47' 27"	179.914
85-lb to 100-lb rail, inclusive; 6¼-in. heel spread		
7–6	3° 44' 35"	89.808
10–0	2° 48' 23"	119.856
15–0	1° 52' 14"	179.904

Frog and Switch Data

(N) Frog No.	(L) Switch Length ft—in.	$\tan\frac{1}{2}(F + S)$	$2\sin\frac{1}{2}(F + S) \times \sin\frac{1}{2}(F - S)$	$\cos\frac{1}{2}(F - S)$	F − S (Radians)
20-lb to 60-lb rail, inclusive; 5-in. heel spread					
2	3–6	.309501	.111566	.9820406	.379614
2	4–0	.301934	.112994	.9807114	.393455
2	5–0	.291410	.114672	.9787751	.412799
2½	4–0	.250711	.072271	.9888984	.298291
2½	5–0	.240456	.073949	.9874150	.317634
3	4–0	.216700	.049402	.9931752	.233797
3	5–0	.206595	.051079	.9920006	.253141
3	6–0	.199890	.051989	.9911674	.266017
4	5–0	.164391	.027794	.9963235	.171551
4	6–0	.157786	.028704	.9957513	.184428
4	7–6	.151196	.029448	.9951381	.197300
5	6–0	.132577	.017736	.9977209	.135055
5	7–6	.126034	.018481	.9972659	.147926
6	7–6	.109277	.012472	.9983510	.114872
6	10–0	.102777	.013050	.9979614	.127729

Complete room turnout, mounted on a Bethlehem Turnout Tie Set.

Frog and Switch Data (continued)

(N) Frog No.	(L) Switch Length ft—in.	$\tan\frac{1}{2}(F+S)$	$2\sin\frac{1}{2}(F+S) \times \sin\frac{1}{2}(F-S)$	$\cos\frac{1}{2}(F-S)$	$F-S$ (Radians)
70-lb and 80-lb rail; 6-in. heel spread					
3	5–0	.215332	.049650	.9930219	.236410
3	7–6	.198986	.052099	.9910516	.267758
4	5–0	.172995	.026365	.9970053	.154820
4	7–6	.156894	.028814	.9956708	.186168
5	7–6	.131692	.017847	.9976618	.136795
5	10–0	.123739	.018703	.9970965	.152445
6	7–6	.114913	.011838	.9986550	.103740
6	10–0	.106992	.012694	.9982188	.119390
6	15–0	.099093	.013303	.9977182	.135025
7	10–0	.095033	.009052	.9988547	.095722
7	15–0	.087158	.009664	.9984518	.111357
8	15–0	.078209	.007295	.9989028	.093584
85-lb to 100-lb rail, inclusive; 6¼-in. heel spread					
3	7–6	.200429	.051923	.9912365	.264970
4	7–6	.158320	.028634	.9957959	.183381
4	10–0	.149958	.029569	.9950208	.199729
5	10–0	.124799	.018603	.9971767	.150355
6	10–0	.108052	.012594	.9982775	.117301
6	15–0	.099791	.013258	.9977660	.133634
7	10–0	.096094	.008953	.9989012	.093632
7	15–0	.087853	.009618	.9984897	.109965
8	15–0	.078903	.007249	.9989353	.092192

TURNOUT DATA FOR 18-IN. GAGE

20-lb to 60-lb A.S.C.E. rail, inclusive

CAST FROG DESIGN 289		SWITCH			ACTUAL LEAD	CLOSURE RAILS			
						CURVED			STRAIGHT
Frog No.	Frog Angle	Length ft-in.	Switch Angle	Vertex Distance in.	ft-in.	Radius ft-in.	M.O. in.	Length ft-in.	Length ft-in.
2½	22° 37′ 12″	3-6	6° 19′ 20″	4	7-5 1/16	11-10⅛	1 7/16	3-4 11/16	3-2 3/16
3	18° 55′ 29″	5-0	4° 25′ 15″	5	9-11½	17-2⅛	1 11/16	4-4 7/16	4-2⅜
4	14° 15′ 00″	5-0	4° 25′ 15″	5	11-3⅝	31-6⅝	1 13/32	5-5⅛	5-3 9/16
5	11° 25′ 16″	7-6	2° 56′ 44″	8	15-8⅛	47-4 13/16	1 9/16	7-0 5/16	6-11 1/16
6	9° 31′ 38″	10-0	2° 12′ 32″	10	20-0	67-1 3/16	1 1/16	8-7	8-5 15/16

TURNOUT DATA FOR 24-IN. GAGE

20-lb to 60-lb A.S.C.E. rail, inclusive

CAST FROG DESIGN 289		SWITCH			ACTUAL LEAD	CLOSURE RAILS			
						CURVED			STRAIGHT
Frog No.	Frog Angle	Length ft-in.	Switch Angle	Vertex Distance in.	ft-in.	Radius ft-in.	M.O. in.	Length ft-in.	Length ft-in.
2	28° 04′ 21″	3-6	6° 19′ 20″	4	8-3⅜	12-1 5/32	2 17/32	4-5 31/32	4-2 3/16
2½	22° 37′ 12″	5-0	4° 25′ 15″	5	11-2 5/16	18-2 9/32	2 1/16	5-8 3/16	5-5 3/16
3	18° 55′ 29″	5-0	4° 25′ 15″	5	12-3¼	27-1 21/32	2½	6-8 13/16	6-6 5/16
		7-6	2° 56′ 44″	8	15-3½	26-2¼	3	7-2½	6-11⅞
4	14° 15′ 00″	5-0	4° 25′ 15″	5	14-2 13/16	50-1 23/32	2⅛	8-4 15/32	8-2½
		7-6	2° 56′ 44″	8	17-5⅞	46-11 15/16	2 21/32	9-1 21/32	8-11 9/16
5	11° 25′ 16″	7-6	2° 56′ 44″	8	19-6¼	75-0 13/16	2 13/32	10-10 15/32	10-8 15/16
		10-0	2° 12′ 32″	10	22-7 21/32	72-5 15/16	2¾	11-5 13/16	11-4 11/32
6	9° 31′ 38″	7-6	2° 56′ 44″	8	21-4⅞	111-7 11/16	2⅛	12-5 25/32	12-4 9/16
		10-0	2° 12′ 32″	10	24-8 9/16	106-1	2 17/32	13-3 23/32	13-2¼

TURNOUT DATA FOR 30-IN. GAGE

LIGHT RAIL — 20-lb to 60-lb A.S.C.E. rail, inclusive

American Mining Congress Standards

FROG						SWITCH					ACTUAL LEAD	CLOSURE RAILS			
												CURVED			STRAIGHT
No.	Angle	Type	Rail Weight lb	Point in.	Actual Toe Length in.	Length ft-in.	Angle	Point in.	Heel Spread in.	Vertex Distance in.	ft-in.	Radius ft-in.	M.O. in.	Length ft-in.	Length ft-in.
2	28° 04′ 21″	Cast	20 to 40	¼	6 11/16	3-6	6° 19′ 20″	⅜	5	4	9-5	13-0	3⅞	5-9½	5-4¼
		R.P.F.	20 to 30	¼	17	3-6	6° 19′ 20″	⅜	5	4	9-5	13-0	2 13/16	4-11	4-6
		R.P.F.	40	⅜	20	3-6	6° 19′ 20″	⅜	5	4	9-5	13-0	2½	4-8¼	4-3
2½	22° 37′ 12″	Cast	20 to 40	¼	8¼	5-0	4° 25′ 15″	⅜	5	5	12-10	21-0	4	7-5¾	7-1¾
		R.P.F.	20 to 30	¼	16½	5-0	4° 25′ 15″	⅜	5	5	12-10	21-0	3 5/16	6-9½	6-5½
		R.P.F.	40	⅜	20	5-0	4° 25′ 15″	⅜	5	5	12-10	21-0	3	6-6	6-2
3	18° 55′ 29″	Cast	20 to 60	¼	8⅜	5-0	4° 25′ 15″	⅜	5	5	14-4	32-0	3¼	8-11	8-7½
		R.P.F.	20 to 30	¼	16½	5-0	4° 25′ 15″	⅜	5	5	14-4	32-0	3 3/16	8-2¾	7-11½
		R.P.F.	40 to 60	⅜	24	5-0	4° 25′ 15″	⅜	5	5	14-4	32-0	2¾	7-7½	7-4
4	14° 15′ 00″	Cast	40 to 60	¼	11 1/16	5-0	4° 25′ 15″	⅜	5	5	17-0	60-0	3⅛	11-3½	11-1
		R.P.F.	40 to 60	⅜	27	5-0	4° 25′ 15″	⅜	5	5	17-0	60-0	2 7/16	9-11½	9-9
5	11° 25′ 16″	Cast	40 to 60	¼	13 13/16	7-6	2° 56′ 44″	⅜	5	8	23-0	93-0	3⅜	14-6¼	14-4¼
		R.P.F.	40 to 60	⅜	30	7-6	2° 56′ 44″	⅜	5	8	23-0	93-0	2 13/16	13-2	13-0
6	9° 31′ 38″	Cast	40 to 60	¼	16 9/16	7-6	2° 56′ 44″	⅜	5	8	25-7	139-0	3 1/16	16-10	16-8½
		R.P.F.	40 to 60	⅜	36	7-6	2° 56′ 44″	⅜	5	8	25-7	139-0	2½	15-2¾	15-1
6	9° 31′ 38″	Cast	40 to 60	¼	16 9/16	10-0	2° 12′ 32″	⅜	5	10	29-0	133-0	3 9/16	17-9	17-7½
		R.P.F.	40 to 60	⅜	36	10-0	2° 12′ 32″	⅜	5	10	29-0	133-0	3	16-1¾	16-0

Note: R.P.F. denotes "Riveted Plate Frog."

TURNOUT DATA FOR 30-IN. GAGE *(continued)*

HEAVY RAIL — 70-lb to 80-lb A.S.C.E. rail, inclusive

American Mining Congress Standards

FROG						SWITCH					ACTUAL LEAD	CLOSURE RAILS			
												CURVED			STRAIGHT
No.	Angle	Type	Rail Weight lb	Point in.	Actual Toe Length in.	Length ft-in.	Angle	Point in.	Heel Spread in.	Vertex Distance in.	ft-in.	Radius ft-in.	M.O. in.	Length ft-in.	Length ft-in.
3	18° 55′ 29″	Cast	70 to 80	½	9½	7-6	3° 35′ 00″	⅜	6	6	16-7	30-0	3⅛	8-6¾	8-3½
		R.B.F.	70 to 80	½	31	7-6	3° 35′ 00″	⅜	6	6	16-7	30-0	2⁵⁄₁₆	6-9¼	6-6
4	14° 15′ 00″	Cast	70 to 80	½	12½	7-6	3° 35′ 00″	⅜	6	6	20-0	55-0	3¹¹⁄₁₆	11-7¹⁵⁄₁₆	11-5½
		R.B.F.	70 to 80	½	40	7-6	3° 35′ 00″	⅜	6	6	20-0	55-0	2⅜	9-4⁷⁄₁₆	9-2
5	11° 25′ 16″	Cast	70 to 80	½	15¹¹⁄₁₆	10-0	2° 41′ 12″	⅜	6	8	25-0	87-0	3⁵⁄₁₆	13-10¼	13-8⁵⁄₁₆
		R.B.F.	70 to 80	½	42½	10-0	2° 41′ 12″	⅜	6	8	25-0	87-0	2⁵⁄₁₆	11-7⁹⁄₁₆	11-5½
6	9° 31′ 38″	Cast	70 to 80	½	18¹³⁄₁₆	10-0	2° 41′ 12″	⅜	6	8	27-6	130-0	3	16-0⅞	15-11³⁄₁₆
		R.B.F.	70 to 80	½	45	10-0	2° 41′ 12″	⅜	6	8	27-6	130-0	2¼	13-10¾	13-9

Note: R.B.F. denotes "Rigid Bolted Frog."

TURNOUT DATA FOR 36-IN. GAGE

LIGHT RAIL — 20-lb to 60-lb A.S.C.E. rail, inclusive

American Mining Congress Standards

FROG						SWITCH					ACTUAL LEAD	CLOSURE RAILS			
												CURVED			STRAIGHT
No.	Angle	Type	Rail Weight lb	Point in.	Actual Toe Length in.	Length ft-in.	Angle	Point in.	Heel Spread in.	Vertex Distance in.	ft-in.	Radius ft-in.	M.O. in.	Length ft-in.	Length ft-in.
2	28° 04′ 21″	Cast	20 to 40	¼	6¹¹⁄₁₆	3-6	6° 19′ 20″	⅜	5	4	11-0	17-0	4⅞	7-5½	6-11¼
		R.P.F.	20 to 30	¼	17	3-6	6° 19′ 20″	⅜	5	4	11-0	17-0	3⅞	6-7¼	6-1
		R.P.F.	40	⅜	20	3-6	6° 19′ 20″	⅜	5	4	11-0	17-0	3⁹⁄₁₆	6-4¼	5-10
2½	22° 37′ 12″	Cast	20 to 40	¼	8¼	5-0	4° 25′ 15″	⅜	5	5	15-0	28-0	5¹⁄₁₆	9-8½	9-3¾
		R.P.F.	20 to 30	¼	16½	5-0	4° 25′ 15″	⅜	5	5	15-0	28-0	4⅜	9-0¼	8-7½
		R.P.F.	40	⅜	20	5-0	4° 25′ 15″	⅜	5	5	15-0	28-0	4¹⁄₁₆	8-8¾	8-4
3	18° 55′ 29″	Cast	20 to 60	¼	8⅜	5-0	4° 25′ 15″	⅜	5	5	16-9	42-0	4⅝	11-4¾	11-0¾
		R.P.F.	20 to 30	¼	16½	5-0	4° 25′ 15″	⅜	5	5	16-9	42-0	4⅛	10-8½	10-4½
		R.P.F.	40 to 60	⅜	24	5-0	4° 25′ 15″	⅜	5	5	16-9	42-0	3⅝	10-1	9-9
4	14° 15′ 00″	Cast	40 to 60	¼	11¹⁄₁₆	5-0	4° 25′ 15″	⅜	5	5	20-0	78-0	3¹⁵⁄₁₆	14-4	14-1
		R.P.F.	40 to 60	⅜	27	5-0	4° 25′ 15″	⅜	5	5	20-0	78-0	3¼	13-0¼	12-9
5	11° 25′ 16″	Cast	40 to 60	¼	13¹³⁄₁₆	7-6	2° 56′ 44″	⅜	5	8	27-0	120-0	4⁵⁄₁₆	18-6¾	18-4¼
		R.P.F.	40 to 60	⅜	30	7-6	2° 56′ 44″	⅜	5	8	27-0	120-0	3¾	17-2½	17-0
6	9° 31′ 38″	Cast	40 to 60	¼	16⁹⁄₁₆	7-6	2° 56′ 44″	⅜	5	8	30-2	179-0	3⅞	21-5½	21-3½
		R.P.F.	40 to 60	⅜	36	7-6	2° 56′ 44″	⅜	5	8	30-2	179-0	3⁵⁄₁₆	19-10	19-8
6	9° 31′ 38″	Cast	40 to 60	¼	16⁹⁄₁₆	10-0	2° 12′ 32″	⅜	5	10	34-0	171-0	4⁹⁄₁₆	22-9½	22-7½
		R.P.F.	40 to 60	⅜	36	10-0	2° 12′ 32″	⅜	5	10	34-0	171-0	3¹⁵⁄₁₆	21-2	21-0

Note: R.P.F. denotes "Riveted Plate Frog."

TURNOUT DATA FOR 36-IN. GAGE *(continued)*

HEAVY RAIL — 70-lb to 100-lb A.S.C.E. rail, inclusive

American Mining Congress Standards

FROG						SWITCH					ACTUAL LEAD	CLOSURE RAILS			
												CURVED			STRAIGHT
No.	Angle	Type	Rail Weight lb	Point in.	Actual Toe Length in.	Length ft-in.	Angle	Point in.	Heel Spread in.	Vertex Distance in.	ft-in.	Radius ft-in.	M.O. in.	Length ft-in.	Length ft-in.
3	18° 55′ 29″	Cast	70 to 80	½	9½	7-6	3° 35′ 00″	⅜	6	6	19-1	39-0	4¾	11-1 7/16	10-9½
		Cast	85 to 100	½	11	7-6	3° 44′ 35″	⅜	6¼	6	18-10⅝	37-7 3/16	4⅝	10-9 9/16	10-5⅝
		R.B.F.	70 to 80	½	31	7-6	3° 35′ 00″	⅜	6	6	19-1	39-0	3⅞	9-3 15/16	9-0
		R.B.F.	85 to 100	½	31	7-6	3° 44′ 35″	⅜	6¼	6	18-10⅝	37-7 3/16	3⅜	9-1 9/16	8-9⅝
4	14° 15′ 00″	Cast	70 to 80	½	12 9/16	7-6	3° 35′ 00″	⅜	6	6	22-5	73-0	4⅛	14-1½	13-10½
		Cast	85 to 100	½	14⅝	7-6	3° 44′ 35″	⅜	6¼	6	22-2½	70-4⅝	4	13-8⅞	13-5⅞
		R.B.F.	70 to 80	½	40	7-6	3° 35′ 00″	⅜	6	6	22-5	73-0	2⅞	11-10	11-7
		R.B.F.	85 to 100	½	40	7-6	3° 44′ 35″	⅜	6¼	6	22-2½	70-4⅝	2⅞	11-7½	11-4½
5	11° 25′ 16″	Cast	70 to 80	½	15 11/16	10-0	2° 41′ 12″	⅜	6	8	29-0	114-0	4¼	17-10 11/16	17-8 5/16
		Cast	85 to 100	½	18 3/16	10-0	2° 48′ 23″	⅜	6¼	8	28-9⅛	110-6	4⅛	17-5⅜	17-2 15/16
		R.B.F.	70 to 80	½	42½	10-0	2° 41′ 12″	⅜	6	8	29-0	114-0	3¼	15-7⅞	15-5½
		R.B.F.	85 to 100	½	42½	10-0	2° 48′ 23″	⅜	6¼	8	28-9⅛	110-6	3¼	15-5 1/16	15-2⅝
6	9° 31′ 38″	Cast	70 to 80	½	18 13/16	10-0	2° 41′ 12″	⅜	6	8	32-2	169-0	3 13/16	20-9 3/16	20-7 3/16
		Cast	85 to 100	½	21 13/16	10-0	2° 48′ 23″	⅜	6¼	8	31-10½	165-4 3/16	3¾	20-2¾	20-0 11/16
		R.B.F.	70 to 80	½	45	10-0	2° 41′ 12″	⅜	6	8	32-2	169-0	3 1/16	18-7 1/16	18-5
		R.B.F.	85 to 100	½	45	10-0	2° 48′ 23″	⅜	6¼	8	31-10½	165-4 3/16	3 1/16	18-3 9/16	18-1½
7	8° 10′ 16″	Cast	70 to 80	½	21 15/16	10-0	2° 41′ 12″	⅜	6	8	35-4 11/16	238-11 11/16	3 9/16	23-8½	23-6¾
		Cast	85 to 100	½	25 7/16	10-0	2° 48′ 23″	⅜	6¼	8	34-9⅜	234-7 15/16	3 5/16	22-9 11/16	22-7 15/16
		R.B.F.	70 to 80	½	56½	10-0	2° 41′ 12″	⅜	6	8	35-4 11/16	238-11 11/16	2¾	20-9 15/16	20-8 3/16
		R.B.F.	85 to 100	½	56½	10-0	2° 48′ 23″	⅜	6¼	8	34-9⅜	234-7 15/16	2⅝	20-2⅝	20-0⅞
8	7° 9′ 10″	Cast	70 to 80	½	25 1/16	15-0	1° 47′ 27″	⅜	6	12	45-8⅞	298-8 11/16	4 3/16	28-9½	28-7 13/16
		Cast	85 to 100	½	29 1/16	15-0	1° 52′ 14″	⅜	6¼	12	45-0⅜	291-9¼	3 15/16	27-8 13/16	27-7 5/16
		R.B.F.	70 to 80	½	61	15-0	1° 47′ 27″	⅜	6	12	45-8⅞	298-8 11/16	3⅜	25-9 11/16	25-7⅞
		R.B.F.	85 to 100	½	61	15-0	1° 52′ 14″	⅜	6¼	12	45-0⅜	291-9¼	3¼	25-0⅞	24-11⅜

Note: R.B.F. denotes "Rigid Bolted Frog."

TURNOUT DATA FOR 42-IN. GAGE

—*The American Mining Congress has adopted 42-in. gage as the standard gage for mines. This gage should be used when it is possible to do so.*

LIGHT RAIL — 20-lb to 60-lb A.S.C.E. rail, inclusive

American Mining Congress Standards

FROG						SWITCH					ACTUAL LEAD	CLOSURE RAILS			
												CURVED			STRAIGHT
No.	Angle	Type	Rail Weight lb	Point in.	Actual Toe Length in.	Length ft-in.	Angle	Point in.	Heel Spread in.	Vertex Distance in.	ft-in.	Radius ft-in.	M.O. in.	Length ft-in.	Length ft-in.
2	28° 04′ 21″	Cast	20 to 40	¼	6 11/16	3-6	6° 19′ 20″	⅜	5	4	12-7	22-0	5⅝	9-1½	8-6¼
		R.P.F.	20 to 30	¼	17	3-6	6° 19′ 20″	⅜	5	4	12-7	22-0	4¾	8-3¼	7-8
		R.P.F.	40	⅜	20	3-6	6° 19′ 20″	⅜	5	4	12-7	22-0	4½	8-0¼	7-5
2½	22° 37′ 12″	Cast	20 to 40	¼	8¼	5-0	4° 25′ 15″	⅜	5	5	16-11	35-0	5 13/16	11-8¼	11-2¾
		R.P.F.	20 to 30	¼	16½	5-0	4° 25′ 15″	⅜	5	5	16-11	35-0	5¼	10-11⅞	10-6½
		R.P.F.	40	⅜	20	5-0	4° 25′ 15″	⅜	5	5	16-11	35-0	4⅞	10-8½	10-3
3	18° 55′ 29″	Cast	20 to 60	¼	8⅜	5-0	4° 25′ 15″	⅜	5	5	19-0	52-0	5½	13-8½	13-3½
		R.P.F.	20 to 30	¼	16½	5-0	4° 25′ 15″	⅜	5	5	19-0	52-0	5	13-0¼	12-7½
		R.P.F.	40 to 60	⅜	24	5-0	4° 25′ 15″	⅜	5	5	19-0	52-0	4 11/16	12-5	12-0
3	18° 55′ 29″	Cast	20 to 60	¼	8⅜	6-0	3° 40′ 59″	⅜	5	6	20-6	51-0	5⅞	14-2¾	13-9½
		R.P.F.	20 to 30	¼	16½	6-0	3° 40′ 59″	⅜	5	6	20-6	51-0	5⅜	13-6	13-1½
		R.P.F.	40 to 60	⅜	24	6-0	3° 40′ 59″	⅜	5	6	20-6	51-0	4⅞	12-10¾	12-6
4	14° 15′ 00″	Cast	40 to 60	¼	11 1/16	6-0	3° 40′ 59″	⅜	5	6	24-7	94-0	5⅛	17-11¼	17-7¾
		R.P.F.	40 to 60	⅜	27	6-0	3° 40′ 59″	⅜	5	6	24-7	94-0	4 7/16	16-7½	16-4
4	14° 15′ 00″	Cast	40 to 60	¼	11 1/16	7-6	2° 56′ 44″	⅜	5	8	26-10	91-0	5¾	18-8¼	18-4¾
		R.P.F.	40 to 60	⅜	27	7-6	2° 56′ 44″	⅜	5	8	26-10	91-0	5	17-4½	17-1
5	11° 25′ 16″	Cast	40 to 60	¼	13 13/16	7-6	2° 56′ 44″	⅜	5	8	31-0	148-0	5 3/16	22-7	22-4¼
		R.P.F.	40 to 60	⅜	30	7-6	2° 56′ 44″	⅜	5	8	31-0	148-0	4 11/16	21-2¾	21-0
6	9° 31′ 38″	Cast	40 to 60	¼	16 9/16	7-6	2° 56′ 44″	⅜	5	8	34-9	220-0	4⅝	26-0¾	25-10½
		R.P.F.	40 to 60	⅜	36	7-6	2° 56′ 44″	⅜	5	8	34-9	220-0	4⅛	24-5½	24-3
6	9° 31′ 38″	Cast	40 to 60	¼	16 9/16	10-0	2° 12′ 32″	⅜	5	10	38-10	210-0	5 7/16	27-7¾	27-5½
		R.P.F.	40 to 60	⅜	36	10-0	2° 12′ 32″	⅜	5	10	38-10	210-0	4¾	26-0¼	25-10

Note: R.P.F. denotes "Riveted Plate Frog."

TURNOUT DATA FOR 42-IN. GAGE *(continued)*

HEAVY RAIL — 70-lb to 100-lb A.S.C.E. rail, inclusive

American Mining Congress Standards

FROG						SWITCH					ACTUAL LEAD	CLOSURE RAILS			
												CURVED			STRAIGHT
No.	Angle	Type	Rail Weight lb	Point in.	Actual Toe Length in.	Length ft-in.	Angle	Point in.	Heel Spread in.	Vertex Distance in.	ft-in.	Radius ft-in.	M.O. in.	Length ft-in.	Length ft-in.
3	18° 55′ 29″	Cast	70 to 80	½	9½	7-6	3° 35′ 00″	⅜	6	6	21-7	49-0	5¾	13-8 1/16	13-3½
		Cast	85 to 100	½	11	7-6	3° 44′ 35″	⅜	6¼	6	21-4 9/16	47-2¾	5⅝	13-4 3/16	12-11 9/16
		R.B.F.	70 to 80	½	31	7-6	3° 35′ 00″	⅜	6	6	21-7	49-0	4 5/16	11-10 9/16	11-6
		R.B.F.	85 to 100	½	31	7-6	3° 44′ 35″	⅜	6¼	6	21-4 9/16	47-2¾	4 5/16	11-8 3/16	11-3 9/16
4	14° 15′ 00″	Cast	70 to 80	½	12 9/16	7-6	3° 35′ 00″	⅜	6	6	25-7	90-0	5	17-4	17-0½
		Cast	85 to 100	½	14⅝	7-6	3° 44′ 35″	⅜	6¼	6	25-4⅜	87-10 3/16	4⅞	16-11 5/16	16-7¾
		R.B.F.	70 to 80	½	40	7-6	3° 35′ 00″	⅜	6	6	25-7	90-0	3¾	15-0½	14-9
		R.B.F.	85 to 100	½	40	7-6	3° 44′ 35″	⅜	6¼	6	25-4⅜	87-10 3/16	3¾	14-9 15/16	14-6⅜
5	11° 25′ 16″	Cast	70 to 80	½	15 11/16	10-0	2° 41′ 12″	⅜	6	8	33-1	140-0	5 3/16	22-0 1/16	21-9 5/16
		Cast	85 to 100	½	18 3/16	10-0	2° 48′ 23″	⅜	6¼	8	32-9¼	137-4 9/16	5	21-5⅞	21-3 1/16
		R.B.F.	70 to 80	½	42½	10-0	2° 41′ 12″	⅜	6	8	33-1	140-0	4 3/16	19-9¼	19-6½
		R.B.F.	85 to 100	½	42½	10-0	2° 48′ 23″	⅜	6¼	8	32-9¼	137-4 9/16	4⅛	19-5 9/16	19-2¾
6	9° 31′ 38″	Cast	70 to 80	½	18 13/16	10-0	2° 41′ 12″	⅜	6	8	36-10	209-0	4⅝	25-5 9/16	25-3 3/16
		Cast	85 to 100	½	21 13/16	10-0	2° 48′ 23″	⅜	6¼	8	36-6	205-0¾	4½	24-10⅝	24-8 3/16
		R.B.F.	70 to 80	½	45	10-0	2° 41′ 12″	⅜	6	8	36-10	209-0	3⅞	23-3⅜	23-1
		R.B.F.	85 to 100	½	45	10-0	2° 48′ 23″	⅜	6¼	8	36-6	205-0¾	3⅞	22-11 7/16	22-9
7	8° 10′ 16″	Cast	70 to 80	½	21 15/16	10-0	2° 41′ 12″	⅜	6	8	40-7 13/16	294-1¾	4 5/16	28-11⅞	28-9⅞
		Cast	85 to 100	½	25 7/16	10-0	2° 48′ 23″	⅜	6¼	8	39-11¾	290-6⅛	4 1/16	28-0 7/16	27-10 5/16
		R.B.F.	70 to 80	½	56½	10-0	2° 41′ 12″	⅜	6	8	40-7 13/16	294-1¾	3½	26-1 5/16	25-11 5/16
		R.B.F.	85 to 100	½	56½	10-0	2° 48′ 23″	⅜	6¼	8	39-11¾	290-6⅛	3⅜	25-5⅜	25-3¼
8	7° 9′ 10″	Cast	70 to 80	½	25 1/16	15-0	1° 47′ 27″	⅜	6	12	52-1⅝	367-3¾	5 1/16	35-2½	35-0 9/16
		Cast	85 to 100	½	29 1/16	15-0	1° 52′ 14″	⅜	6¼	12	51-4 7/16	360-8⅞	4 13/16	34-1⅛	33-11⅜
		R.B.F.	70 to 80	½	61	15-0	1° 47′ 27″	⅜	6	12	52-1⅝	367-3¾	4¼	32-2 9/16	32-0⅝
		R.B.F.	85 to 100	½	61	15-0	1° 52′ 14″	⅜	6¼	12	51-4 7/16	360-8⅞	4⅛	31-5 3/16	31-3 7/16

Note: R.B.F. denotes "Rigid Bolted Frog."

TURNOUT DATA FOR 44-IN. GAGE

LIGHT RAIL — 20-lb to 60-lb A.S.C.E. rail, inclusive

American Mining Congress Standards

FROG						SWITCH					ACTUAL LEAD	CLOSURE RAILS			
												CURVED			STRAIGHT
No.	Angle	Type	Rail Weight lb	Point in.	Actual Toe Length in.	Length ft-in.	Angle	Point in.	Heel Spread in.	Vertex Distance in.	ft-in.	Radius ft-in.	M.O. in.	Length ft-in.	Length ft-in.
2	28° 04′ 21″	Cast	20 to 40	¼	6 11/16	3-6	6° 19′ 20″	⅜	5	4	13-2	24-0	5 15/16	9-8¾	9-1¼
		R.P.F.	20 to 30	¼	17	3-6	6° 19′ 20″	⅜	5	4	13-2	24-0	4 15/16	8-10½	8-3
		R.P.F.	40	⅜	20	3-6	6° 19′ 20″	⅜	5	4	13-2	24-0	4⅝	8-7½	8-0
2½	22° 37′ 12″	Cast	20 to 40	¼	8¼	5-0	4° 25′ 15″	⅜	5	5	17-7	37-0	6 3/16	12-4½	11-10¾
		R.P.F.	20 to 30	¼	16½	5-0	4° 25′ 15″	⅜	5	5	17-7	37-0	5 9/16	11-8¼	11-2½
		R.P.F.	40	⅜	20	5-0	4° 25′ 15″	⅜	5	5	17-7	37-0	5¼	11-4¾	10-11
3	18° 55′ 29″	Cast	20 to 60	¼	8⅜	5-0	4° 25′ 15″	⅜	5	5	19-11	55-0	5 13/16	14-7¼	14-2½
		R.P.F.	20 to 30	¼	16½	5-0	4° 25′ 15″	⅜	5	5	19-11	55-0	5 5/16	13-11¼	13-6½
		R.P.F.	40 to 60	⅜	24	5-0	4° 25′ 15″	⅜	5	5	19-11	55-0	4⅞	13-4	12-11
4	14° 15′ 00″	Cast	40 to 60	¼	11 1/16	6-0	3° 40′ 49″	⅜	5	6	25-8	99-0	5½	19-0½	18-8¾
		R.P.F.	40 to 60	⅜	27	6-0	3° 40′ 49″	⅜	5	6	25-8	99-0	5 1/16	18-3	17-4½
4	14° 15′ 00″	Cast	40 to 60	¼	11 1/16	7-6	2° 56′ 44″	⅜	5	8	28-0	97-0	6⅛	19-10¼	19-6¾
		R.P.F.	40 to 60	⅜	27	7-6	2° 56′ 44″	⅜	5	8	28-0	97-0	5 5/16	18-6¾	18-3
5	11° 25′ 16″	Cast	40 to 60	¼	13 13/16	7-6	2° 56′ 44″	⅜	5	8	32-3	156-0	5 7/16	23-10	23-7
		R.P.F.	40 to 60	⅜	30	7-6	2° 56′ 44″	⅜	5	8	32-3	156-0	4⅞	22-6	22-3
6	9° 31′ 38″	Cast	40 to 60	¼	16 9/16	7-6	2° 56′ 44″	⅜	5	8	36-3	233-0	4⅞	27-6¾	27-4¼
		R.P.F.	40 to 60	⅜	36	7-6	2° 56′ 44″	⅜	5	8	36-3	233-0	4 5/16	25-11½	25-9
6	9° 31′ 38″	Cast	40 to 60	¼	16 9/16	10-0	2° 12′ 32″	⅜	5	10	40-5	223-0	5¾	29-2½	29-0¼
		R.P.F.	40 to 60	⅜	36	10-0	2° 12′ 32″	⅜	5	10	40-5	223-0	5⅛	27-7½	27-5

Note: R.P.F. denotes "Riveted Plate Frog."

TURNOUT DATA FOR 44-IN. GAGE *(continued)*

HEAVY RAIL — 70-lb to 100-lb A.S.C.E. rail, inclusive

American Mining Congress Standards

FROG						SWITCH					ACTUAL LEAD	CLOSURE RAILS			
												CURVED			STRAIGHT
No.	Angle	Type	Rail Weight lb	Point in.	Actual Toe Length in.	Length ft-in.	Angle	Point in.	Heel Spread in.	Vertex Distance in.	ft-in.	Radius ft-in.	M.O. in.	Length ft-in.	Length ft-in.
3	18° 55′ 29″	Cast	70 to 80	½	9½	7-6	3° 35′ 00″	⅜	6	6	22-6	52-0	6⅛	14-7¼	14-2½
		Cast	85 to 100	½	11	7-6	3° 44′ 35″	⅜	6¼	6	22-2 9/16	50-5 5/16	5 15/16	14-2⅜	13-9 9/16
		R.B.F.	70 to 80	½	31	7-6	3° 35′ 00″	⅜	6	6	22-6	52-0	4¾	12-10	12-5
		R.B.F.	85 to 100	½	31	7-6	3° 44′ 35″	⅜	6¼	6	22-2 9/16	50-5 5/16	4 11/16	12-6⅜	12-1 9/16
4	14° 15′ 00″	Cast	70 to 80	½	12 9/16	7-6	3° 35′ 00″	⅜	6	6	26-10	96-0	5⅜	18-7	18-3½
		Cast	85 to 100	½	14⅝	7-6	3° 44′ 35″	⅜	6¼	6	26-5	93-8 1/16	5 3/16	18-0⅛	17-8⅜
		R.B.F.	70 to 80	½	40	7-6	3° 35′ 00″	⅜	6	6	26-10	96-0	4 3/16	16-3¾	16-0
		R.B.F.	85 to 100	½	40	7-6	3° 44′ 35″	⅜	6¼	6	26-5	93-8 1/16	4 1/16	15-10¾	15-7
5	11° 25′ 16″	Cast	70 to 80	½	15 11/16	10-0	2° 41′ 12″	⅜	6	8	34-7	149-0	5 9/16	23-6	23-3¼
		Cast	85 to 100	½	18 3/16	10-0	2° 48′ 23″	⅜	6¼	8	34-1¼	146-4 1/16	5 5/16	22-10 1/16	22-7 1/16
		R.B.F.	70 to 80	½	42½	10-0	2° 41′ 12″	⅜	6	8	34-7	149-0	4 9/16	21-3½	21-0½
		R.B.F.	85 to 100	½	42½	10-0	2° 48′ 23″	⅜	6¼	8	34-1¼	146-4 1/16	4 7/16	20-9¾	20-6¾
6	9° 31′ 38″	Cast	70 to 80	½	18 13/16	10-0	2° 41′ 12″	⅜	6	8	38-8	222-0	5 1/16	27-3½	27-1
		Cast	85 to 100	½	21 13/16	10-0	2° 48′ 23″	⅜	6¼	8	38-0½	218-3⅜	4 13/16	26-5 5/16	26-2 11/16
		R.B.F.	70 to 80	½	45	10-0	2° 41′ 12″	⅜	6	8	38-8	222-0	4¼	25-1½	24-11
		R.B.F.	85 to 100	½	45	10-0	2° 48′ 23″	⅜	6¼	8	38-0½	218-3⅜	4⅛	24-6⅛	24-3½
7	8° 10′ 16″	Cast	70 to 80	½	21 15/16	10-0	2° 41′ 12″	⅜	6	8	42-4⅞	312-7 7/16	4 9/16	30-9⅛	30-6 15/16
		Cast	85 to 100	½	25 7/16	10-0	2° 48′ 23″	⅜	6¼	8	41-8⅝	309-1½	4 5/16	29-9 5/16	29-7 3/16
		R.B.F.	70 to 80	½	56½	10-0	2° 41′ 12″	⅜	6	8	42-4⅞	312-7 7/16	3¾	27-10 9/16	27-8⅜
		R.B.F.	85 to 100	½	56½	10-0	2° 48′ 23″	⅜	6¼	8	41-8⅝	309-1½	3⅝	27-2¼	27-0⅛
8	7° 9′ 10″	Cast	70 to 80	½	25 1/16	15-0	1° 47′ 27″	⅜	6	12	54-3 3/16	390-2 1/16	5⅜	37-4 3/16	37-2⅛
		Cast	85 to 100	½	29 1/16	15-0	1° 52′ 14″	⅜	6¼	12	53-5¾	383-8 11/16	5⅛	36-2 9/16	36-0 11/16
		R.B.F.	70 to 80	½	61	15-0	1° 47′ 27″	⅜	6	12	54-3 3/16	390-2 1/16	4½	34-4¼	34-2 3/16
		R.B.F.	85 to 100	½	61	15-0	1° 52′ 14″	⅜	6¼	12	53-5¾	383-8 11/16	4 7/16	33-6⅜	33-4¾

Note: R.B.F. denotes "Rigid Bolted Frog."

TURNOUT DATA FOR 48-IN. GAGE

LIGHT RAIL — 20-lb to 60-lb A.S.C.E. rail, inclusive

American Mining Congress Standards

FROG						SWITCH					ACTUAL LEAD	CLOSURE RAILS			
												CURVED			STRAIGHT
No.	Angle	Type	Rail Weight lb	Point in.	Actual Toe Length in.	Length ft-in.	Angle	Point in.	Heel Spread in.	Vertex Distance in.	ft-in.	Radius ft-in.	M.O. in.	Length ft-in.	Length ft-in.
2	28° 04′ 21″	Cast	20 to 40	¼	6 11/16	3-6	6° 19′ 20″	⅜	5	4	14-3	26-0	6¾	10-10¼	10-2¼
		R.P.F.	20 to 30	¼	17	3-6	6° 19′ 20″	⅜	5	4	14-3	26-0	5¾	10-0¼	9-4
		R.P.F.	40	⅜	20	3-6	6° 19′ 20″	⅜	5	4	14-3	26-0	5½	9-9¼	9-1
2½	22° 37′ 12″	Cast	20 to 40	¼	8¼	5-0	4° 25′ 15″	⅜	5	5	19-0	41-0	7	13-10¼	13-3¾
		R.P.F.	20 to 30	¼	16½	5-0	4° 25′ 15″	⅜	5	5	19-0	41-0	6 5/16	13-2	12-7½
		R.P.F.	40	⅜	20	5-0	4° 25′ 15″	⅜	5	5	19-0	41-0	6 1/16	12-10½	12-4
3	18° 55′ 29″	Cast	20 to 60	¼	8⅜	5-0	4° 25′ 15″	⅜	5	5	21-7	62-0	6 7/16	16-4	15-10½
		R.P.F.	20 to 30	¼	16½	5-0	4° 25′ 15″	⅜	5	5	21-7	62-0	5 15/16	15-8	15-2½
		R.P.F.	40 to 60	⅜	24	5-0	4° 25′ 15″	⅜	5	5	21-7	62-0	5½	15-0½	14-7
4	14° 15′ 00″	Cast	40 to 60	¼	11 1/16	7-6	2° 56′ 44″	⅜	5	8	30-2	108-0	6¾	22-0½	21-8¾
		R.P.F.	40 to 60	⅜	27	7-6	2° 56′ 44″	⅜	5	8	30-2	108-0	6 5/16	20-9	20-5
5	11° 25′ 16″	Cast	40 to 60	¼	13 13/16	7-6	2° 56′ 44″	⅜	5	8	35-0	174-0	6 1/16	26-7½	26-4¼
		R.P.F.	40 to 60	⅜	30	7-6	2° 56′ 44″	⅜	5	8	35-0	174-0	5½	25-3¼	25-0
6	9° 31′ 38″	Cast	40 to 60	¼	16 9/16	7-6	2° 56′ 44″	⅜	5	8	39-4	260-0	5 7/16	30-8¼	30-5½
		R.P.F.	40 to 60	⅜	36	7-6	2° 56′ 44″	⅜	5	8	39-4	260-0	4⅞	29-0¾	28-10
6	9° 31′ 38″	Cast	40 to 60	¼	16 9/16	10-0	2° 12′ 32″	⅜	5	10	43-8	248-0	6 7/16	32-6¼	32-3½
		R.P.F.	40 to 60	⅜	36	10-0	2° 12′ 32″	⅜	5	10	43-8	248-0	5¾	30-10¼	30-8

Note: R.P.F. denotes "Riveted Plate Frog."

TURNOUT DATA FOR 48-IN. GAGE *(continued)*

HEAVY RAIL — 70-lb to 100-lb A.S.C.E. rail, inclusive

American Mining Congress Standards

FROG						SWITCH					ACTUAL LEAD	CLOSURE RAILS			
												CURVED			STRAIGHT
No.	Angle	Type	Rail Weight lb	Point in.	Actual Toe Length in.	Length ft-in.	Angle	Point in.	Heel Spread in.	Vertex Distance in.	ft-in.	Radius ft-in.	M.O. in.	Length ft-in.	Length ft-in.
3	18° 55′ 29″	Cast	70 to 80	½	9½	7-6	3° 35′ 00″	⅜	6	6	24-1	58-0	6 13/16	16-2 13/16	15-9½
		Cast	85 to 100	½	11	7-6	3° 44′ 35″	⅜	6¼	6	23-10½	56-10 5/16	6 11/16	15-10 13/16	15-5½
		R.B.F.	70 to 80	½	31	7-6	3° 35′ 00″	⅜	6	6	24-1	58-0	5⅜	14-5¼	14-0
		R.B.F.	85 to 100	½	31	7-6	3° 44′ 35″	⅜	6¼	6	23-10½	56-10 5/16	5⅜	14-2 13/16	13-9½
4	14° 15′ 00″	Cast	70 to 80	½	12 9/16	7-6	3° 35′ 00″	⅜	6	6	28-10	107-0	5 15/16	20-7 9/16	20-3½
		Cast	85 to 100	½	14⅝	7-6	3° 44′ 35″	⅜	6¼	6	28-6¼	105-3¾	5¾	20-1¾	19-9⅝
		R.B.F.	70 to 80	½	40	7-6	3° 35′ 00″	⅜	6	6	28-10	107-0	4¾	18-4 1/16	18-0
		R.B.F.	85 to 100	½	40	7-6	3° 44′ 35″	⅜	6¼	6	28-6¼	105-3¾	4⅝	18-0⅜	17-8¼
5	11° 25′ 16″	Cast	70 to 80	½	15 11/16	10-0	2° 41′ 12″	⅜	6	8	37-1	167-0	6⅛	26-0½	25-9 5/16
		Cast	85 to 100	½	18 3/16	10-0	2° 48′ 23″	⅜	6¼	8	36-9 5/16	164-3⅛	5 15/16	25-6⅜	25-3⅛
		R.B.F.	70 to 80	½	42½	10-0	2° 41′ 12″	⅜	6	8	37-1	167-0	5 1/16	23-9¾	23-6½
		R.B.F.	85 to 100	½	42½	10-0	2° 48′ 23″	⅜	6¼	8	36-9 5/16	164-3⅛	5 1/16	23-6 1/16	23-2 13/16
6	9° 31′ 38″	Cast	70 to 80	½	18 13/16	10-0	2° 41′ 12″	⅜	6	8	41-6	248-0	5½	30-1 15/16	29-11 3/16
		Cast	85 to 100	½	21 13/16	10-0	2° 48′ 23″	⅜	6¼	8	41-1½	244-9 5/16	5⅜	29-6 9/16	29-3 11/16
		R.B.F.	70 to 80	½	45	10-0	2° 41′ 12″	⅜	6	8	41-6	248-0	4¾	27-11¾	27-9
		R.B.F.	85 to 100	½	45	10-0	2° 48′ 23″	⅜	6¼	8	41-1½	244-9 5/16	4 11/16	27-7⅜	27-4½
7	8° 10′ 16″	Cast	70 to 80	½	21 13/16	10-0	2° 41′ 12″	⅜	6	8	45-10 15/16	349-4 7/16	5 1/16	34-3 5/16	34-1
		Cast	85 to 100	½	25 7/16	10-0	2° 48′ 23″	⅜	6¼	8	45-2¼	346-4¼	4 13/16	33-3 3/16	33-0 13/16
		R.B.F.	70 to 80	½	56½	10-0	2° 41′ 12″	⅜	6	8	45-10 15/16	349-4 7/16	4¼	31-4¾	31-2 7/16
		R.B.F.	85 to 100	½	56½	10-0	2° 48′ 23″	⅜	6¼	8	45-2¼	346-4¼	4 1/16	30-8⅛	30-5¾
8	7° 9′ 10″	Cast	70 to 80	½	25 1/16	15-0	1° 47′ 27″	⅜	6	12	58-6 5/16	435-10¾	5⅝	41-7½	41-5¼
		Cast	85 to 100	½	29 1/16	15-0	1° 52′ 14″	⅜	6¼	12	57-8 7/16	429-8 7/16	5¾	40-5⅜	40-3⅜
		R.B.F.	70 to 80	½	61	15-0	1° 47′ 27″	⅜	6	12	58-6 5/16	435-10¾	5 1/16	38-7 9/16	38-5 5/16
		R.B.F.	85 to 100	½	61	15-0	1° 52′ 14″	⅜	6¼	12	57-8 7/16	429-8 7/16	5	37-9 7/16	37-7 7/16

Note: R.B.F. denotes "Rigid Bolted Frog."

TURNOUT DATA FOR 56½-IN. GAGE

LIGHT RAIL — 20-lb to 60-lb A.S.C.E. rail, inclusive

American Mining Congress Standards

FROG						SWITCH					ACTUAL LEAD	CLOSURE RAILS			
												CURVED			STRAIGHT
No.	Angle	Type	Rail Weight lb	Point in.	Actual Toe Length in.	Length ft-in.	Angle	Point in.	Heel Spread in.	Vertex Distance in.	ft-in.	Radius ft-in.	M.O. in.	Length ft-in.	Length ft-in.
2	28° 04′ 21″	Cast	20 to 40	¼	6 11/16	3-6	6° 19′ 20″	⅜	5	4	16-7	33-0	8 1/16	13-4	12-6¼
		R.P.F.	20 to 30	¼	17	3-6	6° 19′ 20″	⅜	5	4	16-7	33-0	7 1/16	12-5¾	11-8
		R.P.F.	40	⅜	20	3-6	6° 19′ 20″	⅜	5	4	16-7	33-0	6¾	12-2¾	11-5
2½	22° 37′ 12″	Cast	20 to 40	¼	8¼	5-0	4° 25′ 15″	⅜	5	5	22-0	51-0	8 7/16	16-11¼	16-3¾
		R.P.F.	20 to 30	¼	16½	5-0	4° 25′ 15″	⅜	5	5	22-0	51-0	7¾	16-3	15-7½
		R.P.F.	40	⅜	20	5-0	4° 25′ 15″	⅜	5	5	22-0	51-0	7½	15-11½	15-4
3	18° 55′ 29″	Cast	20 to 60	¼	8⅜	5-0	4° 25′ 15″	⅜	5	5	25-0	76-0	7¾	19-10	19-3½
		R.P.F.	20 to 30	¼	16½	5-0	4° 25′ 15″	⅜	5	5	25-0	76-0	7¼	19-1¾	18-7½
		R.P.F.	40 to 60	⅜	24	5-0	4° 25′ 15″	⅜	5	5	25-0	76-0	6¾	18-6½	18-0
4	14° 15′ 00″	Cast	40 to 60	¼	11 1/16	7-6	2° 56′ 44″	⅜	5	8	34-10	132-0	8 3/16	26-9½	26-4¾
		R.P.F.	40 to 60	⅜	27	7-6	2° 56′ 44″	⅜	5	8	34-10	132-0	7 11/16	25-6	25-1¼
5	11° 25′ 16″	Cast	40 to 60	¼	13 13/16	7-6	2° 56′ 44″	⅜	5	8	40-7	212-0	7⅜	32-3	31-11¼
		R.P.F.	40 to 60	⅜	30	7-6	2° 56′ 44″	⅜	5	8	40-7	212-0	6¾	30-10¾	30-7
6	9° 31′ 38″	Cast	40 to 60	¼	16 9/16	7-6	2° 56′ 44″	⅜	5	8	45-10	316-0	6 9/16	37-2¾	36-11½
		R.P.F.	40 to 60	⅜	36	7-6	2° 56′ 44″	⅜	5	8	45-10	316-0	6	35-7¼	35-4
6	9° 31′ 38″	Cast	40 to 60	¼	16 9/16	10-0	2° 12′ 32″	⅜	5	10	50-7	302-0	7¾	39-5½	39-2½
		R.P.F.	40 to 60	⅜	36	10-0	2° 12′ 32″	⅜	5	10	50-7	302-0	7⅛	37-10¼	37-7

Note: R.P.F. denotes "Riveted Plate Frog."

TURNOUT DATA FOR 56½-IN. GAGE *(continued)*

HEAVY RAIL — 70-lb to 100-lb A.S.C.E. rail, inclusive

American Mining Congress Standards

FROG						SWITCH					ACTUAL LEAD	CLOSURE RAILS			
												CURVED			STRAIGHT
No.	Angle	Type	Rail Weight lb	Point in.	Actual Toe Length in.	Length ft-in.	Angle	Point in.	Heel Spread in.	Vertex Distance in.	ft-in.	Radius ft-in.	M.O. in.	Length ft-in.	Length ft-in.
3	18° 55′ 29″	Cast	70 to 80	½	9½	7-6	3° 35′ 00″	⅜	6	6	27-8	72-0	8¼	19-10¾	19-4½
		Cast	85 to 100	½	11	7-6	3° 44′ 35″	⅜	6¼	6	27-4 15/16	70-6 1/16	8 1/16	19-6 3/16	18-11 15/16
		R.B.F.	70 to 80	½	31	7-6	3° 35′ 00″	⅜	6	6	27-8	72-0	6 13/16	18-1¼	17-7
		R.B.F.	85 to 100	½	31	7-6	3° 44′ 35″	⅜	6¼	6	27-4 15/16	70-6 1/16	6¾	17-10 3/16	17-3 15/16
4	14° 15′ 00″	Cast	70 to 80	½	12 9/16	7-6	3° 35′ 00″	⅜	6	6	33-4	132-0	7 3/16	25-2 5/16	24-9½
		Cast	85 to 100	½	14⅝	7-6	3° 44′ 35″	⅜	6¼	6	32-11 15/16	130-0⅝	7	24-8 3/16	24-3 5/16
		R.B.F.	70 to 80	½	40	7-6	3° 35′ 00″	⅜	6	6	33-4	132-0	5 15/16	22-10 13/16	22-6
		R.B.F.	75 to 100	½	40	7-6	3° 44′ 35″	⅜	6¼	6	32-11 15/16	130-0⅝	5⅞	22-6 13/16	22-1 15/16
5	11° 25′ 16″	Cast	70 to 80	½	15 11/16	10-0	2° 41′ 12″	⅜	6	8	42-10	205-0	7 7/16	31-10 1/16	31-6 5/16
		Cast	85 to 100	½	18 3/16	10-0	2° 48′ 23″	⅜	6¼	8	42-5 7/16	202-4⅛	7¼	31-3 1/16	30-11¼
		R.B.F.	70 to 80	½	42½	10-0	2° 41′ 12″	⅜	6	8	42-10	205-0	6 7/16	29-7¼	29-3½
		R.B.F.	85 to 100	½	42½	10-0	2° 48′ 23″	⅜	6¼	8	42-5 7/16	202-4⅛	6⅜	29-2¾	28-10 15/16
6	9° 31′ 38″	Cast	70 to 80	½	18 13/16	10-0	2° 41′ 12″	⅜	6	8	48-2	304-0	6¾	36-10 7/16	36-7 3/16
		Cast	85 to 100	½	21 13/16	10-0	2° 48′ 23″	⅜	6¼	8	47-8 3/16	301-0½	6½	36-1¾	35-10⅜
		R.B.F.	70 to 80	½	45	10-0	2° 41′ 12″	⅜	6	8	48-2	304-0	5 15/16	34-8¼	34-5
		R.B.F.	85 to 100	½	45	10-0	2° 48′ 23″	⅜	6¼	8	47-8 3/16	301-0½	5 13/16	34-2 9/16	33-11 3/16
7	8° 10′ 16″	Cast	70 to 80	½	21 15/16	10-0	2° 41′ 12″	⅜	6	8	53-4 7/16	427-7¼	6⅛	41-9 3/16	41-6½
		Cast	85 to 100	½	25 7/16	10-0	2° 48′ 23″	⅜	6¼	8	52-6 11/16	425-5 11/16	5⅞	40-8 1/16	40-5¼
		R.B.F.	70 to 80	½	56½	10-0	2° 41′ 12″	⅜	6	8	53-4 7/16	427-7¼	5 9/16	38-10⅝	38-7 15/16
		R.B.F.	85 to 100	½	56½	10-0	2° 48′ 23″	⅜	6¼	8	52-6 11/16	425-5 11/16	5⅛	38-1	37-10 3/16
8	7° 9′ 10″	Cast	70 to 80	½	25 1/16	15-0	1° 47′ 27″	⅜	6	12	67-7	533-0¾	7¼	50-8⅝	50-5 15/16
		Cast	85 to 100	½	29 1/16	15-0	1° 52′ 14″	⅜	6¼	12	66-8 3/16	527-4⅞	7	49-5½	49-3⅛
		R.B.F	70 to 80	½	61	15-0	1° 47′ 27″	⅜	6	12	67-7	533-0¾	6 7/16	47-8 11/16	47-6
		R.B.F.	85 to 100	½	61	15-0	1° 52′ 14″	⅜	6¼	12	66-8 3/16	527-4⅞	6¼	46-9 9/16	46-7 3/16

Note: R.B.F. denotes "Rigid Bolted Frog."

DATA FOR TURNOUTS WITH LONG SWITCHES

LIGHT RAIL — 20-lb to 60-lb A.S.C.E. rail, inclusive. With Cast Frogs

American Mining Congress Standards

Frog No.	Gage	SWITCH		ACTUAL LEAD	CLOSURE RAILS			
					CURVED			STRAIGHT
	in.	Length ft-in.	Vertex Distance in.	ft-in.	Radius ft-in.	M.O. in.	Length ft-in.	Length ft-in.
3	36	6-0	6	18-0	41-0	4 15/16	11-7½	11-3½
	42	6-0	6	20-6	51-0	5 15/16	14-2¾	13-9½
	44	6-0	6	21-4	54-0	6¼	15-0¼	14-7½
	48	6-0	6	23-0	60-0	7	16-8¾	16-3½
	56½	6-0	6	26-6	74-0	8⅜	20-3¾	19-9½
3	36	7-6	8	19-10	40-0	5⅜	11-11¼	11-7½
	42	7-6	8	22-5	50-0	6 7/16	14-7	14-2½
	44	7-6	8	23-4	53-0	6 13/16	15-6¼	15-1½
	48	7-6	8	25-0	59-0	7 9/16	17-2¾	16-9½
	56½	7-6	8	28-8	73-0	9	20-11½	20-5½
4	36	6-0	6	21-5	76-0	4 5/16	14-8¾	14-5¾
	42	6-0	6	24-7	94-0	5⅛	17-11¼	17-7¾
	44	6-0	6	25-8	99-0	5½	19-0½	18-8¾
	48	6-0	6	27-10	111-0	6⅛	21-2¾	20-10¾
	56½	6-0	6	32-3	136-0	7 5/16	25-8½	25-3¾
4	36	7-6	8	23-7	74-0	4 13/16	15-4½	15-1¾
	42	7-6	8	26-10	91-0	5¾	18-8¼	18-4¾
	44	7-6	8	28-0	97-0	6⅛	19-10¼	19-6¾
	48	7-6	8	30-2	108-0	6¾	22-0½	21-8¾
	56½	7-6	8	34-10	132-0	8 3/16	26-9½	26-4¾
5	36	10-0	10	30-5	116-0	4⅞	19-5¼	19-3
	42	10-0	10	34-8	143-0	5 15/16	23-8¾	23-6
	44	10-0	10	36-0	151-0	6¼	25-0¾	24-10
	48	10-0	10	38-10	169-0	6 15/16	27-11	27-8
	56½	10-0	10	44-9	206-0	8⅜	33-10¾	33-7

DATA FOR TURNOUTS WITH LONG SWITCHES (continued)
HEAVY RAIL — 70-lb to 100-lb A.S.C.E. rail, inclusive. With Cast Frogs
American Mining Congress Standards

Frog No.	Gage in.	Length ft.-in.	Vertex Distance in.	ACTUAL LEAD		CLOSURE RAILS			
				Rail Weight lb	ft.-in.	CURVED			STRAIGHT
						Radius ft.-in.	M.O. in.	Length ft.-in.	Length ft.-in.
6	36	15-0	12	70 to 80	39-0 1/16	161-2 7/16	4 13/16	22-7 1/4	22-5 1/4
		15-0	12	85 to 100	38-5 11/16	156-11 15/16	4 9/16	21-9 13/16	21-7 7/8
	42	15-0	12	70 to 80	44-0 5/8	198-9 5/8	5 13/16	27-8 1/2	27-5 13/16
		15-0	12	85 to 100	43-5 13/16	194-8 7/16	5 9/16	26-10 1/4	26-8
	44	15-0	12	70 to 80	45-8 3/4	211-4	6 1/2	29-4 7/16	29-1 15/16
		15-0	12	85 to 100	45-1 1/8	207-3 5/16	5 15/16	28-6 7/16	28-4 1/16
	48	15-0	12	70 to 80	49-1 1/8	236-4 3/8	6 13/16	32-9 1/16	32-6 5/16
		15-0	12	85 to 100	48-5 15/16	232-4 15/16	6 5/8	31-10 3/4	31-8 1/8
	56 1/2	15-0	12	70 to 80	56-2 15/16	289-7 13/16	8 5/16	39-11 3/8	39-8 1/8
		15-0	12	85 to 100	55-7 1/8	285-10	8	39-0 3/8	38-9 5/16
7	36	15-0	12	70 to 80	42-5 7/16	223-10 1/16	4 1/2	25-9 1/8	25-7 1/2
		15-0	12	85 to 100	41-10	218-5 1/4	4 1/4	24-10 1/4	24-8 9/16
	42	15-0	12	70 to 80	48-2 1/4	275-6 15/16	5 7/16	31-6 1/4	31-4 5/16
		15-0	12	85 to 100	47-6 5/16	270-5 1/16	5 3/16	30-6 7/8	30-4 7/8
	44	15-0	12	70 to 80	50-1 3/16	292-9 5/8	5 3/4	33-5 5/16	33-3 1/4
		15-0	12	85 to 100	49-5 1/16	287-9 1/16	5 1/2	32-5 3/4	32-3 5/8
	48	15-0	12	70 to 80	53-11 1/16	327-3 13/16	6 1/2	37-3 7/16	37-1 1/8
		15-0	12	85 to 100	53-2 1/2	322-4 15/16	6 3/8	36-3 1/2	36-1 3/16
	56 1/2	15-0	12	70 to 80	62-0 5/8	400-7 3/8	7 3/4	45-5 3/8	45-2 11/16
		15-0	12	85 to 100	61-3 1/8	396-0 11/16	7 1/2	44-4 11/16	44-1 15/16

Bethlehem Heavy-Duty Main Haulage Turnout near mine portals. Every loaded and empty trip passes over this turnout.

A.R.E.A. PRACTICAL LEADS FOR TURNOUTS
FOR HEAVY RAIL ON STANDARD GAGE (4′-8½″) ONLY

	PROPERTIES OF FROGS					PROPERTIES OF SWITCHES		PRACTICAL LEADS						
Frog No.	Total Length	Toe Length to ½″ Point	Frog Angle	Toe Spread	Heel Spread	Length of Switch Rail	Thickness of Point = ¼″ Heel Spread = 6¼″ Switch Angle	Lead = Distance Actual Point of Switch Rail to Frog ½″	CLOSURE RAILS Number of Rails and Lengths in Feet and Inches Straight Rail	Curved Rail	LEAD CURVE Radius of Center Line	Degree of Curve	Tangent Adjacent to Switch Rail	Tangent Adjacent to Toe of Frog
	Ft.–In.	Ft.–In.		In.	In.	Ft.–In.		Ft.–In.	Ft.–In.	Ft.–In.	Feet		Feet	Feet
5	9-0	3-6½	11° 25′ 16″	7 15/16	13 9/16	11-0	2° 39′ 34″	42-6½	28-0	28-4	177.80	32° 39′ 56″	0.00	0.78
6	10-0	3-9	9° 31′ 38″	7	13	11-0	2° 39′ 34″	47-6	32-9	33-0	258.57	22° 17′ 58″	0.00	1.75
7	12-0	4-8½	8° 10′ 16″	7 9/16	13	16-6	1° 46′ 22″	62-1	40-10½	41-1¼	365.59	15° 43′ 16″	0.01	0.00
8	13-0	5-1	7° 09′ 10″	7⅛	12⅜	16-6	1° 46′ 22″	68-0	46-5	46-7½	487.28	11° 46′ 44″	0.64	0.00
9	16-0	6-4½	6° 21′ 35″	8	13 5/16	16-6	1° 46′ 22″	72-3½	49-5	49-7¼	615.12	9° 19′ 30″	0.00	0.17
10	16-6	6-5	5° 43′ 29″	7 3/16	12⅝	16-6	1° 46′ 22″	78-9	55-10	56-0	779.39	7° 21′ 24″	2.08	0.00
11	18-8½	7-0	5° 12′ 18″	7⅛	13¼	22-0	1° 19′ 46″	91-10¼	62-10¼	63-0	927.27	6° 10′ 56″	0.00	0.13
12	20-4	7-9½	4° 46′ 19″	7 5/16	13 1/16	22-0	1° 19′ 46″	96-8	66-10½	67-0	1104.63	5° 11′ 20″	0.00	0.50
14	23-7	8-7½	4° 05′ 27″	6⅞	13 5/16	22-0	1° 19′ 46″	107-0¾	76-5¼	76-6¾	1581.20	3° 37′ 28″	0.24	0.00
15	24-4½	9-5	3° 49′ 06″	7	12 7/16	30-0	0° 58′ 30″	126-4½	86-11½	87-0¾	1720.77	3° 19′ 48″	1.56	0.00
16	26-0	9-5	3° 34′ 47″	6 9/16	12 15/16	30-0	0° 58′ 30″	131-4	91-11	92-0	2007.12	2° 51′ 18″	0.66	0.00
18	29-3	11-0½	3° 10′ 56″	6⅞	12⅝	30-0	0° 58′ 30″	140-11½	99-11	100-0	2578.79	2° 13′ 20″	0.57	0.00
20	30-10½	11-0½	2° 51′ 51″	6⅛	12⅜	30-0	0° 58′ 30″	151-11½	110-11	111-0	3289.29	1° 44′ 32″	2.47	0.00

Turnouts Recommended

For Main Line High Speed Movements, No. 16 or No. 20.
For Main Line Slow Speed Movements, No. 12 or No. 10.
For Yards and Sidings, to meet General Conditions, No. 8.

A group of Bethlehem Turnouts and Model 1217 Switch Stands in a ladder track for a mine locomotive shed.

This big, heavy double-crossover on a fine West Virginia haulway was built from rails accurately pre-cut to length, curves preformed to proper radii, and frogs, switches and other components pre-assembled at Bethlehem's plant.

PREFABRICATED TRACK LAYOUTS

Bethlehem Prefabricated Track is planned in detail, precut and precurved in the Bethlehem shops to fit the transportation system of a mine or industrial location. Prefabricated track can be made for any weight of rail.

Bethlehem engineers visit the location with the customer, and assist in designing the layout best suited to that particular operation. The track plan is worked out in minute detail, so the track can be "custom built" to specifications. When desired, plans and specifications are sent to the customer for approval before track fabrication is begun.

MINE LAYOUTS

Prefabricated track simplifies the installation and removal of mine tracks, speeds up the movement of mining equipment, and promotes the efficiency of the mining system. It can be quickly and easily assembled or dismantled by a small crew of men, using ordinary tools.

Because of variations in physical conditions and established practices at different mines, it is usually necessary to design a track system for each individual mine. All the technical problems are considered, such as entry, room, and crosscut centers, the angle of driving crosscuts, roof and bottom conditions, size and wheel-base of cars, locomotives, and other equipment, size of turnouts, radii of curves, and other pertinent data.

INDUSTRIAL YARD LAYOUTS

Bethlehem Prefabricated Track can be designed for any industrial or mine-yard layout, for placement in a permanent or temporary location, for use with light or heavy equipment.

Prefabricated track is the most efficient that can be used for industrial locations of all types. The track comes to the plant "knocked down," complete to the last bolt and nut, marked for quick, easy assembly. A yard layout "tailored to your needs," makes possible faster and safer haulage, reduces derailments, and lowers the haulage cost per ton handled.

DRAWINGS INCLUDED

Prefabricated track is shipped to the customer ready for installation. All rails are numbered to facilitate identification. In tem-

Bethlehem Prefabricated Track Layouts are thoroughly checked on the shop floor before shipment.

porary installations, the rails are marked with a bead-weld number on both sides of the web at the center of each rail. However, for permanent installations, each rail is stamped on the head at each end with its identifying number.

Maintenance of track is simplified by giving a set of detailed drawings to the customer when the track is ready for installation. Then, in case a section of track has to be replaced later on, it is ordered by part and plan number, and will fit perfectly when received.

MAXIMUM FLEXIBILITY

A Bethlehem Prefabricated Temporary Track system is extremely flexible. By using various combinations of rails, the track may be changed to suit almost any situation. Room and crosscut centers may be changed by increments of a few feet. On the other hand, if certain fixed combinations of rails and turnouts are adhered to, a uniform mining pattern will result.

Should occasion arise, the angle of driving crosscuts may be altered, for example from 60 deg to 90 deg, with very little change, usually by adding not more than two rails. Track-layers soon become accustomed to the system, and automatically use certain rail combinations to accomplish the desired results.

One of the main features of Bethlehem Prefabricated Track is that the same units may be used in driving main entries as well as for room-and-pillar mining and pillar recovery, resulting in great economies.

An 85-lb ASCE track layout completely prefabricated by Bethlehem for a large mine.

IT'S BETTER TRACK

The initial cost of a Bethlehem Prefabricated Track Layout is very little more than it costs to obtain an equivalent amount of ordinary trackwork items such as turnouts, steel ties, turnout tie sets, joints and straight rails.

When plain materials are bought, trackmen spend much of their time cutting, drilling, bending and rebending rails. This work is usually done under unfavorable conditions, with makeshift equipment. One result is a confusion of off-standard curves which can only be used in certain locations. Under this method much rail waste occurs in the form of short ends of rails broken by curving and recurving in a haphazard manner.

Compare this method with that used by Bethlehem: After the design of the layout has been approved by the customer, Bethlehem cuts the rails to proper length and curves them to the correct radii. Turnouts and curves are made so accurately that they are interchangeable for various locations.

By using a Bethlehem Prefabricated Track Layout as a nucleus, an efficient, concentrated system of mining can be evolved, and a considerable amount of rail can be saved.

GREATER SAFETY, TOO

Loads can be run faster and more safely over Bethlehem Prefabricated Tracks because they are rugged and durable. They materially reduce the hazard of derailments, speed up haulage, and save equipment from costly damage.

Bethlehem specializes in heavy-duty prefabricated trackwork for mines and industrial plants.

BETHLEHEM 20-LB TO 100-LB STEEL RAILS

Bethlehem rolls rails for all requirements, including rails for mine and industrial purposes, crane rails, girder rails, and standard tee rails for railroad use. Bethlehem can also furnish formed rail circles for such applications as rotary car dumpers, swing bridges, turntables, etc.

Only blooms of new steel are used for rolling Bethlehem rails. All rail sections shown in this catalog conform to standards established and approved by the American Society of Civil Engineers (ASCE). Light rails (60 lb per yard and under) are furnished to manufacturers' specifications and tolerances. Rails above 60 lb per yard, are known as standard tee rails, and are furnished in accordance with ASTM rail specifications.

20-lb to 100-lb STEEL RAILS

On the following pages, full-size sections of rails weighing from 20-lb to 100-lb per yd are shown, together with accompanying splice or angle-bars.

Details of standard rail drilling, splice-bar punching, track spikes and bolts, together with such other pertinent data, such as properties of standard T-rails, rails and accessories for one mile of track, etc., are covered on pages 128 to 137, inclusive. Other information on these items, and details of rails of other sizes and types, will be furnished upon application to the nearest Bethlehem sales office.

ORDERING RAILS

When ordering Bethlehem Rails, please specify the weight per yard, lengths required, and all necessary information for drilling.

RAIL SECTION NO. 20-AS

AMERICAN SOCIETY OF CIVIL ENGINEERS' TYPE

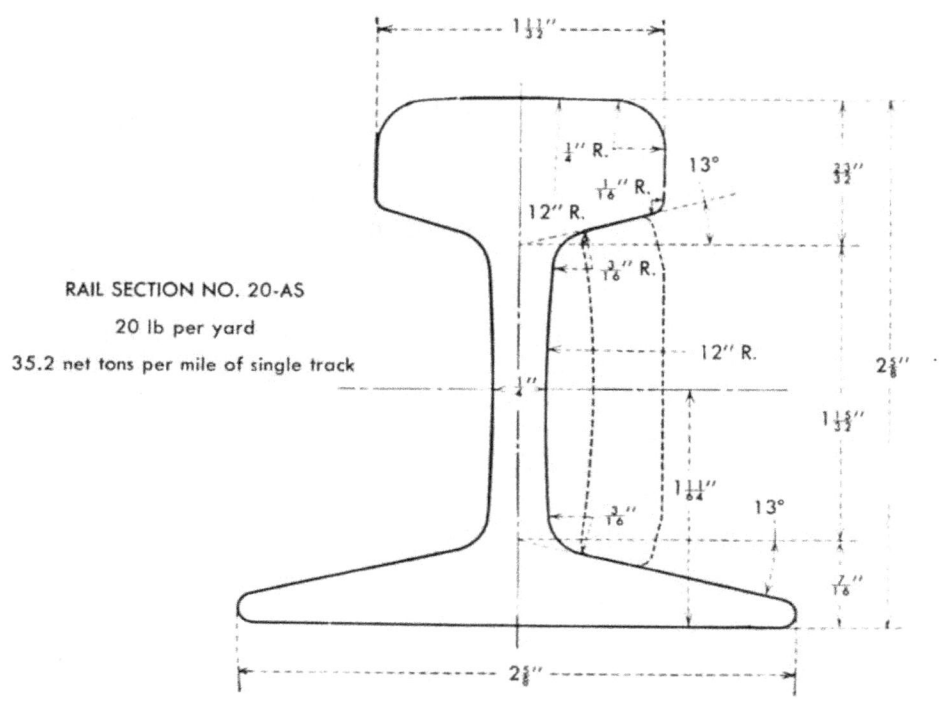

RAIL SECTION NO. 20-AS
20 lb per yard
35.2 net tons per mile of single track

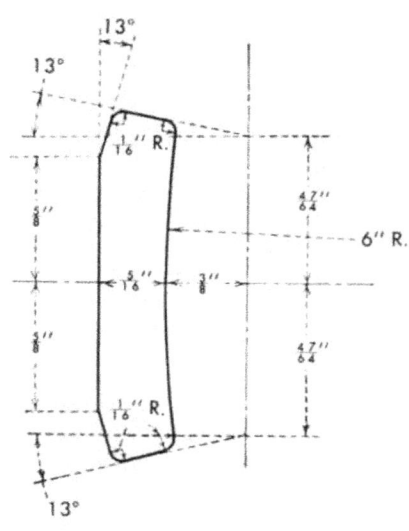

PLAIN SPLICE BAR SECTION NO. P-20-AS
4.86 lb per pair
Length of bar, 16 1/8 in.

RAIL SECTION NO. 25-AS

AMERICAN SOCIETY OF CIVIL ENGINEERS' TYPE

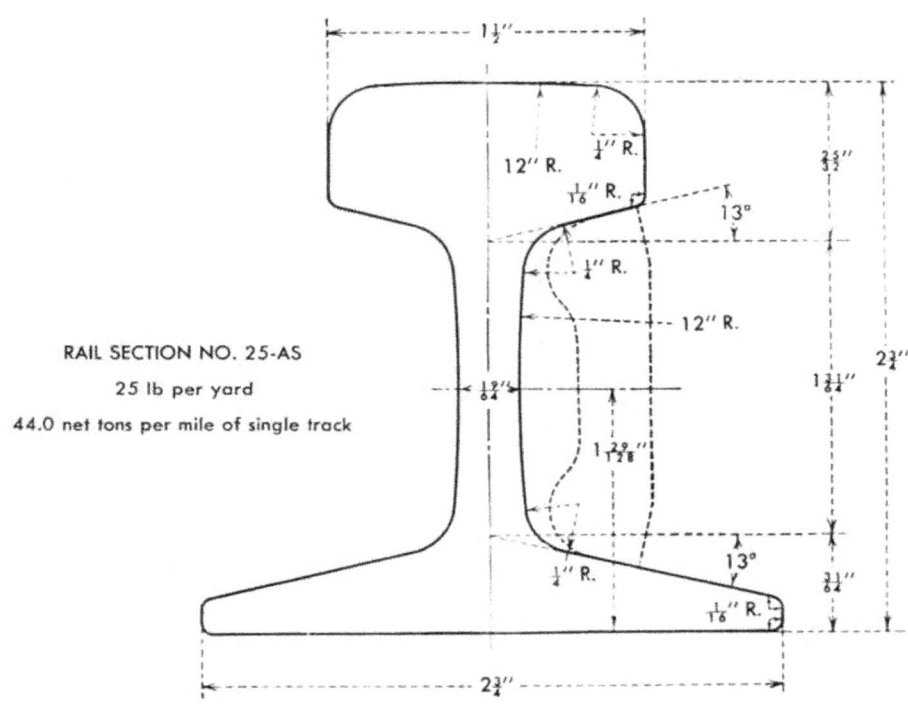

RAIL SECTION NO. 25-AS
25 lb per yard
44.0 net tons per mile of single track

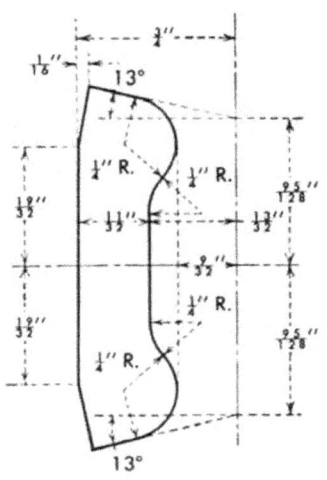

SPLICE BAR SECTION NO. P-25-AS
5.70 lb per pair
Length of bar, 16⅛ in.

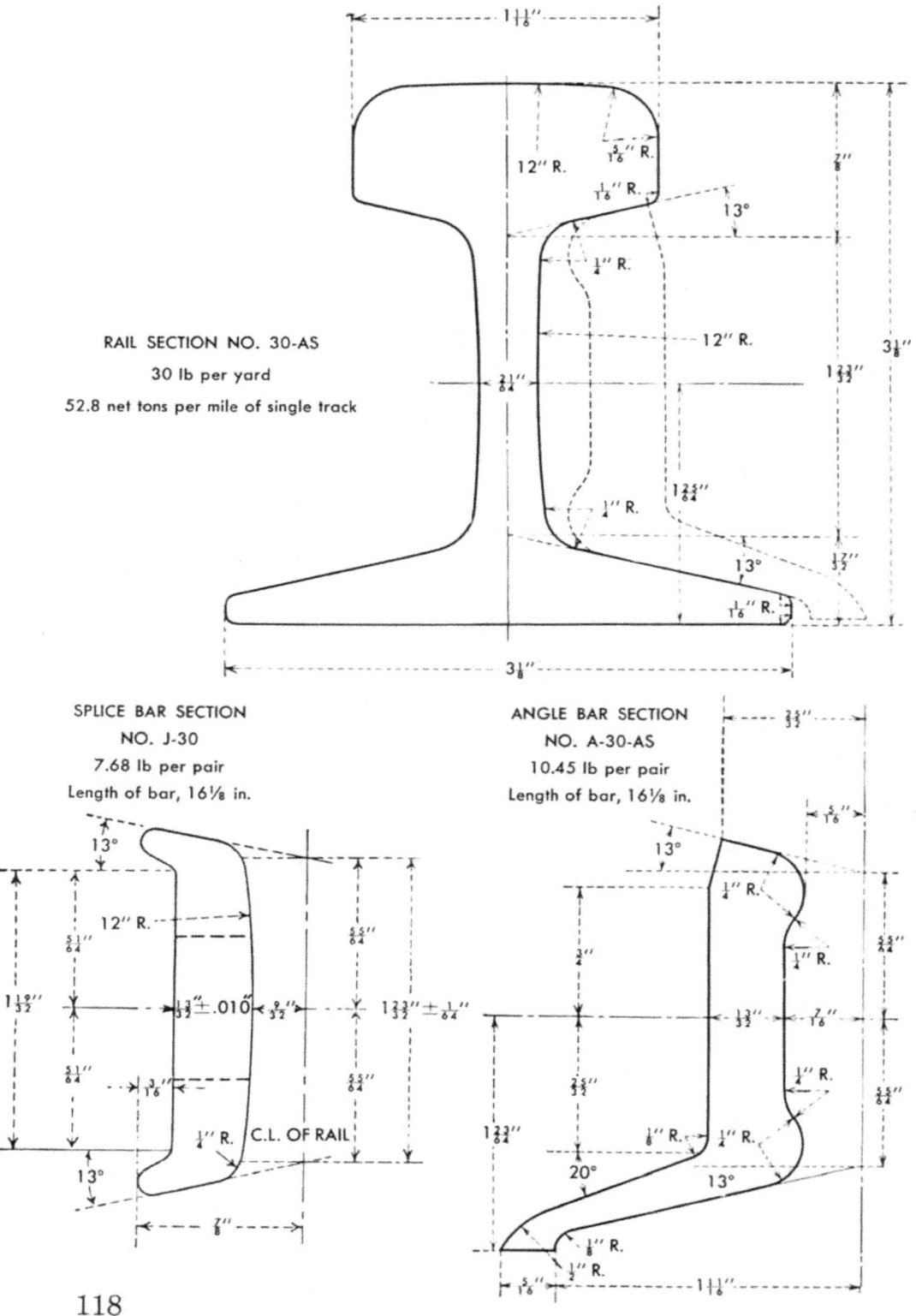

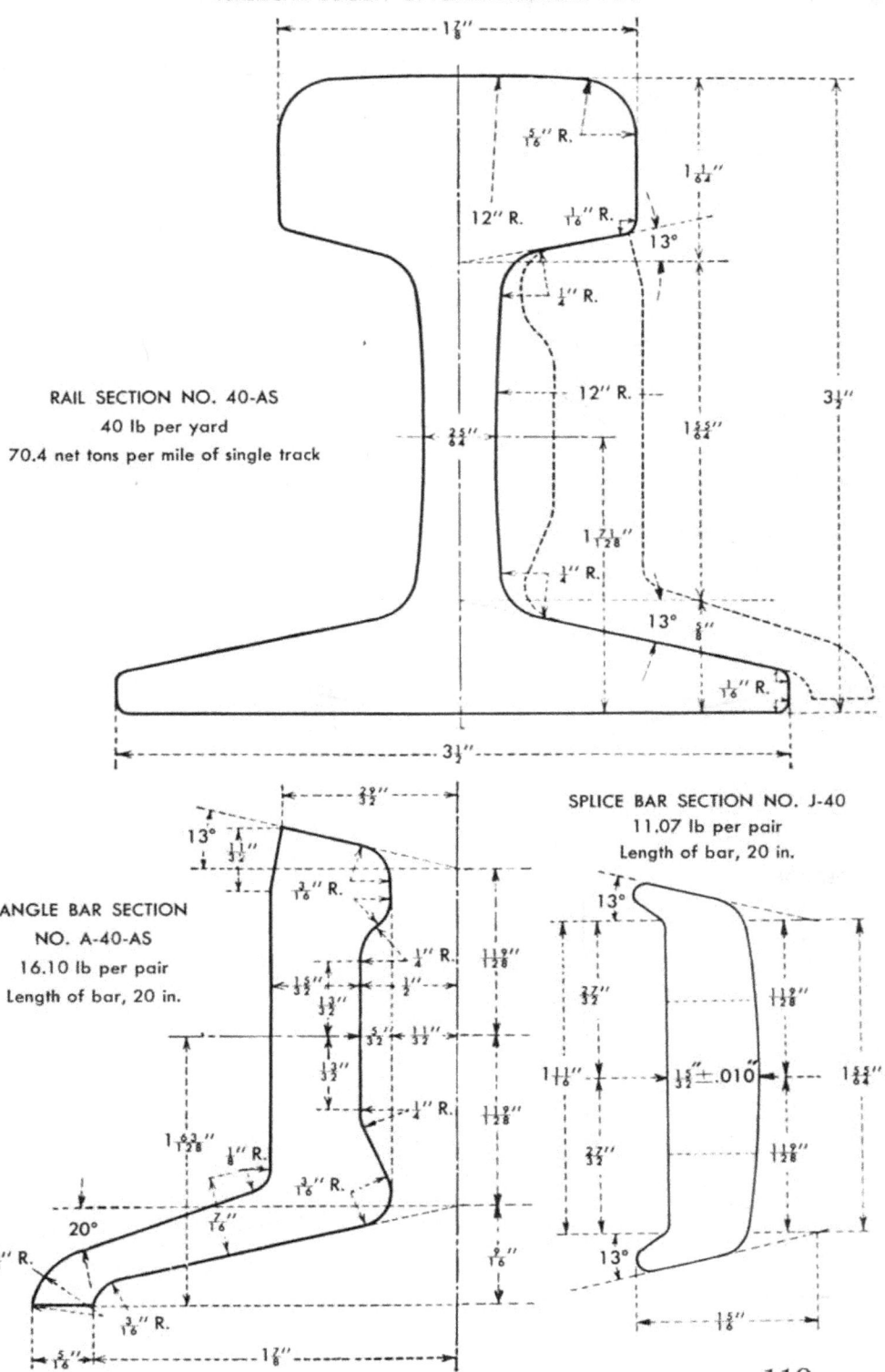

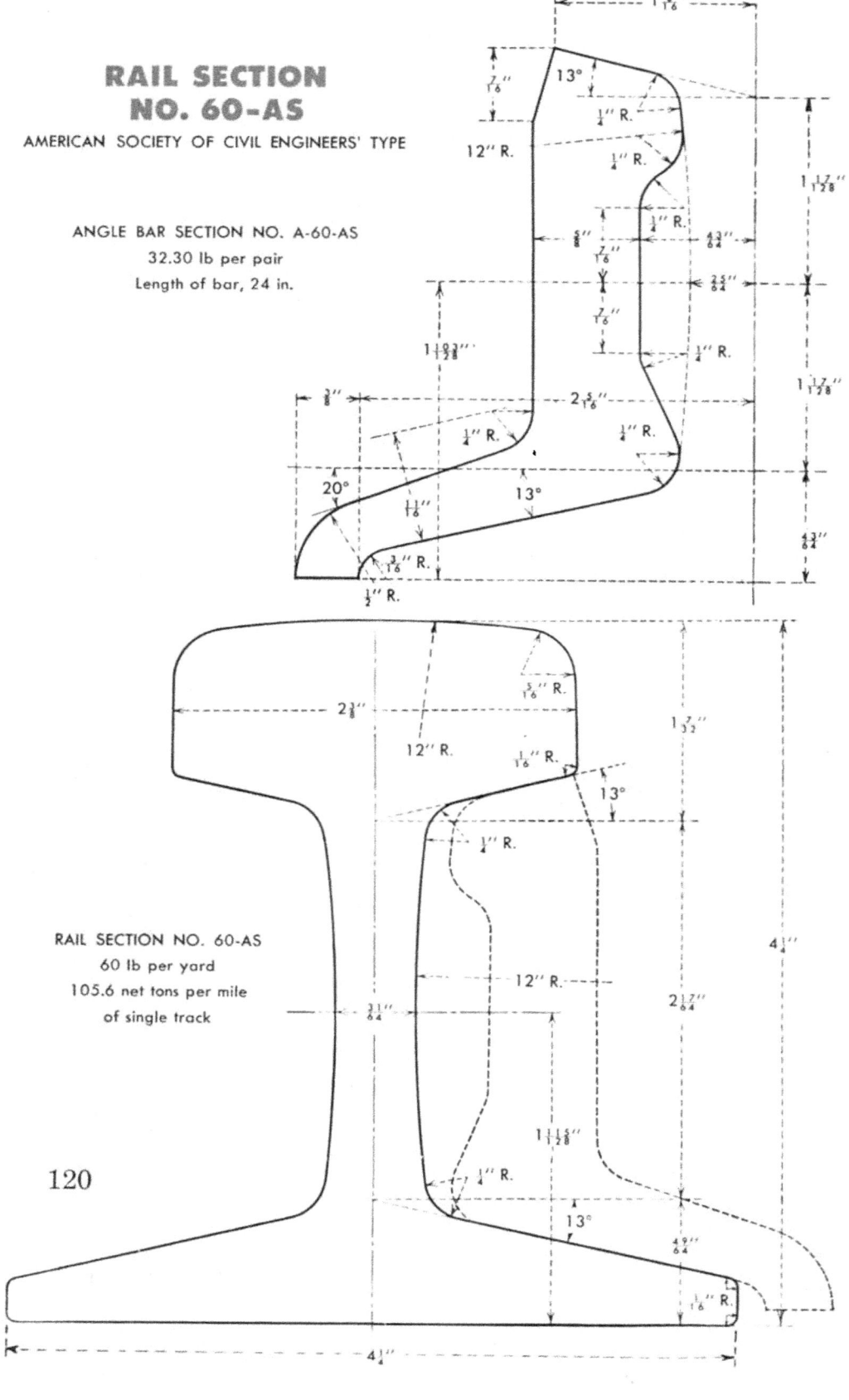

RAIL SECTION NO. 70-AS

AMERICAN SOCIETY OF CIVIL ENGINEERS' TYPE

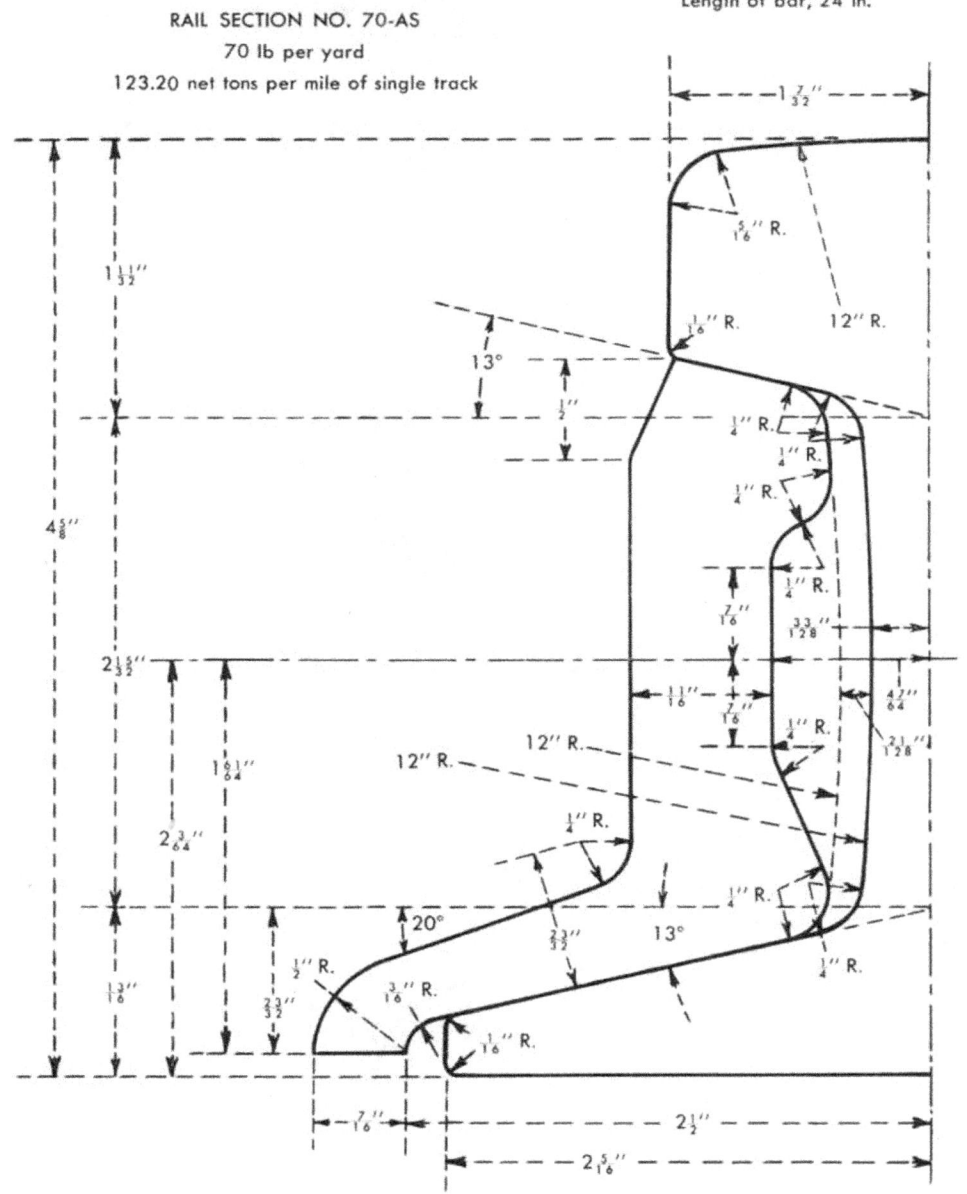

RAIL SECTION NO. 75-AS

AMERICAN SOCIETY OF CIVIL ENGINEERS' TYPE

RAIL SECTION NO. 75-AS
75 lb per yard
132.00 net tons per mile of single track

ANGLE BAR SECTION NO. A-75-AS
41.28 lb per pair
Length of bar, 24 in.

RAIL SECTION NO. 80-AS

AMERICAN SOCIETY OF CIVIL ENGINEERS' TYPE

ANGLE BAR SECTION NO. A-80-AS
45.0 lb per pair
Length of bar, 24 in.

RAIL SECTION NO. 80-AS
80 lb per yard
140.80 net tons per mile of single track

123

RAIL SECTION NO. 85-AS

AMERICAN SOCIETY OF CIVIL ENGINEERS' TYPE

RAIL SECTION NO. 85-AS
85 lb per yard
149.60 net tons per mile of single track

ANGLE BAR SECTION NO. A-85-AS
47.94 lb per pair
Length of bar, 24 in.

RAIL SECTION NO. 90-AS

AMERICAN SOCIETY OF CIVIL ENGINEERS' TYPE

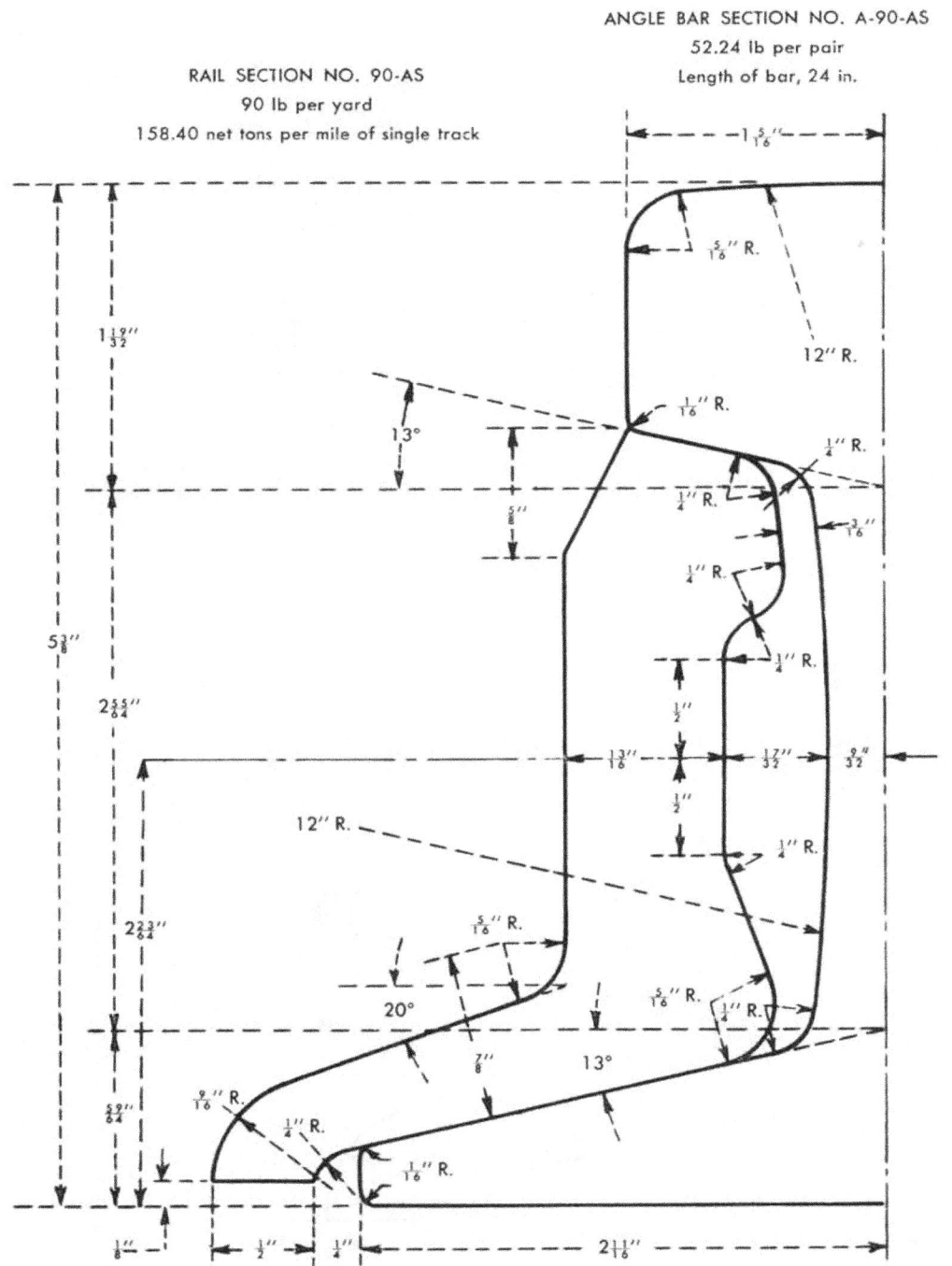

125

RAIL SECTION NO. 100-AS

AMERICAN SOCIETY OF CIVIL ENGINEERS' TYPE

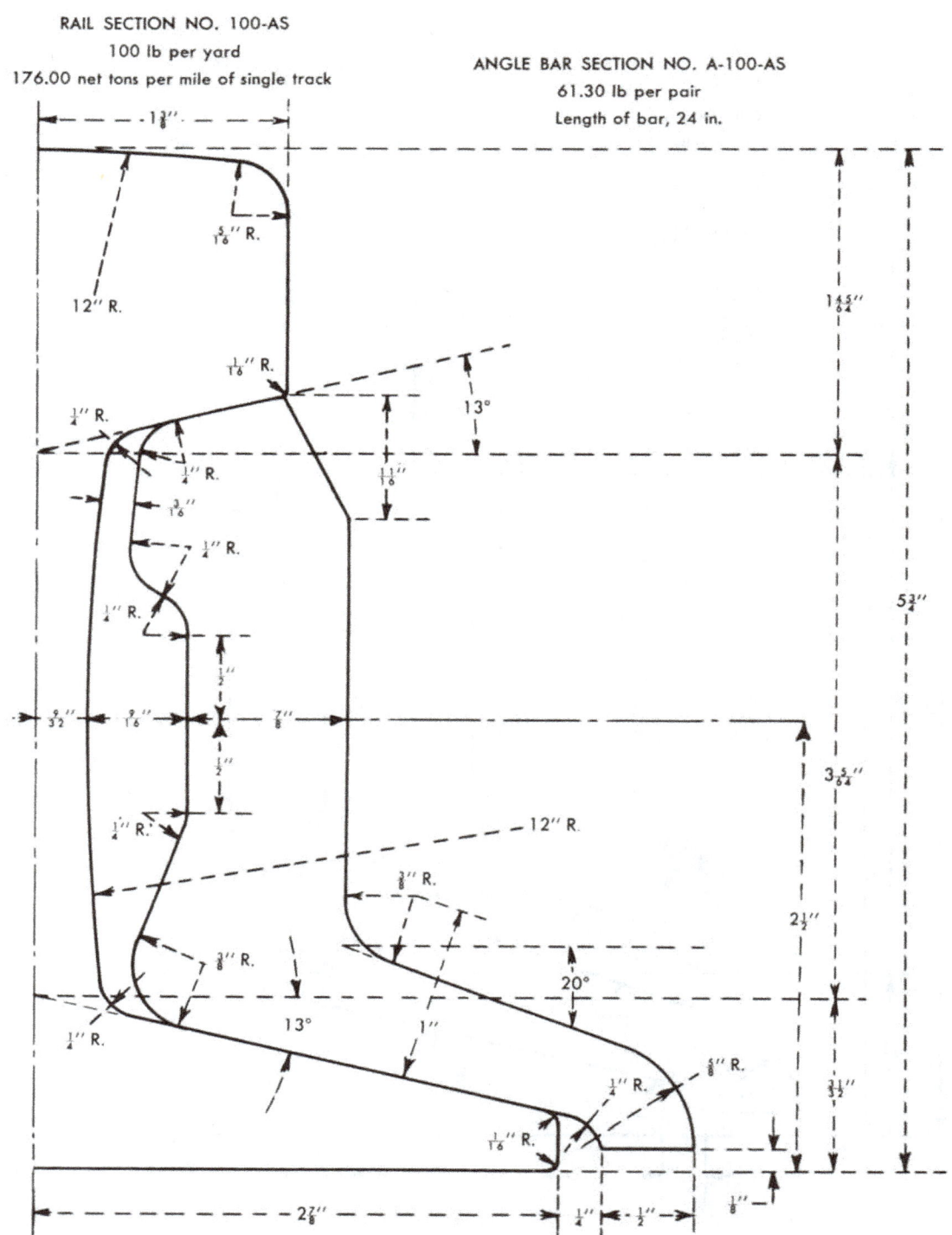

RAIL SECTION NO. 100-AS
100 lb per yard
176.00 net tons per mile of single track

ANGLE BAR SECTION NO. A-100-AS
61.30 lb per pair
Length of bar, 24 in.

PROPERTIES AND PRINCIPAL DIMENSIONS OF T-RAILS, 20-LB TO 100-LB, INCLUSIVE

AMERICAN SOCIETY OF CIVIL ENGINEERS' TYPE

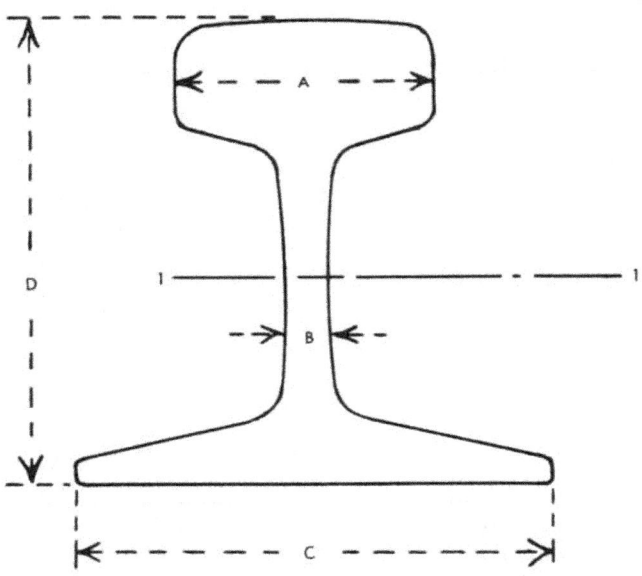

Section No.	Weight Per Yard lb	Total Area sq in.	A in.	B in.	C in.	D in.	AXIS 1—1	
							Moment of inertia in.⁴	Section modulus, head in.³
20-AS	20	2.00	1 11/32	1/4	2 5/8	2 5/8	1.93	1.41
25-AS	25	2.40	1 1/2	19/64	2 3/4	2 3/4	2.50	1.76
30-AS	30	3.00	1 11/16	21/64	3 1/8	3 1/8	4.10	2.55
40-AS	40	3.94	1 7/8	25/64	3 1/2	3 1/2	6.54	3.59
60-AS	60	5.93	2 3/8	31/64	4 1/4	4 1/4	14.60	6.67
70-AS	70	6.81	2 7/16	33/64	4 5/8	4 5/8	19.70	8.23
75-AS	75	7.33	2 15/32	17/32	4 13/16	4 13/16	22.86	9.11
80-AS	80	7.86	2 1/2	35/64	5	5	26.38	10.07
85-AS	85	8.33	2 9/16	9/16	5 3/16	5 3/16	30.10	11.08
90-AS	90	8.83	2 5/8	9/16	5 3/8	5 3/8	34.40	12.20
100-AS	100	9.84	2 3/4	9/16	5 3/4	5 3/4	44.00	14.60

See preceding pages for full-size sections and detailed dimensions of rails with splice bars.

STANDARD DRILLING FOR RAILS AND SPLICE-BAR PUNCHING

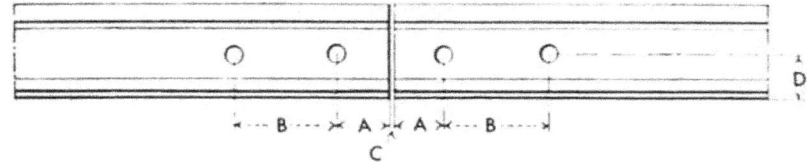

RAIL DRILLING

Rail Section	Size of Bolt Holes in.	A in.	B in.	C in.	D in.
20-AS	5/8	2	4	1/8	1 11/64
25-AS	5/8	2	4	1/8	1 29/128
30-AS	3/4	2	4	1/8	1 25/64
40-AS	7/8	2 1/2	5	1/8	1 71/128
60-AS	1	2 1/2	5	1/8	1 115/128
70-AS	1	2 1/2	5	1/8	2 3/64
75-AS	1 1/8	2 1/2	5	1/8	2 1/8
80-AS	1 1/8	2 1/2	5	1/8	2 3/16
85-AS	1 1/8	2 1/2	5	1/8	2 17/64
90-AS	1 1/8	2 1/2	5	1/8	2 23/64
100-AS	1 1/4	2 1/2	5	1/8	2 1/2

If rail-bond drilling is desired, we can furnish as specified on the order.

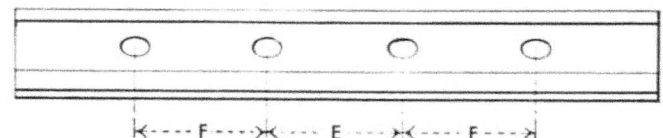

SPLICE-BAR PUNCHING

Rail Section	Size of Bolt Holes in.	Length of Splice Bar in.	F in.	E in.	F in.
20-AS	9/16 x 3/4	16 1/8	4	4 1/8	4
25-AS	9/16 x 3/4	16 1/8	4	4 1/8	4
30-AS	11/16 x 15/16	16 1/8	4	4 1/8	4
40-AS	13/16 x 1 1/8	20	5	5 1/8	5
60-AS	13/16 x 1 1/8	24	5	5 1/8	5
70-AS	7/8 x 1 1/8	24	5	5 1/8	5
75-AS	1 x 1 1/4	24	5	5 1/8	5
80-AS	1 x 1 1/4	24	5	5 1/8	5
85-AS	1 x 1 1/4	24	5	5 1/8	5
90-AS	1 x 1 1/4	24	5	5 1/8	5
100-AS	1 1/8 x 1 7/16	24	5	5 1/8	5

BETHLEHEM CRANE RAILS

Bethlehem Crane Rails are used throughout industry to carry all types of flanged-wheel vehicles. They are actually classed as tee rails, but they differ substantially in design from those used in railroad track. Crane rails can be obtained in the heat-treated condition, when specified.

Overhead cranes are by far the largest single application for crane rails. Shipyards and naval drydocks are also big users of these rails. Circle rails, made up of crane rails, are frequently used on turret plates of large power shovels, turntables, swing bridges, rotary car dumpers, on aircraft carriers, and the like. There are crane rails in use at the numerous locks of the St. Lawrence Seaway, and in speed-testing runways for missiles and rockets.

Send for Catalog. Bethlehem has prepared a comprehensive 24-page catalog containing information on how to select and order crane rail sections, how to specify the drilling of crane rails and the punching of joint bars, and how to apply clips and holders to fasten the rails to the runway, and other data. Steel specifications are given for all crane rail sections. Ask for Catalog 464, "Bethlehem Crane Rails."

BETHLEHEM CRANE RAIL SECTIONS

Bethlehem Crane Rails are available in four sections: 104-CR, 135-CR, 171-CR and 175-CR. The numerals indicate the weight-per-yard of the rail. Detail drawings of these sections and their joint bars are shown on the following pages. Standard lengths of Bethlehem Crane Rails are 33 ft, 39 ft, and 60 ft. Other lengths up to 60 ft can be furnished, if desired.

Typical crane rail installation for overhead crane in structural steel shipping yard. Rail is anchored to runway by Bethlehem forged double clips and holders.

Bethlehem also makes a complete line of Crane Rail Clips for fastening the rails to supporting beams. These are made in two types: (1) forged crane rail clip and holder (single and double); and (2) pressed steel clip and reversible filler (single and double). Both types are available for any of the four rail sections.

CRANE RAIL SECTION 104-CR
Joint Bar Section A-104-CR

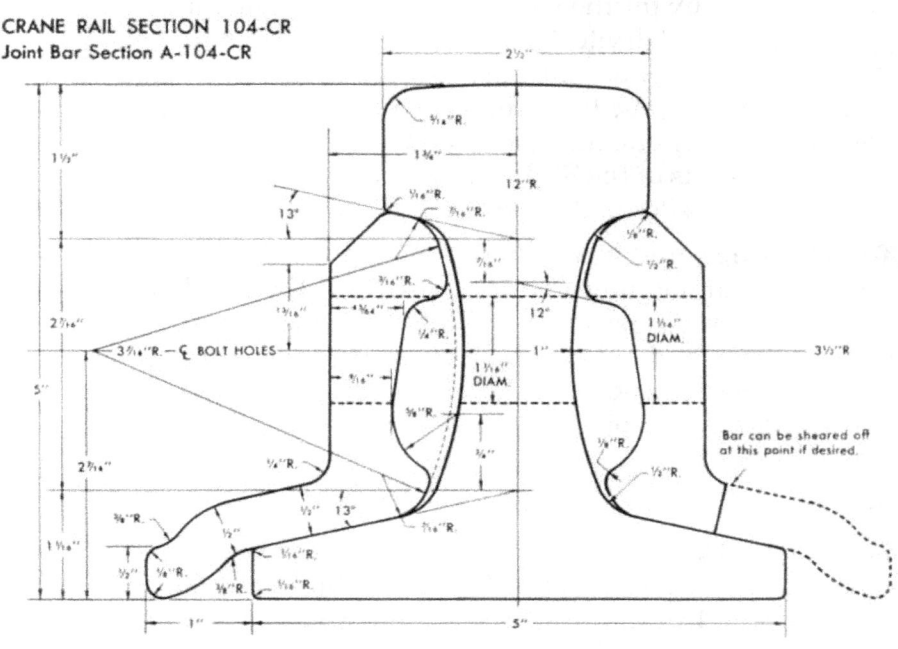

CRANE RAIL SECTION 135-CR
Joint Bar Section P-135-CR

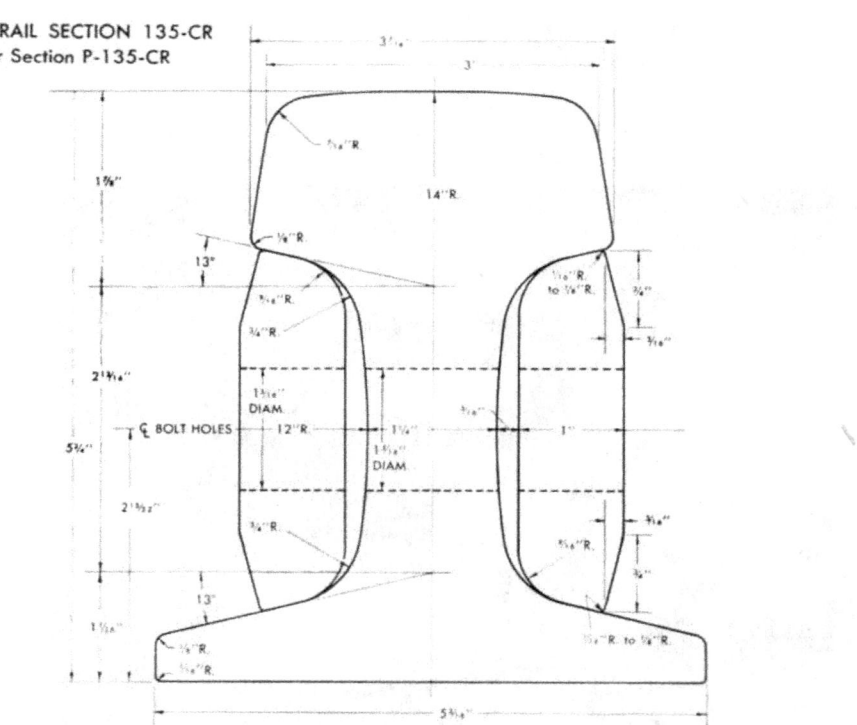

CRANE RAIL SECTION 171-CR
Joint Bar Section P-171-CR

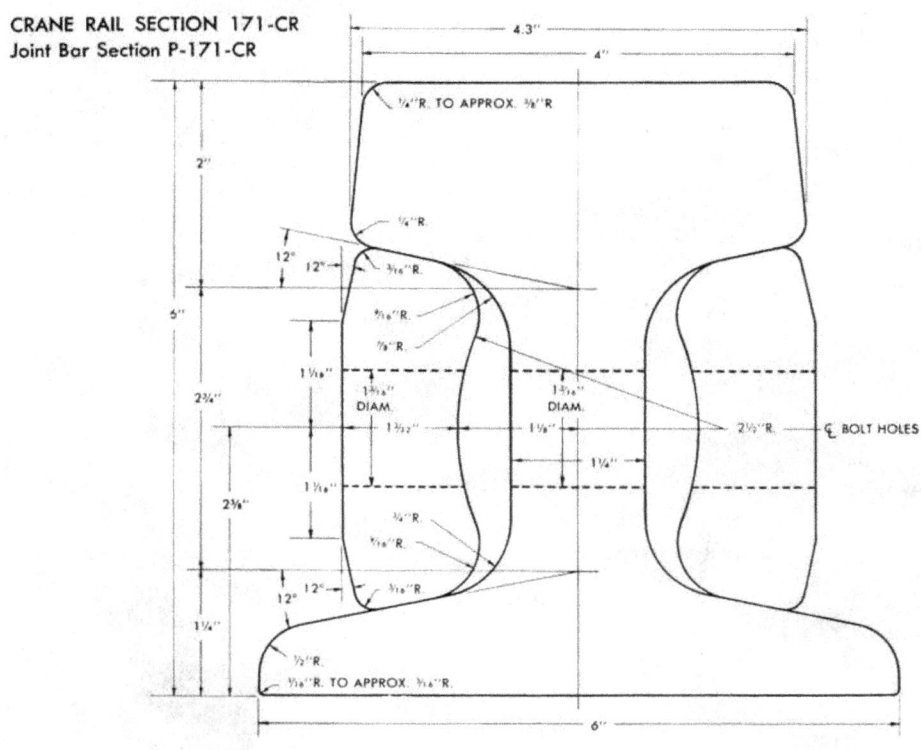

CRANE RAIL SECTION 175-CR
Joint Bar Section P-175-CR

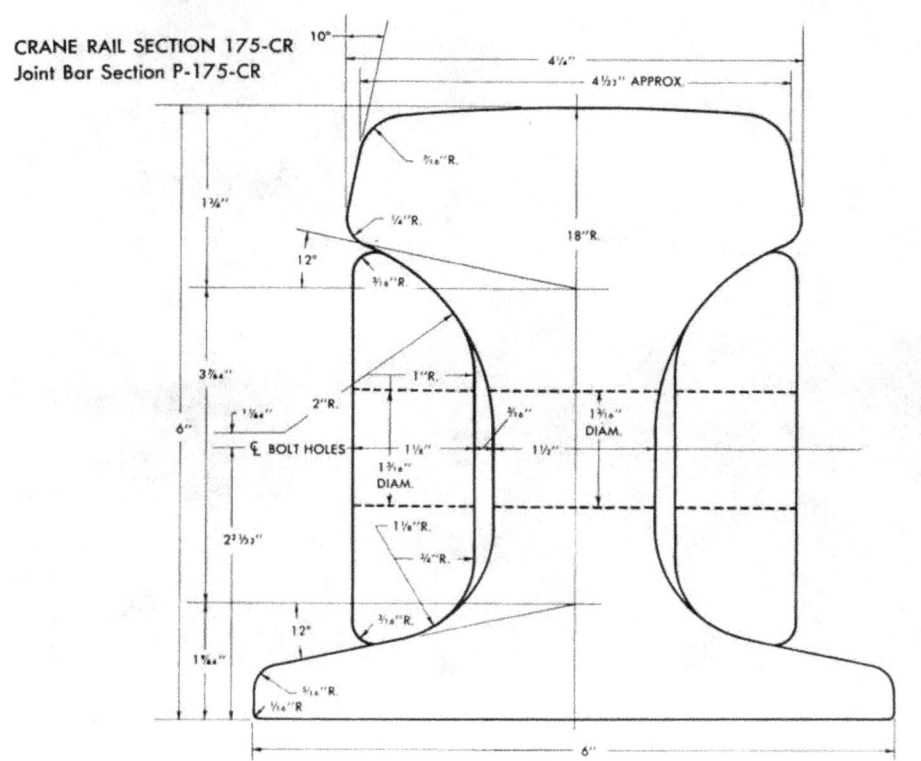

There are no stronger, sturdier joints than those held by Bethlehem Track Bolts and Nuts.

BETHLEHEM SPIKES AND BOLTS

CUT TRACK SPIKES

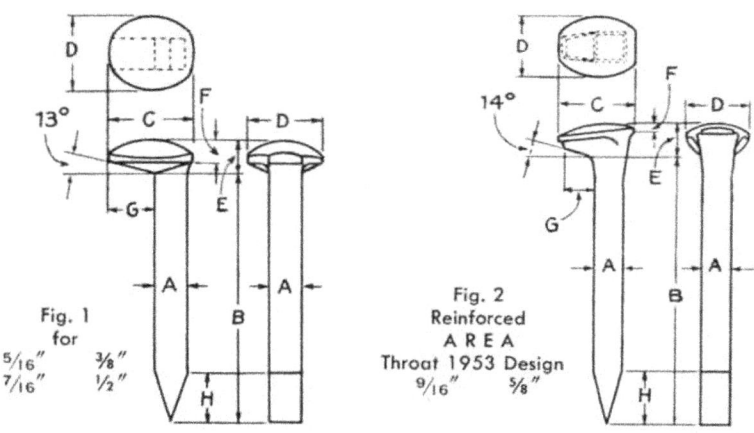

Fig. 1 for 5/16" 3/8" 7/16" 1/2"

Fig. 2 Reinforced AREA Throat 1953 Design 9/16" 5/8"

DIMENSIONS AND QUANTITIES

	SIZE OF SPIKE		HEAD				Length Of Taper Of Point	Approximate Number Per Keg Of 200 lb	Kegs Per Mile Of Single Track	Used With Rails Of Weight Per Yard
	Thickness	Length	Length	Width	Thickness	Thickness Of Heel	Length Of Hook			
	A	B	C	D	E	F	G	H		
	in.	in.	in.	in.	in.	in.	in.	in.	Number	lb
Fig. 1	5/16	2	13/16	3/4	5/16	7/32	7/16	1/2	2440	4.35	12 to 16
	5/16	2½	13/16	3/4	5/16	7/32	7/16	1/2	2050	5.15	12 to 16
	3/8	2	1 1/16	7/8	3/8	1/4	9/16	5/8	1778	5.98	12 to 16
	3/8	2½	1 1/16	7/8	3/8	1/4	9/16	5/8	1470	7.18	12 to 16
	3/8	3	1 1/16	7/8	3/8	1/4	9/16	5/8	1270	8.32	12 to 16
	3/8	3½	1 1/16	7/8	3/8	1/4	9/16	5/8	1135	9.30	12 to 16
	3/8	4	1 1/16	7/8	3/8	1/4	9/16	5/8	974	10.90	16 to 20
	7/16	2½	1 3/16	1	7/16	5/16	5/8	3/4	1084	9.80	16 to 20
	7/16	3	1 3/16	1	7/16	5/16	5/8	3/4	920	11.48	16 to 20
	7/16	3½	1 3/16	1	7/16	5/16	5/8	3/4	810	13.05	16 to 20
	7/16	4	1 3/16	1	7/16	5/16	5/8	3/4	725	14.55	16 to 20
	7/16	4½	1 3/16	1	7/16	5/16	5/8	3/4	653	16.15	20 to 30
	1/2	3	1 5/16	1 1/8	1/2	5/16	11/16	7/8	700	15.10	20 to 30
	1/2	3½	1 5/16	1 1/8	1/2	5/16	11/16	7/8	638	16.55	20 to 30
	1/2	4	1 5/16	1 1/8	1/2	5/16	11/16	7/8	550	17.20	20 to 30
	1/2	4½	1 5/16	1 1/8	1/2	5/16	11/16	7/8	505	20.90	30 to 40
	1/2	5	1 5/16	1 1/8	1/2	5/16	11/16	7/8	460	23.00	30 to 40
Fig. 2	9/16	4½	1½	1¼	5/8	5/32	5/8	1 1/8	408	25.80	40 to 50
	9/16	5	1½	1¼	5/8	5/32	5/8	1 1/8	365	29.90	40 to 60
	9/16	5½	1½	1¼	5/8	5/32	5/8	1 1/8	335	34.40	65 to 100
	9/16	6	1½	1¼	5/8	5/32	5/8	1 1/8	302	38.20	65 to 100
	5/8	4½	1 9/16	1 5/16	11/16	5/32	11/16	1¼	312	33.80	40 to 60
	5/8	5	1 9/16	1 5/16	11/16	5/32	11/16	1¼	286	40.40	75 to 100
	5/8	5½	1 9/16	1 5/16	11/16	5/32	11/16	1¼	264	43.70	75 to 130
	5/8	6	1 9/16	1 5/16	11/16	5/32	11/16	1¼	244	47.30	75 to 130

Number of spikes in this table based on tie spacing of 24-in. for rails up to and including 60 lb and 22-in. for rails 65 lb and heavier.

TRACK BOLTS

With Oval Necks, Rolled Threads and Either Heavy Square or Heavy Hexagon Nuts.

FOR RAILS 20 lb to 100 lb Per Yd

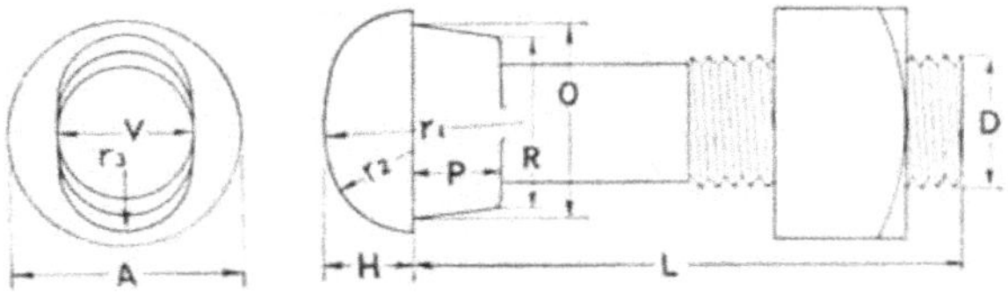

DIMENSIONS

Diam (D) in.	Length (L) in.	Head: A in.	Head: H in.	Head: r_1 in.	Head: r_2 in.	*Neck: O in.	*Neck: R in.	*Neck: P in.	Length Thread in.	Nuts: Thickness in.	Nuts: Short diam of square and hexagon in.
½	1½ to 3	⅞	5/16	11/16	9/32	⅝	19/32	5/16	1⅛	½	⅞
⅝	2¼ to 3½	1 5/64	25/64	59/64	23/64	13/16	25/32	⅜	1¼	⅝	1 1/16
¾	2½ to 5½	1 9/32	15/32	1 5/32	7/16	1 1/16	1 1/32	7/16	1¾	¾	1¼
⅞	3 to 4½	1 31/64	35/64	1 25/64	33/64	1 7/32	1 3/16	½	2	⅞	1 7/16
1	3 to 5	1 11/16	⅝	1⅝	19/32	1⅜	1 11/32	9/16	2¼	1	1⅝

**Dimensions r_3 equal ½ body diameter of bolt. Dimension V equals body diameter of bolt.*

Every rail joint should have a full complement of Bethlehem Track Bolts.

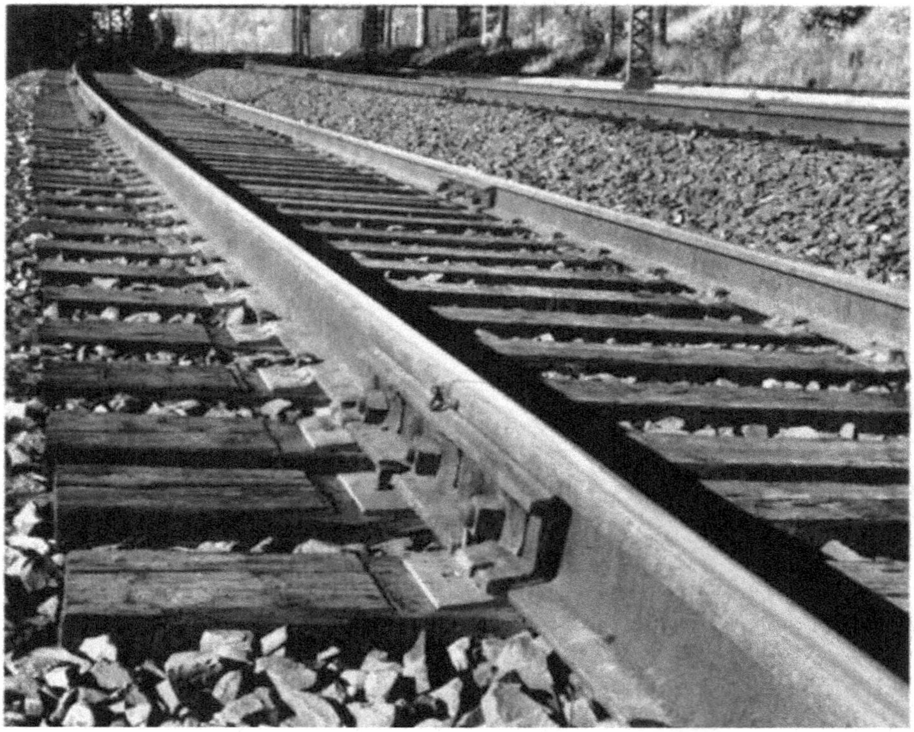

WEIGHTS AND QUANTITIES

Diam in.	Length in.	With Heavy Square Nuts			With Heavy Hexagon Nuts			Used with rails of weight per yard lb
		Weight lb per 100	Number in 200-lb Keg	Number of kegs per mile of Track	Weight lb per 100	Number in 200-lb Keg	Number of Kegs per mile of Track	
½	1½	18.9	1058	1.36	17.7	1130	1.27	12 to 16
	1¾	20.0	1000	1.44	18.8	1064	1.35	12 to 16
	1⅞	20.6	971	1.48	19.4	1031	1.40	12 to 20
	2	21.1	948	1.52	19.9	1004	1.43	16 to 25
	2¼	22.2	901	1.60	21.0	952	1.51	20 to 25
	2½	23.3	858	1.67	22.1	904	1.59	25
	3	25.4	787	1.83	24.2	823	1.75	25
⅝	2¼	36.7	545	2.64	34.2	585	2.46	30 to 35
	2½	38.5	520	2.76	36.0	555	2.59	30 to 35
	2¾	40.3	497	2.89	37.8	528	2.72	30 to 35
	3	42.1	476	3.02	39.6	505	2.84	30 to 35
	3½	45.7	438	3.28	43.2	463	3.11	30 to 35
¾	2½	63.0	317	4.53	59.2	338	4.25	40 to 45
	3	68.3	293	4.92	64.4	311	4.62	40 to 45
	3¼	70.9	282	5.09	67.0	299	4.81	45 to 55
	3½	73.5	272	5.29	69.6	288	4.98	50 to 60
	3¾	76.1	263	4.94	72.2	277	4.70	65 to 70
	4	78.7	254	5.12	74.8	268	4.85	70 to 75
	4¼	81.3	246	5.28	77.4	259	5.02	70 to 75
	4½	84.0	238	5.46	80.1	250	5.20	70 to 75
	5½	94.5	212	6.13	90.6	221	5.88	70 to 75
⅞	3	101.0	198	6.57	94.8	211	6.16	80
	3¼	104.5	192	6.78	98.3	203	6.40	80
	3½	108.2	185	7.03	102.0	196	6.63	80
	3¾	112.8	178	7.30	106.6	188	6.92	80
	4	115.5	173	7.52	109.3	183	7.10	80
	4¼	119.1	168	7.74	112.9	177	7.34	80 to 85
	4½	122.8	163	7.98	116.6	172	7.56	80 to 90
1	3	141.0	142	9.15	132.0	152	8.55	100
	3¼	146.0	137	9.48	137.0	146	8.91	100
	3½	151.0	133	9.78	142.0	141	9.22	100
	3¾	156.0	129	10.07	147.0	136	9.56	100
	4	161.0	124	10.49	152.0	132	9.85	100
	4¼	165.5	121	10.75	156.5	128	10.16	100
	4½	170.5	117	11.11	161.5	124	10.49	100
	4¾	175.5	114	11.40	166.5	120	10.83	100
	5	180.0	111	11.70	171.0	117	11.11	100
	6	200.0	100	13.00	191.0	105	12.38	100

Based on four bolts per joint.
Kegs required per mile of track are based on rails of 60-lb and under 30 ft long (10 pct shorter lengths varying by one foot down to 20 ft); rails of 65-lb and over being 33 ft long (10 pct shorter lengths varying by one foot down to 24 ft).

RAILS AND ACCESSORIES FOR ONE MILE OF TRACK AND ACCESSORIES FOR 1000 NET TONS OF RAILS

This data is based on: Rail 70 lb and over, 33-ft lengths with 10 pct shorts to 25 ft; Ties, 2,880 per mile spaced on 22-in. centers; Bolt lengths include ¼ in. extra for spring washers. Rail 60 lb and under, 30-ft lengths with 10 pct shorts to 20 ft; Ties, 2,640 per mile spaced on 24-in. centers.

If spring washers are used, add ¼ in. to bolt lengths.

Weight and Section of Rail	Height of Rail	Base of Rail	Length of Splice Bars	Size of Bolts	Size of Spikes	FOR ONE RAIL JOINT				
						Section Number of Splice Bar	Weight of One Pair of Splice Bars	Number and Weight of Bolts & Nuts		Total Weight Complete
	in.	in.	in.	in.	in.		lb	No.	lb	lb
100AREA	6	5⅜	24	1 x 5¼	⅝ x 6	H3-100-RE	62.90	4	7.40	70.30
100ASCE	5¾	5¾	24	1 x 5	⅝ x 6	A-100-AS	61.30	4	7.20	68.50
100ARA"A"	6	5½	24	1 x 5	⅝ x 6	A-100-RA	71.00	4	7.20	78.20
100ARA"B"	5 41/64	5 9/64	24	1 x 5	⅝ x 6	A-100-RB	61.00	4	7.20	68.20
90ASCE	5⅜	5⅜	24	⅞ x 4¾	9/16 x 5½	A-90-AS	52.24	4	5.06	57.30
90ARA"A"	5⅝	5⅛	24	⅞ x 4¾	9/16 x 5½	A-90-RA	64.00	4	5.06	69.06
85ASCE	5 3/16	5 3/16	24	⅞ x 4½	9/16 x 5½	A-85-AS	47.94	4	4.91	52.85
80ASCE	5	5	24	⅞ x 4½	9/16 x 5½	A-80-AS	45.00	4	4.91	49.91
75ASCE	4 13/16	4 13/16	24	⅞ x 4¼	9/16 x 5½	A-75-AS	41.28	4	4.76	46.04
70ASCE	4⅝	4⅝	24	¾ x 4	9/16 x 5½	A-70-AS	38.56	4	3.15	41.71
60ASCE	4¼	4¼	24	¾ x 3½	9/16 x 5	A-60-AS	32.30	4	2.94	35.24
50ASCE	3⅞	3⅞	24	¾ x 3¼	9/16 x 4½	A-50-AS	25.50	4	2.84	28.34
40ASCE	3½	3½	20	¾ x 3	9/16 x 4½	A-40-AS	16.10	4	2.73	18.83
30ASCE	3⅛	3⅛	16⅛	⅝ x 2½	½ x 4½	A-30-AS	10.45	4	1.54	11.99
25ASCE	2¾	2¾	16⅛	½ x 2¼	½ x 4	P-25-AS	5.70	4	.88	6.58
20ASCE	2⅝	2⅝	16⅛	½ x 2	½ x 3½	P-20-AS	4.86	4	.84	5.70

FOR ONE MILE OF SINGLE TRACK

Weight and Section of Rail	Pairs of Splice Bars	Bolts and Nuts	Spikes 4 per Tie	Splice Bars	Bolts and Nuts	Spring Washers	Spikes	Total Accessories	Rails	Total Rails and Accessories
	Estimated Number			Estimated Weight in Net Tons						
100AREA	325	1,300	11,520	10.22	1.20	.12	4.73	16.27	176.00	192.27
100ASCE	325	1,300	11,520	9.96	1.17	.12	4.73	15.98	176.00	191.98
100ARA"A"	325	1,300	11,520	11.54	1.17	.12	4.73	17.56	176.00	193.56
100ARA"B"	325	1,300	11,520	9.91	1.17	.12	4.73	15.93	176.00	191.93
90ASCE	325	1,300	11,520	8.49	.82	.04	3.44	12.79	158.40	171.19
90ARA"A"	325	1,300	11,520	10.40	.82	.04	3.44	14.70	158.40	173.10
85ASCE	325	1,300	11,520	7.79	.80	.04	3.44	12.07	149.60	161.67
80ASCE	325	1,300	11,520	7.31	.80	.04	3.44	11.59	140.80	152.39
75ASCE	325	1,300	11,520	6.71	.77	.04	3.44	10.96	132.00	142.96
70ASCE	325	1,300	11,520	6.27	.51	.03	3.44	10.25	123.20	133.45
60ASCE	359	1,436	10,560	5.80	.53	.03	2.89	9.25	105.60	114.85
50ASCE	359	1,436	10,560	4.58	.51	.03	2.58	7.70	88.00	95.70
40ASCE	359	1,436	10,560	2.89	.49	.03	2.58	5.99	70.40	76.39
30ASCE	359	1,436	10,560	1.88	.28	.02	2.09	4.27	52.80	57.07
25ASCE	359	1,436	10,560	1.02	.16	.01	1.92	3.11	44.00	47.11
20ASCE	359	1,436	10,560	.87	.15	.01	1.66	2.69	35.20	37.89

FOR 1,000 NET TONS OF RAILS

Weight and Section of Rail	Pairs of Splice Bars	Bolts and Nuts	Spikes 4 Per Tie	Splice Bars	Bolts and Nuts	Spring Washers	Spikes	Total Accessories
	Estimated Number			Estimated Weight in Net Tons				
100AREA	1,844	7,376	65,460	57.99	6.82	.68	26.83	92.32
100ASCE	1,844	7,376	65,460	56.52	6.64	.68	26.83	90.67
100ARA"A"	1,844	7,376	65,460	65.46	6.64	.68	26.83	99.61
100ARA"B"	1,844	7,376	65,460	56.24	6.64	.68	26.83	90.39
90ASCE	2,048	8,192	72,730	53.49	5.18	.25	21.76	80.68
90ARA"A"	2,048	8,192	72,730	65.54	5.18	.25	21.76	92.73
85ASCE	2,168	8,672	77,010	51.97	5.32	.27	22.99	80.55
80ASCE	2,304	9,216	81,820	51.84	5.66	.28	24.42	82.20
75ASCE	2,458	9,832	87,280	50.73	5.85	.30	26.05	82.93
70ASCE	2,634	10,536	93,510	50.78	4.15	.24	27.91	83.08
60ASCE	3,396	13,584	100,000	54.85	4.99	.37	27.40	87.61
50ASCE	4,074	16,296	120,000	51.94	5.79	.45	29.40	87.58
40ASCE	5,094	20,376	150,000	41.01	6.95	.56	36.75	85.27
30ASCE	6,790	27,160	200,000	35.48	5.22	.30	39.59	80.59
25ASCE	8,150	32,600	240,000	23.23	3.59	.20	43.64	70.66
20ASCE	10,186	40,744	300,000	24.75	4.28	.25	47.01	76.29

Three-way turnout mounted on steel ties punched with weep-holes for imbedding in concrete.

STEEL TIES — for Heavy-Duty Track

Developments in mine mechanization have had an important effect on transportation systems. Larger capacity cars, track-type mechanical coal-cutting and loading machines and excavating machines, have brought about the use of stronger track equipment and heavier rails. The use of 30-lb and 40-lb rails for room track, 60-lb rails in butt entries, and rails 85-lb and over for main haulage track, shows that heavier rails are being placed in service by low-cost producers.

Keeping pace with the changes in transportation requirements, Bethlehem has redesigned its entire group of steel ties. Sections have been made stronger and weights have been proportioned in relation to maximum physical properties. Rail fasteners have been strengthened to afford greater bearing area on rail bases. These new Bethlehem steel ties of all types make possible economical construction of strong, true-to-gage track that will safely transport machines and heavily-loaded cars without danger of derailment, and with minimum track maintenance.

BETHLEHEM STEEL TIES AND THEIR APPLICATION

Bethlehem Steel Ties have a decided advantage over wood ties. They hold the rails securely, keeping them true to gage and the track in alignment. They have unusually long life, even under severe service conditions, and can never become spike-killed or rotted; and they are not a fire hazard.

Bethlehem Steel Ties are produced from six similar sections, rolled especially for the purpose intended, and differing from each other only in weight and strength to accommodate the different load and bottom conditions. All sections are designed to get the maximum physical properties consistent with minimum weight by means of a reinforcing rib through the longitudinal center.

FOR MINE USE

While over ninety per cent of the steel ties manufactured are used in coal mines, steel ties are also used extensively by companies mining materials such as gypsum, potash, limestone, copper, lead, iron and zinc. Bethlehem Steel Ties for room and secondary-haulage tracks are very popular. The ties are light compared to wood. One man can handle a bundle of five ties easily. Ties are relatively shallow in section, thereby saving valuable head-room in low seams.

The heavier ties are sometimes used for main-haulage tracks, and are often used in conjunction with wood ties in place of gage rods, by spacing them between every third or fourth tie.

All Bethlehem Steel Ties may be furnished with holes for mounting on wood bases.

FOR INDUSTRIAL USE

Bethlehem Steel Ties are widely used in industrial applications. Their strong light sections lend themselves particularly well to all kinds of narrow-gage, light-rail track. They are used in laying track in factories, mills, quarries, plantations, and in tunnels and other construction projects. In factories and mills where track is often laid in concrete, the ties hold the rails in alignment and to gage while the concrete is being poured. The shallow depth of steel ties reduces the amount of excavation and concrete required for the track bed.

Contractors have found that Bethlehem Steel Ties with bolted rail fastenings have many applications on construction jobs. These ties are strong and light in weight, and they take up much less storage space than wood ties. They can be used over and over again.

HOW TO ORDER BETHLEHEM STEEL TIES

When ordering steel ties, please give the following information:

1. The Number of Bethlehem Steel Tie: whether No. 2-OSC*, No. 3-SC*, No. 432, etc.

2. The rail weight per yd. If ties are to fit two weights of rail, advise weights and types.

3. The type of rail: whether AS or RB.

4. The gage of track.

Straight end ties are furnished unless otherwise specified. If depressed ends are wanted, mark the order "DE" (depressed ends).

---

*OSC (outside stationary clip) ties have the stationary clips placed on the outside of the rail at each end of the tie.

SC (staggered clip) ties have one stationary clip placed on the inside of rail at one end of tie, and one stationary clip placed on the outside of the rail at the opposite end of the tie.

BETHLEHEM STEEL TIES

Steel ties are manufactured in six weights by Bethlehem. The range of weights permits selection of the tie best fitted for the job. More freedom of choice is secured by a wide selection of clips that can be used. On any tie section, for example, several different clips can be used, in order to accommodate rails from 16 lb to 100 lb per yd, or different types of rail, or the use of two different types of rails at one time.

The choice of a steel tie is influenced by factors such as the condition of the bottom, weight of cars and equipment, amount and speed of traffic, and permanency of trackage. Also to be considered are the weight and type, or types, of rail used.

No. 2 OSC Tie. For 16-lb to 30-lb rails.

No. 3 OSC Tie. For 25-lb to 40-lb rails.

No. 4 OSC Tie. For 30-lb to 40-lb rails.

No. 5 OSC Tie. For 30-lb to 60-lb rails.

No. 6 OSC Tie. For 40-lb to 60-lb rails.

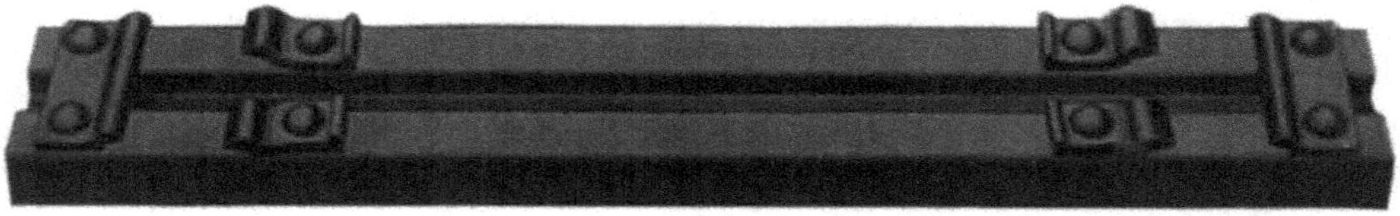

No. 9 OSC Tie. For 60-lb to 100-lb rails.

DIMENSIONS AND WEIGHTS

Tie Section	Depth of Section in.	Width of Section		Thickness of Section in.	Nomina Weight per Foot lb
		Top in.	Bottom in.		
No. 2	1 1/16	3⅜	4⅛	0.122	2.50
No. 3	13/16	4⅛	5	0.130	3.25
No. 4	55/64	4⅛	5	0.176	4.00
No. 5	1 1/16	4½	5½	0.176	5.00
No. 6	1⅞	4¾	6⅛	0.168	6.00
No. 9	1⅞	4¾	6⅛	0.271	9.00

PROPERTIES OF TIE SECTIONS

Tie Section	Area of Section sq in.	Weight of Section lb/ft	Horizontal Axis		
			Moment of Inertia in.^{4}	Section Modulus in.^{3}	Neutral Axis from Base in.
No. 2	0.736	2.500	0.0376	0.0891	0.422
No. 3	0.956	3.250	0.080	0.171	0.471
No. 4	1.177	4.000	0.099	0.201	0.495
No. 5	1.471	5.000	0.196	0.321	0.610
No. 6	1.765	6.000	0.578	0.464	1.203
No. 9	2.647	9.000	0.753	0.624	1.206

Steel Tie Sections

No. 2, No. 3, No. 4 and No. 5

The design of No. 2, No. 3, No. 4 and No. 5 Steel Tie Sections is characterized by a large rail-bearing area on top of the tie and a deep center rib and turned-down sides running lengthwise of the tie. This design affords high strength and stiffness for great load-bearing capacity, and gives the tie stability and "grip" in the mine bottom.

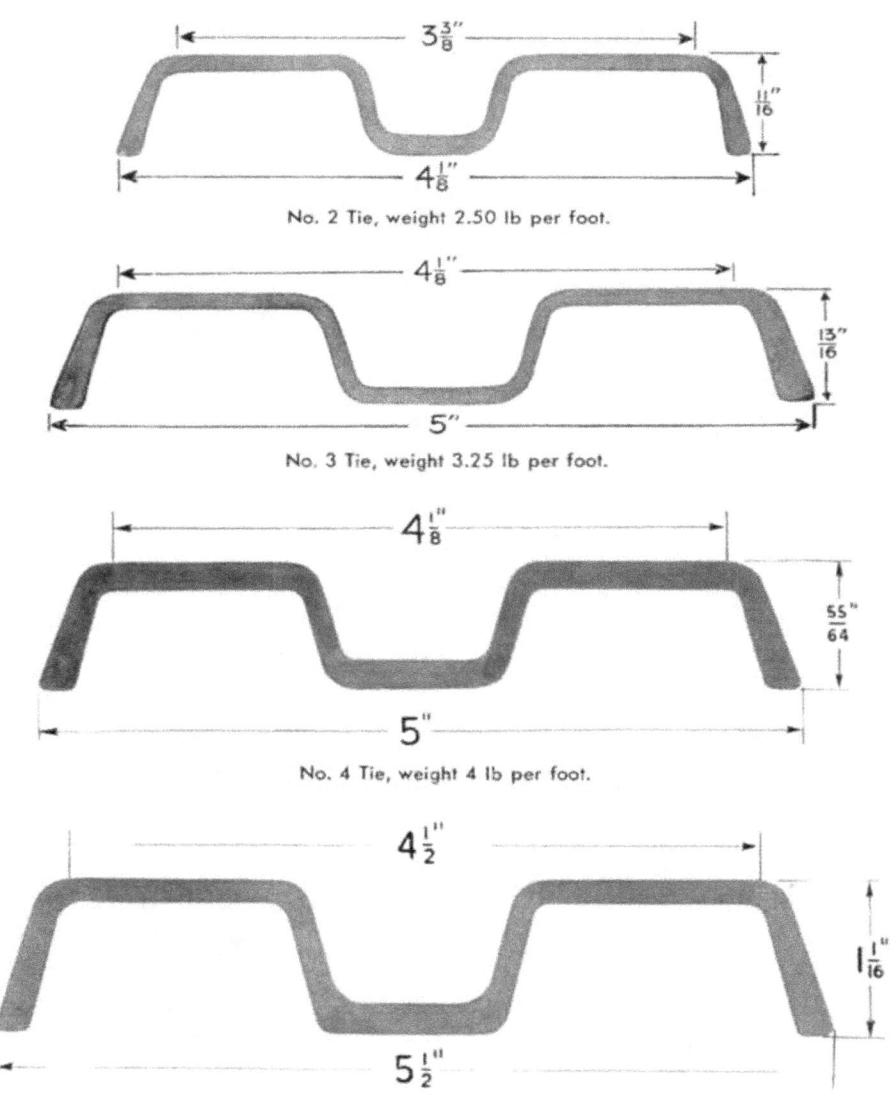

No. 2 Tie, weight 2.50 lb per foot.

No. 3 Tie, weight 3.25 lb per foot.

No. 4 Tie, weight 4 lb per foot.

No. 5 Tie, weight 5 lb per foot.

Steel Tie Sections
No. 6 and No. 9

The design of No. 6 and No. 9 Steel Tie Sections is similar to that of No. 2, No. 3, No. 4 and No. 5, but the weights are considerably greater. The sides are deeper and end in a reinforcing bulb, greatly strengthening the ties and providing larger wearing and gripping surfaces.

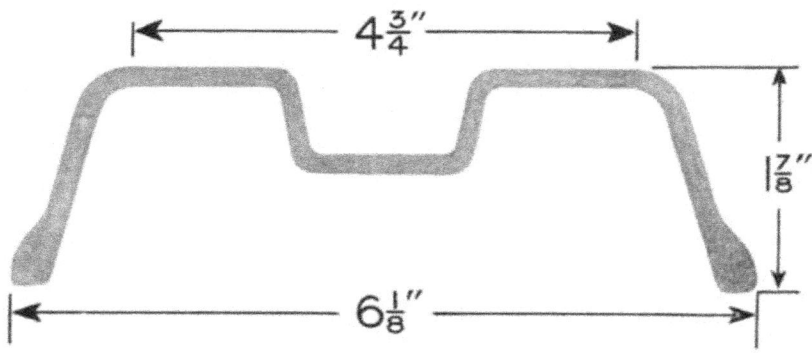

No. 6 Tie, weight 6 lb per foot.

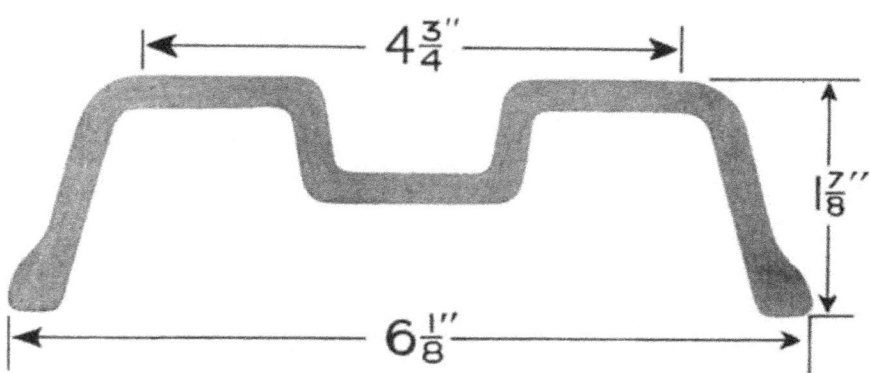

No. 9 Tie, weight 9 lb per foot.

No. 2 Steel Ties

The Bethlehem No. 2 Steel Tie, weighing 2.5 lb per ft, is designed for use with 16-lb, 20-lb, 25-lb and 30-lb rails in locations where the loads are light and bottom conditions are good.

No. 2—OSC Tie

The most widely used No. 2 tie is the OSC (outside stationary clip) tie. It is equipped with four rolled steel movable clips, and two stationary clips placed on the outside ends, as illustrated. The clips are spaced to fit one particular rail section. This tie is usually carried in stock by supply companies who distribute Bethlehem Ties.

No. 2—SC Tie

Next in popularity is the SC (staggered clip) tie, which is equipped with four rolled-steel movable clips and two stationary clips, with a stationary clip on the inside at one end, and on the outside at the other end. This feature is especially useful when it is desired to insert or remove a tie without disturbing the track gage. The clips are spaced to fit one particular rail section.

No. 232 Tie

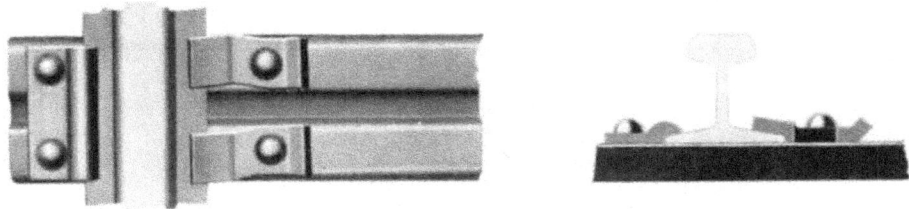

Bethlehem Steel Tie No. 232 is the No. 2 tie section equipped with two No. 32 forged-steel movable clips, and one stationary clip per rail. The No. 32 clip has a long bearing surface on both the tie and rail base, enabling it to fit either AS or RB rails of the same weight. It can also be used for two rail sections having a difference of 5 lb per yd. This tie is furnished only in the OSC (outside stationary clip) design.

No. 242 Tie

No. 242 tie is the No. 2 tie section equipped with one No. 42 forged-steel movable clip and one stationary clip per rail. The No. 42 clip is a double-end, double-utility clip. It is punched and riveted off-center, to fit two different weights of rail. This tie is furnished only in the OSC (outside stationary clip) design.

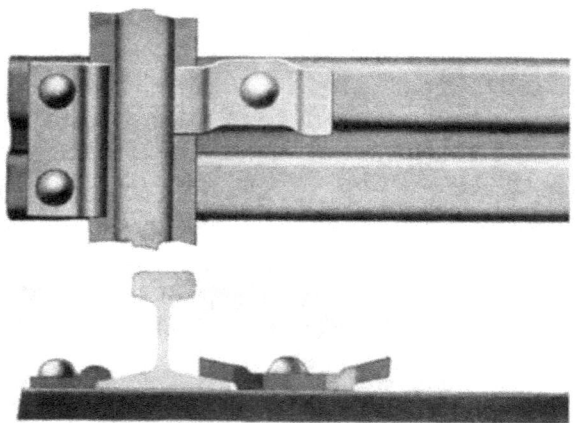

No. 27 Tie

No. 27 tie is the No. 2 tie section equipped with two No. 7 forged-steel clips and two bolts per rail. T-head bolts, which fit into slots in the ties, hold the clips and rail in place. This tie is often used for industrial and construction projects. The No. 7 clips may be used for 16-lb or 20-lb rail.

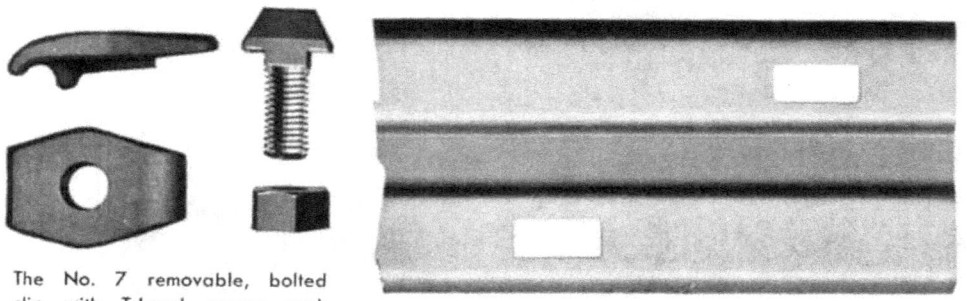

The No. 7 removable, bolted clip with T-head square neck bolt and hexagon nut. The No. 8 clip is of larger size.

Top view of a tie showing the slots for T-head, square neck bolts and the projecting lugs of clip.

No. 28 Tie

No. 28 tie is similar to the No. 27 tie, illustrated above. It is equipped, however, with No. 8 forged-steel clips for 25-lb or 30-lb rail.

No. 3 Steel Ties

The Bethlehem No. 3 Steel Tie Section, weighing 3.25 lb per ft, is designed for use with 25-lb, 30-lb and 40-lb rails for medium loads and fair bottom conditions.

No. 3—OSC Tie

The most widely used No. 3 tie is the OSC (outside stationary clip) tie. It is equipped with four rolled-steel movable clips, and two stationary clips placed on the outside ends, as illustrated. The clips are spaced to fit one particular rail section. This tie is usually carried in stock by supply companies who distribute Bethlehem Ties.

No. 3—SC Tie

Next in popularity is the SC (staggered clip) tie, which is equipped with four rolled-steel movable clips and two stationary clips, with a stationary clip on the inside at one end, and on the outside at the other end. This feature is especially useful when it is desired to insert or remove a tie without disturbing the track gage. The clips are spaced to fit one particular rail section.

No. 332 Tie

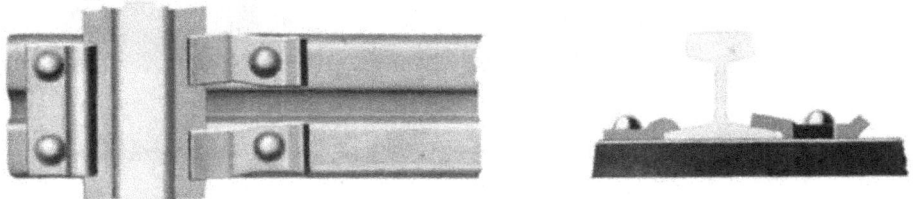

No. 332 tie is the No. 3 tie section equipped with two No. 32 forged-steel movable clips and one stationary clip per rail. The No. 32 clip has a long bearing surface on both the tie and rail base, enabling it to fit either AS or RB rails of the same weight. It can also be used for two rail sections having a difference of 5-lb per yd. This tie is furnished only in the OSC (outside stationary clip) design.

No. 342 Tie

Bethlehem Tie No. 342 is the No. 3 tie section equipped with one No. 42 forged-steel movable clip and one stationary clip per rail. The No. 42 clip is a double-end, double-utility clip. It is punched and riveted off center, to fit two different weights of rail. This tie is furnished only in the OSC (outside stationary clip) design.

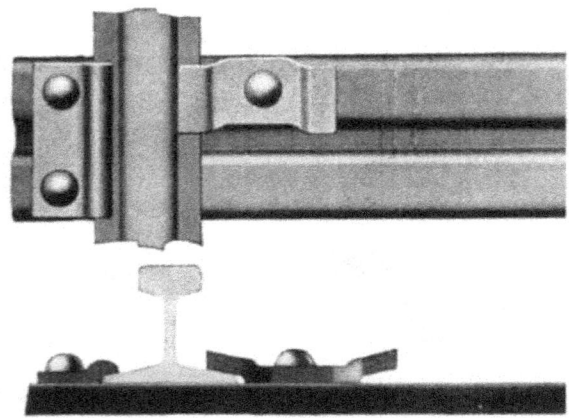

No. 37 Tie

Bethlehem No. 37 Tie is the No. 3 tie section equipped with two No. 7 forged-steel clips and two bolts per rail. T-head bolts, which fit into slots in the ties, hold the clips and rail in place. This tie is widely used for industrial and construction projects. The No. 7 clips may be used for 16-lb or 20-lb rail.

The No. 7 removable, bolted clip with T-head square neck bolt and hexagon nut. The No. 8 clip is of larger size.

Top view of a tie showing the slots for T-head, square neck bolts and the projecting lugs of clip.

No. 38 Tie

No. 38 tie is similar to the No. 37, illustrated above. However, it is equipped with No. 8 forged-steel clips which may be used for 25-lb or 30-lb rails.

No. 4 Steel Ties

The Bethlehem No. 4 Steel Tie Section, weighing 4.00 lb per ft, is designed for use with 30-lb to 40-lb rails, where loads are heavy and bottom uneven.

No. 4—OSC Tie

The most widely used No. 4 tie is the OSC (outside stationary clip) tie. It is equipped with four rolled-steel movable clips, and two stationary clips placed on the outside ends, as illustrated. The clips are spaced to fit one particular rail section. This tie is usually carried in stock by supply companies who distribute Bethlehem Ties.

No. 4—SC Tie

Next in popularity is the SC (staggered clip) tie, which is equipped with four rolled-steel movable clips and two stationary clips, with a stationary clip on the inside at one end, and on the outside at the other end. This feature is especially useful when it is desired to insert or remove a tie without disturbing the track gage. The clips are spaced to fit one particular rail section.

No. 432 Tie

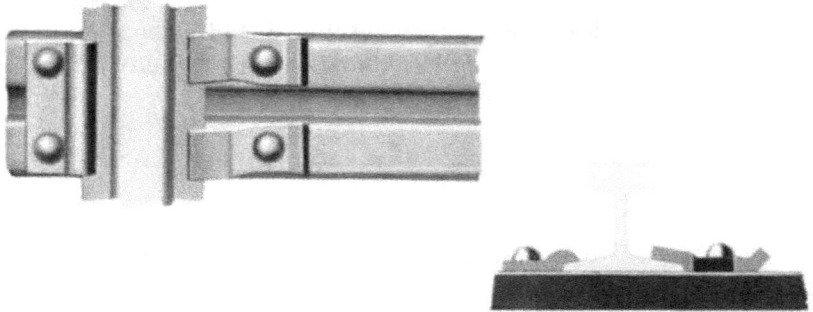

Bethlehem Tie No. 432 is the No. 4 tie section equipped with two No. 32 forged steel movable clips and one stationary clip per rail. The No. 32 clip has a long bearing surface on both the tie and rail base, enabling it to fit either AS or RB rails of the same weight. It can also be used for two rail sections having a difference of 5 lb per yd. This tie is furnished only in the OSC (outside stationary clip) design.

No. 442 Tie

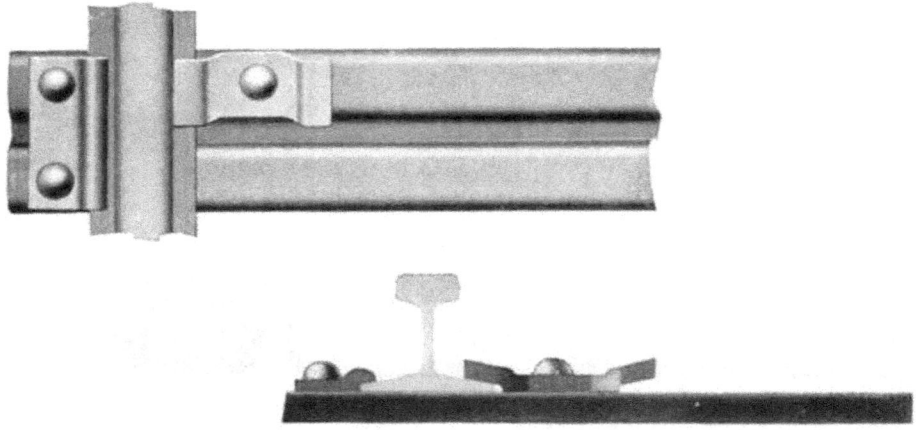

Bethlehem Tie No. 442 is the No. 4 tie section equipped with one No. 42 forged-steel movable clip and one stationary clip per rail. The No. 42 clip is a double-end, double-utility clip. It is punched and riveted off center, to fit two different weights of rail. This tie is furnished only in the OSC (outside stationary clip) design.

No. 5 Steel Ties

Bethlehem No. 5 Steel Tie Section, weighing 5.00 lb per ft, is designed for use with 30-lb to 60-lb rails where very heavy mechanical equipment is used and bottom conditions are rugged.

No. 5—OSC Tie

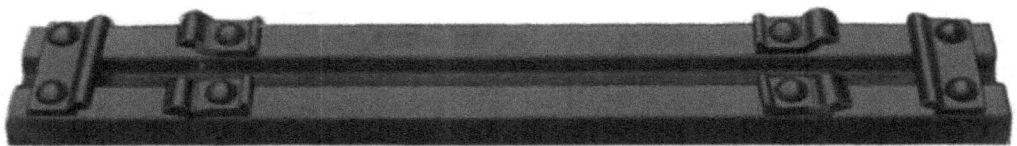

The most widely used No. 5 tie is the OSC (outside stationary clip) tie. It is equipped with four rolled steel movable clips, and two stationary clips placed on the outside ends, as illustrated. The clips are spaced to fit one particular rail section. This tie is usually carried in stock by supply companies who distribute Bethlehem Ties.

No. 5—SC Tie

Next in popularity is the SC (staggered clip) tie, which is equipped with four rolled steel movable clips and two stationary clips, with a stationary clip on the inside at one end, and on the outside at the other end. This feature is especially useful when it is desired to insert or remove a tie without disturbing the track gage. The clips are spaced to fit one particular rail section.

No. 532 Tie

No. 532 tie is the No. 5 tie section equipped with two No. 32 forged-steel movable clips and one stationary clip per rail. The No. 32 clip has a long bearing surface on both the tie and rail base, enabling it to fit either AS or RB rails of the same weight. It can also be used for two rail sections having a difference of 5 lb per yd. This tie is furnished only in the OSC (outside stationary clip) design.

No. 542 Tie

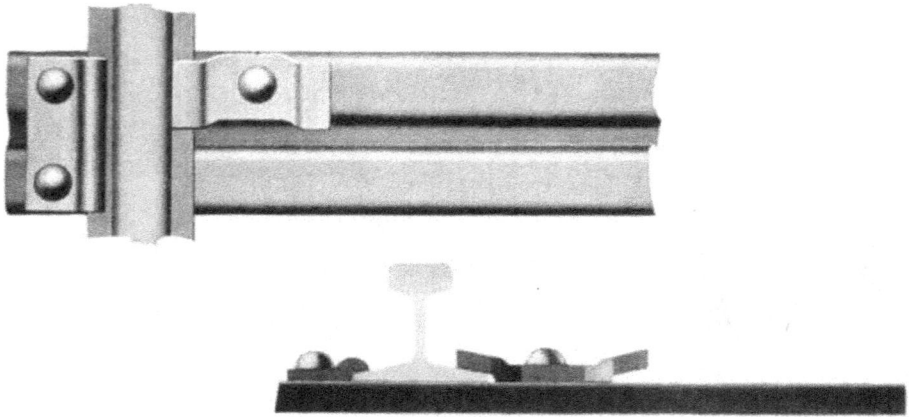

No. 542 tie is the No. 5 tie section equipped with one No. 42 forged-steel movable clip and one stationary clip per rail. The No. 42 clip is a double-end, double-utility clip. It is punched and riveted off center, to fit two different weights of rail. This tie is furnished only in the OSC (outside stationary clip) design.

No. 6 Steel Ties

Bethlehem No. 6 Steel Tie Section, weighing 6.00 lb per ft, is designed for use with 40-lb to 60-lb rails where traffic conditions are severe or wherever track is to be laid in a permanent installation.

No. 6—OSC Tie

The most widely used No. 6 tie is the OSC (outside stationary clip) tie. It is equipped with four rolled-steel movable clips, and two stationary clips placed on the outside ends, as illustrated. The clips are spaced to fit one particular rail section.

No. 6—SC Tie

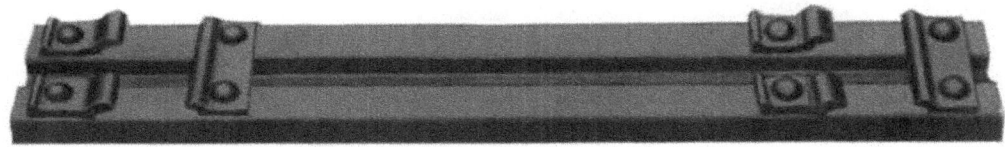

Next in popularity is the SC (staggered clip) tie, which is equipped with four rolled-steel movable clips and two stationary clips, with a stationary clip on the inside at one end, and on the outside at the other end. This feature is especially useful when it is desired to insert or remove a tie without disturbing the track gage. The clips are spaced to fit one particular rail section.

No. 632 Tie

No. 632 tie is the No. 6 tie section equipped with two No. 32 forged-steel movable clips and one stationary clip per rail. The No. 32 clip has a long bearing surface on both the tie and rail base, enabling it to fit either AS or RB rails of the same weight. It can also be used for two rail sections having a difference of 5 lb per yd. This tie is furnished only in the OSC (outside stationary clip) design.

No. 642 Tie

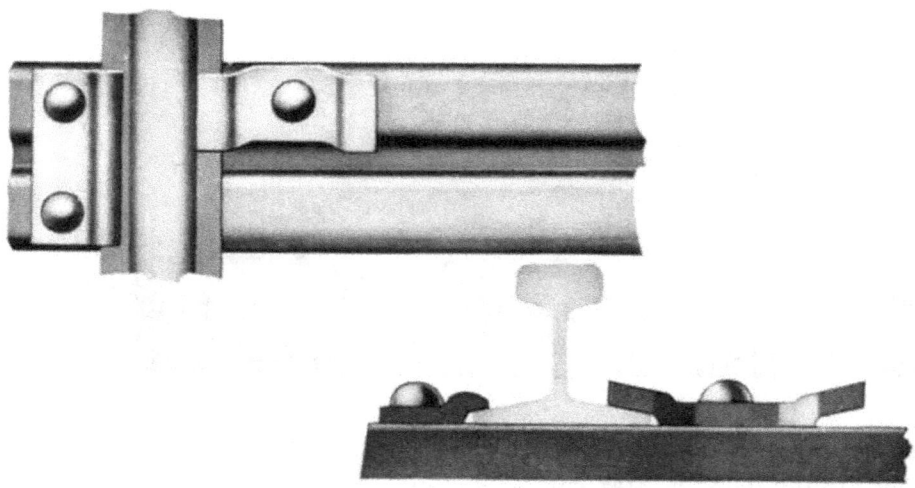

No. 642 tie is the No. 6 tie section equipped with one No. 42 forged-steel movable clip and one stationary clip per rail. It is punched and riveted off center, to fit two different weights of rail. This tie is furnished only in the OSC (outside stationary clip) design.

No. 611 Tie

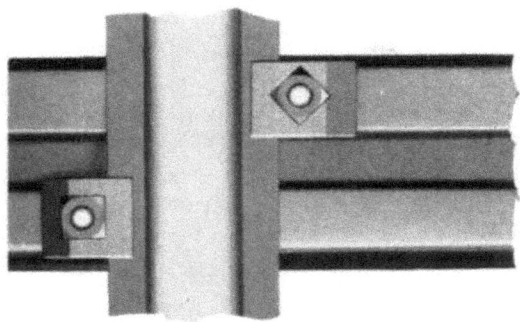

Top view of No. 611 Tie with No. 11-S and No. 11-L removable (bolted) clips.

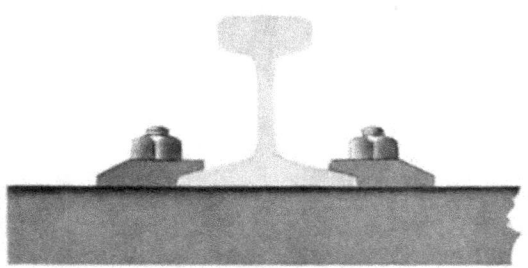

Side view of No. 611 Tie.

Top view showing slots for bolts and clips.

No. 611 tie is the No. 6 tie section punched with four rectangular holes to accommodate one No. 11-S (short) and one No. 11-L (long) clip for each rail. By interchanging the clips the gage may be varied ¼ in. at each rail, providing a total increase of ½ in. in track gage. Each clip is held in place by a T-head, square-neck bolt, inserted from the top of the tie. A shoulder on the bottom of each clip fits into a hole in the tie section to relieve the bolt of shearing stress.

No. 69 Tie

Top view of No. 69 Tie with No. 9-S and No. 9-L removable (bolted) clips.

Side view of No. 69 Tie with No. 9-S and No. 9-L removable (bolted) clips.

Top view of tie showing slotted tie plate spot-welded to tie.

The rib on the bottom of the clip fits into the slot in the tie plate and the shoulder on the bottom of the clip fits against the rail base. The clips are fastened with 5/8-inch bolt and square hot-forged nuts.

No. 69 tie is the No. 6 tie section equipped with heavy tie plates slotted to accommodate one No. 9-S (short) and one 9-L (long) clip for each rail. By interchanging the clips the gage may be varied ¼ in. at each rail, providing a total increase of ½ in. in track gage. This variation is sufficient for widening the gage at curves as required in most tracks. Each clip is held in place by a heavy bolt and nut inserted from the top of the tie. The square head of the bolt is large enough to prevent turning in the central tie groove. The design of the clip is such that it transmits the lateral thrust of the rail direct to the tie plate, relieving the bolt of shearing stress.

No. 9 Steel Ties

Bethlehem No. 9 Steel Tie Section, weighing 9.00 lb per ft, is designed for 60-lb to 100-lb rails where traffic is extremely heavy and wherever track is to be laid in a permanent installation.

No. 9—OSC Tie

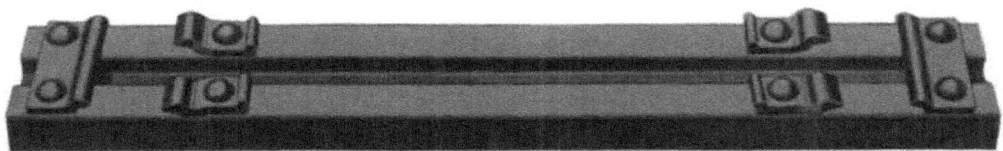

The most widely used No. 9 tie is the OSC (outside stationary clip) tie. It is equipped with four rolled-steel movable clips, and two stationary clips placed on the outside ends, as illustrated. The clips are spaced to fit one particular rail section.

No. 9—SC Tie

Next in popularity is the SC (staggered clip) tie, which is equipped with four rolled-steel movable clips and two stationary clips, with a stationary clip on the inside at one end, and on the outside at the other end. This feature is especially useful when it is desired to insert or remove a tie without disturbing the track gage. The clips are spaced to fit one particular rail section.

No. 932 Tie

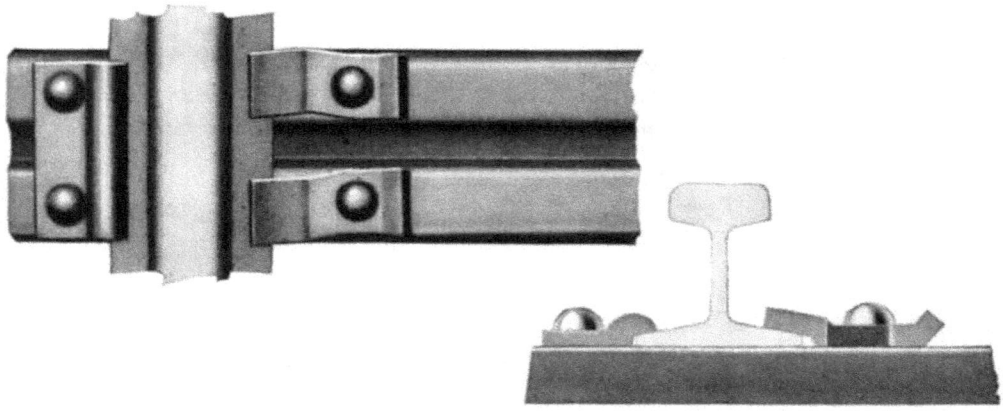

No. 932 tie is the No. 9 tie section equipped with two No. 32 forged-steel movable clips and one stationary clip per rail. The No. 32 clip has a long bearing surface on both the tie and rail base, enabling it to fit either AS or RB rails of the same weight. It can also be used for two rail sections having a difference of 5 lb per yd. This tie is furnished only in the OSC (outside stationary clip) design.

No. 942 Tie

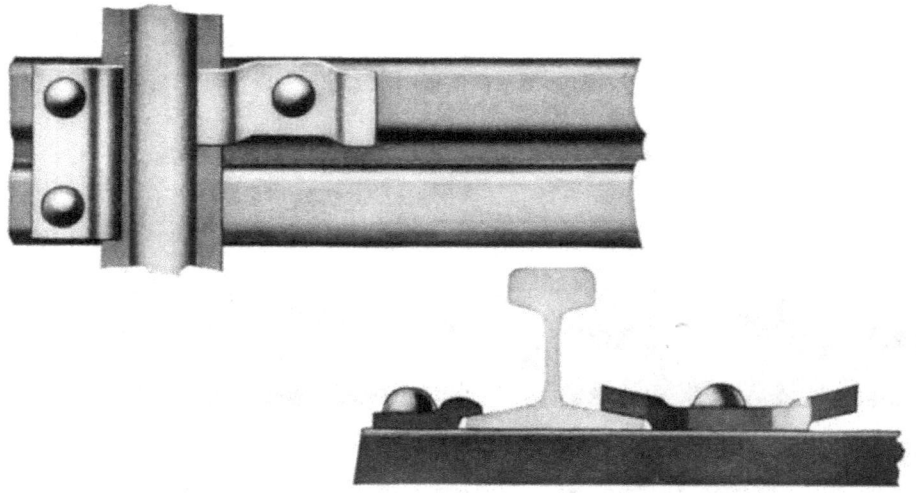

No. 942 tie is the No. 9 tie section equipped with one No. 42 forged-steel movable clip and one stationary clip per rail. The No. 42 clip is a double-end, double-utility clip. It is punched and riveted off center, to fit two different weights of rail. This tie is furnished only in the OSC (outside stationary clip) design.

No. 911 Tie

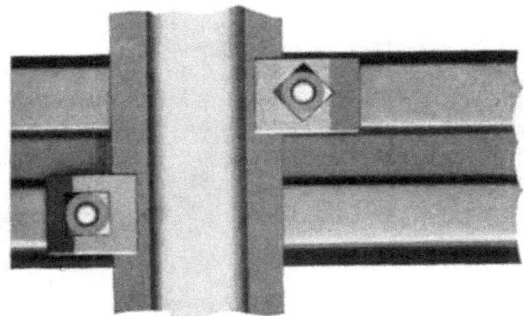

Top view of No. 911 Tie with No. 11-S and No. 11-L removable (bolted) clips.

Side view of No. 911 Tie.

Top view showing slots for bolts and clips.

No. 911 tie is the No. 9 tie section punched with four rectangular holes to accommodate one No. 11-S (short) and one No. 11-L (long) clip for each rail. By interchanging the clips the gage may be varied ¼ in. at each rail, providing a total increase of ½ in. in track gage. Each clip is held in place by a T-head, square-neck bolt inserted from the top of the tie. A shoulder on the bottom of each clip fits into a hole in the tie section to relieve the bolt of shearing stress.

No. 99 Tie

Top view of No. 99 Tie with No. 9-S and No. 9-L removable (bolted) clips.

Side view of No. 99 Tie with No. 9-S and No. 9-L removable (bolted) clips

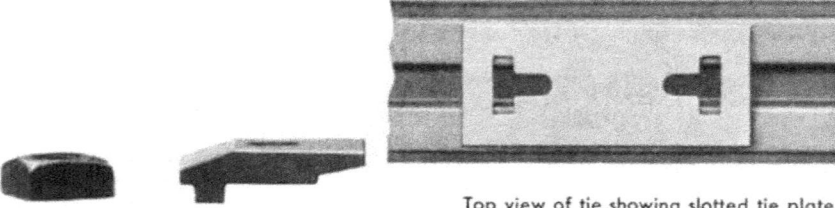

Top view of tie showing slotted tie plate spot-welded to tie.

The rib on the bottom of the clip fits into the slot in the tie plate and the shoulder on the bottom of the clip fits against the rail base. The clips are fastened with ⅝-inch bolt and square hot-forged nuts.

No. 99 tie is the No. 9 tie section equipped with heavy tie plates slotted to accommodate one No. 9-S (short) clip and one No. 9-L (long) clip for each rail. By interchanging the clips the gage may be varied ¼ in. at each rail, providing a total increase of ½ in. in track gage. This variation is sufficient for widening the gage at curves as required in most tracks. Each clip is held in place by a heavy bolt and nut inserted from the top of the tie. The square head of the bolt is large enough to prevent turning in the central tie groove. The design of the clip is such that it transmits the lateral thrust of the rail directly to the tie plate, relieving the bolt of shearing stress.

Steel Ties with Depressed Ends

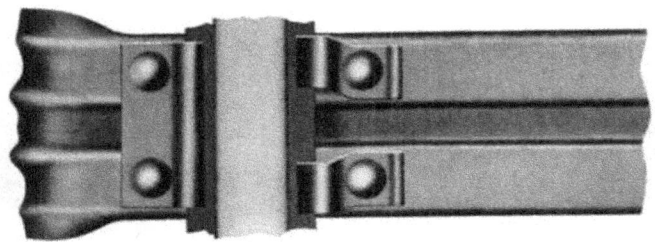

Top view of a tie with depressed ends and movable and stationary (riveted) clips.

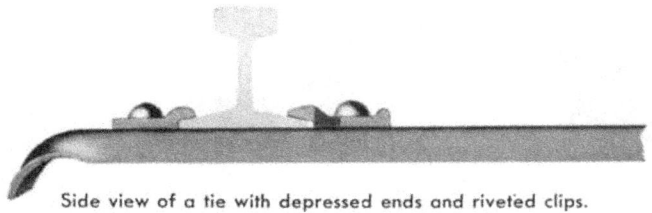

Side view of a tie with depressed ends and riveted clips.

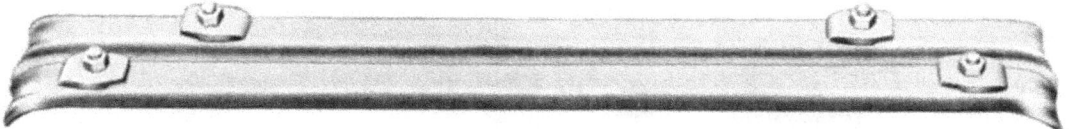

No. 28 Tie with depressed ends.

No. 99 Tie with depressed ends, completely assembled.

Any of the ties shown in the foregoing pages can be furnished with depressed ends. Depressed-end ties are often furnished for main haulage tracks where track is ballasted. They are also specified for room and butt-entry tracks where the mine bottom is soft enough for the ends to dig in and prevent lateral movement of the track, but are not recommended for mines having a hard bottom.

Riveted Clips

STATIONARY (Riveted) CLIPS   **MOVABLE (Riveted) CLIPS**

No. 1-A. Stationary Clip.   For 16- and 20-lb rails.   No. 1. Movable Clip

No. 2-A. Stationary Clip.   For 25- and 30-lb rails.   No. 2 Movable Clip.

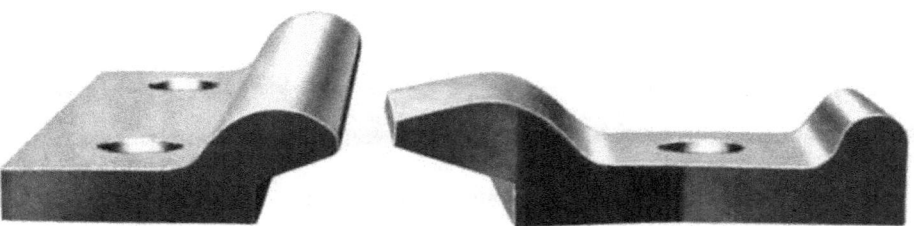

No. 3-A. Stationary Clip.   For 40- and 45-lb rails.   No. 3. Movable Clip.

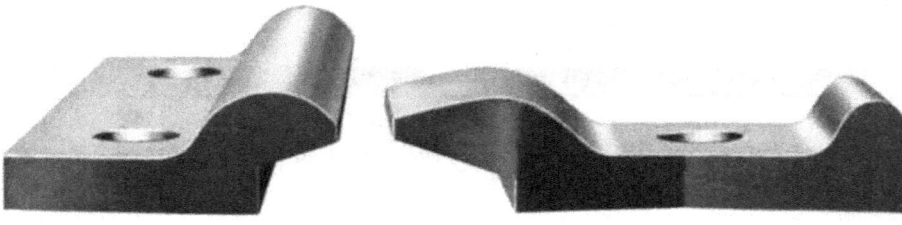

No. 4-A. Stationary Clip.   For 50- and 60-lb rails.   No. 4. Movable Clip

Clips are made of rolled steel, carefully shaped to fit snugly on the base of the rail. Four different sizes are made to fit 16-lb to 60-lb rails. Stationary clips are firmly riveted to the tie with two rivets. Movable clips are snugly fastened with one rivet, and only a hammer is required to turn them into locking position over the rail base.

Special Riveted Clips (Movable)

A number of rail clips have been designed for use with various ties in order to meet special conditions. They are made of rolled or forged steel, and will fit snugly over the base of rails.

No. 32 Clip

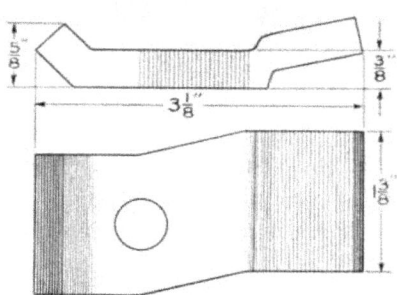

No. 32 clip is a medium-length clip. This clip has a long lip so that it can be used with 25-lb to 60-lb AS or RB rails. It can be used with No. 2, No. 3, No. 4, No. 5, No. 6 and No. 9 ties in combination with stationary clips. The weight of the clip is 0.45 lb.

No. 42 Clip

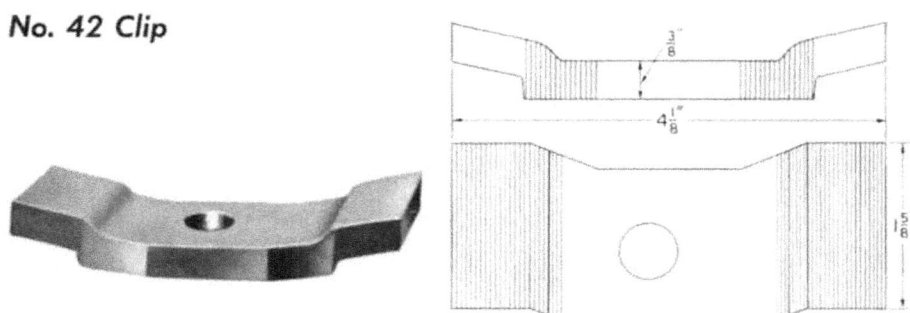

No. 42 clip is a double-ended clip for use with various combinations of any two weights of rail from 25-lb to 60-lb. One end of the clip fits one weight of rail, while the other end will fit the second weight rail. The usual combinations of rail weights for which this clip is made are the following:

>   20 AS and 25 AS   20 AS and 30 AS
>   25 AS and 30 AS   30 AS and 40 AS
>   40 AS and 50 AS   50 AS and 60 AS

The No. 42 clip can be used with No. 2, No. 3, No. 4, No. 5, No. 6 and No. 9 ties in combination with stationary clips. The weight of the clip is 0.68 lb.

Bolted Clips (Removable)

No. 7 Clip

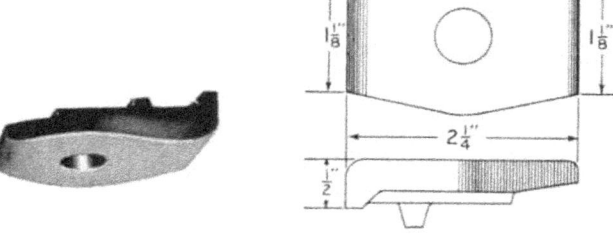

This is a forged-steel, bolted clip that is widely used with ties in industrial track service. It is used with 16-lb and 20-lb rails. Four of these clips are used per tie, and no stationary clips are used with them. The No. 7 clip can be used with No. 2 and No. 3 ties. The clip is fastened with Type L bolts. The weight of the No. 7 clip is 0.29 lb.

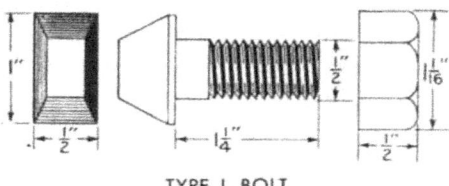

TYPE L BOLT

Type L bolt is used with the No. 7 clip, above, for 16-lb and 20-lb rails. Made with T-head, square neck, hexagon nut, ½ x 1¼ in. Wt. of Bolt is .15 lb.

No. 8 Clip

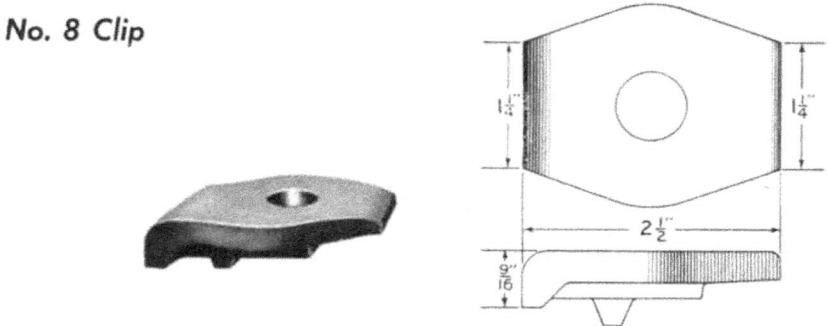

This is a forged-steel, bolted clip similar to and larger than the No. 7 clip for similar service. It is used with 25-lb to 40-lb rails. Four of these clips are used per tie, and no stationary clips are used with them. The No. 8 clip can be used with No. 2 and No. 3 ties. The clip is fastened with Type H bolts. The weight of the No. 8 clip is 0.43 lb.

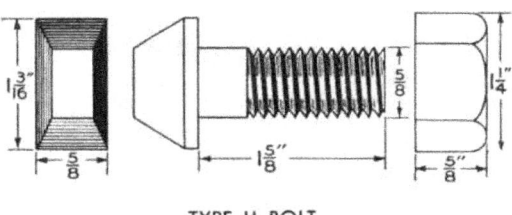

TYPE H BOLT

Type H bolt is used with No. 8 clip, above, for 25-lb to 40-lb rails. Made with T-head, square neck, hexagon nut, ⅝ in. x 1⅝ in. Weight of bolt is .30 lb.

No. 9-S (short) and No. 9-L (long) Clips

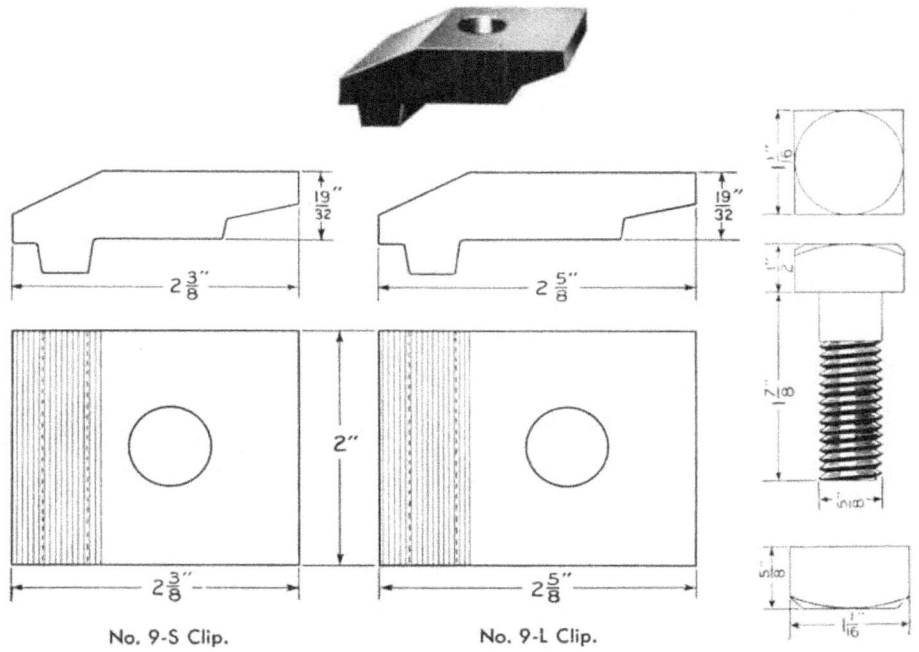

No. 9-S Clip.   No. 9-L Clip.

The No. 9-S (short) and No. 9-L (long) clips are the regular removable (bolted) clips furnished with No. 69 and No. 99 ties. Each tie is equipped with two short and two long clips. They are used with 30-lb to 100-lb rails.

Stationary clips are not used in connection with these clips. By reversing the position of the long and short clips, the gage of track can be increased from ¼ in. to ½ in. Square-head bolts with square nuts, as illustrated, are used to fasten the clips. Weight of bolt is .34 lb. The weight of the No. 9-S clip is 0.70 lb. The weight of the No. 9-L clip is 0.78 lb.

No. 11-S (short) and No. 11-L (long) Clips

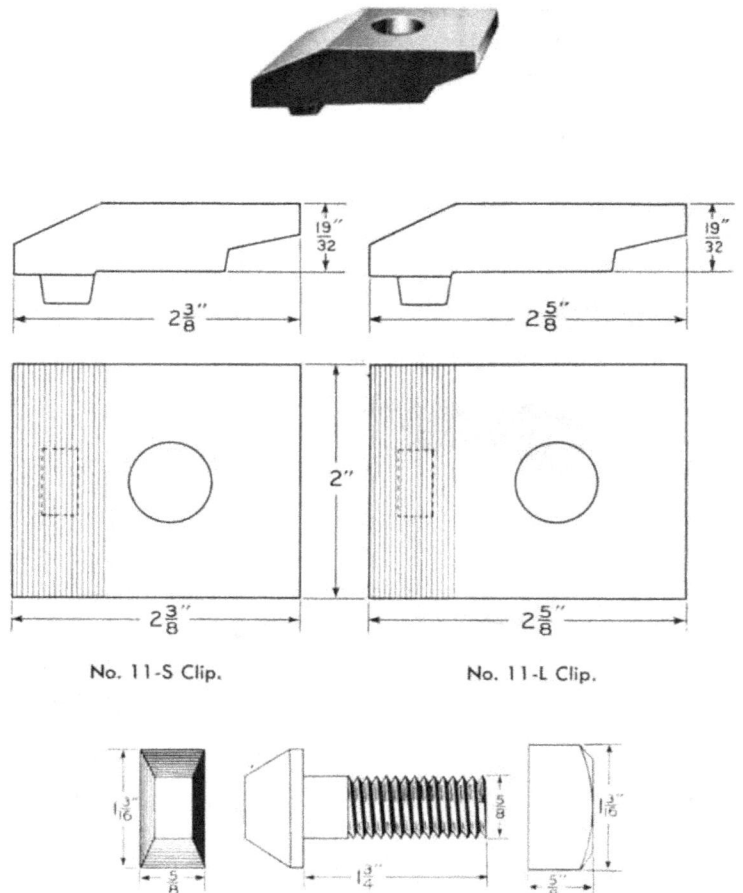

No. 11-S Clip.   No. 11-L Clip.

The No. 11-S (short) and No. 11-L (long) clips are the special removable (bolted) clips used in connection with the No. 611 and No. 911 ties. Each tie is fitted with two short and two long clips. for 30-lb and 100-lb rails.

Stationary clips are not used in connection with these clips. By reversing the position of the long and short clips the gage of track can be increased from ¼ in. to ½ in. over gage. T-head, square-neck bolts with square nuts, as illustrated, are used to fasten the clips. The weight of the No. 11-S clip is 0.67 lb. The weight of the No. 11-L clip is 0.75 lb. Weight of bolt is .31 lb.

No. 62 Rail Clip

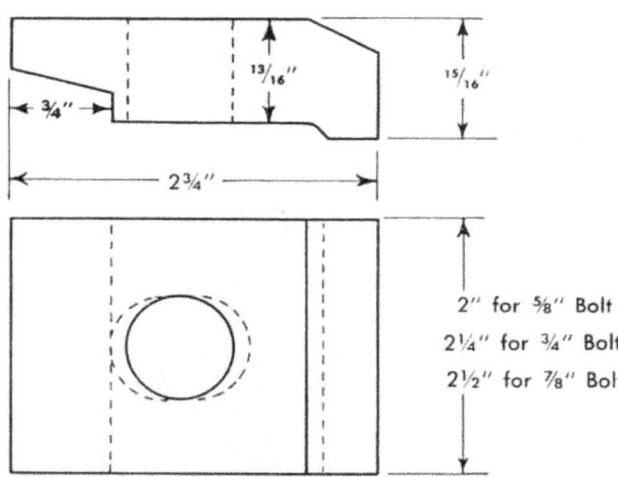

The No. 62 clip is made of a rolled section which may be sheared to lengths required. It is designed for use with heavy rails. When ordering, please give the following information.

1. Rail section.
2. Hole size.
3. Round or Oval Holes.
4. Hole location.
5. Diameter of bolt to be used.

Installing Steel Ties

No. 2, No. 3, No. 4, No. 5, No. 6 and No. 9

The installation of Bethlehem Steel Ties with riveted clips is simple and easy. Whether the ties are straight or depressed-end, they are installed in the same manner.

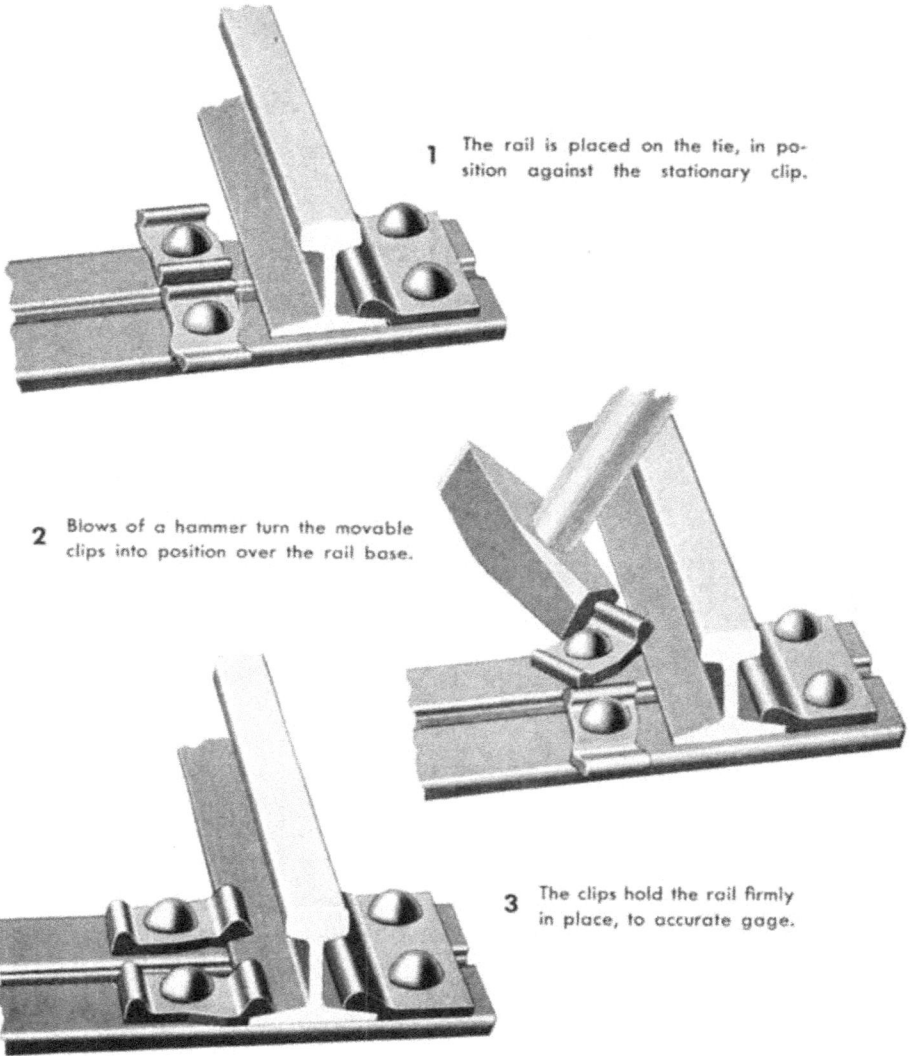

1. The rail is placed on the tie, in position against the stationary clip.

2. Blows of a hammer turn the movable clips into position over the rail base.

3. The clips hold the rail firmly in place, to accurate gage.

In many cases, only one clip need be hammered over the rail base. This allows the other clip to be held in reserve. Track is laid easily and quickly. The gaging of track is eliminated as the ties are to accurate gage.

Installing Bethlehem No. 5 Steel Mine Ties close to the coal face.

Notice how Bethlehem Steel Ties dig into the mine bottom to hold alignment and save headroom. In addition, they eliminate a fire hazard.

MISCELLANEOUS EQUIPMENT

Numerous other products are manufactured by Bethlehem Steel Company for use in mine and industrial track. Among these products are the following:

> Gage Rods
> Tie Plates
> Rail Braces
> Compromise Joints
>   etc.

The products are described briefly in the following pages. A list of other Bethlehem Steel Company products is given on page 186. For more complete information on any product, write to the nearest Bethlehem Steel Company sales office.

GAGE RODS

Bethlehem gage rods represent an improved type of rod, designed for use with all sizes of rail.

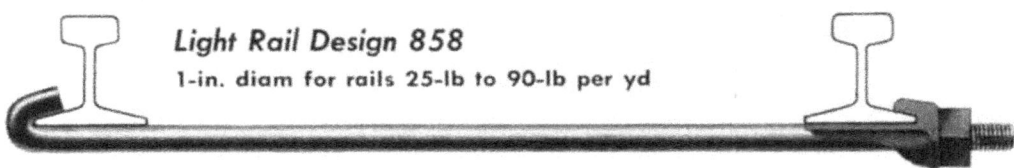

Light Rail Design 858
1-in. diam for rails 25-lb to 90-lb per yd

Gage Rod Design 858 for light rails is made of $^{29}/_{32}$ in. diam rod with a forged hook on one end and a malleable adjustable clip with a square nut and spring lock washer on the other end. This rod has 1-in. diam rolled threads.

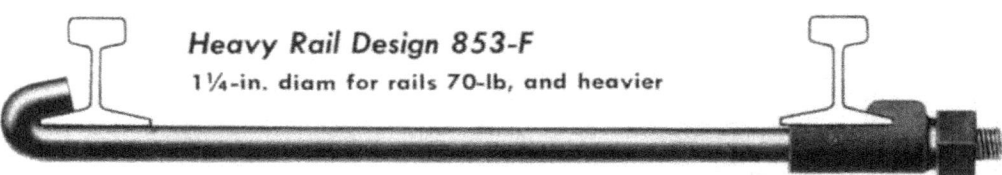

Heavy Rail Design 853-F
1¼-in. diam for rails 70-lb, and heavier

Gage Rod Design 853-F for heavier rails is 1¼-in. diam with a bent hook on one end, and a forged adjustable clip with square nut and spring lock washer on the other end.

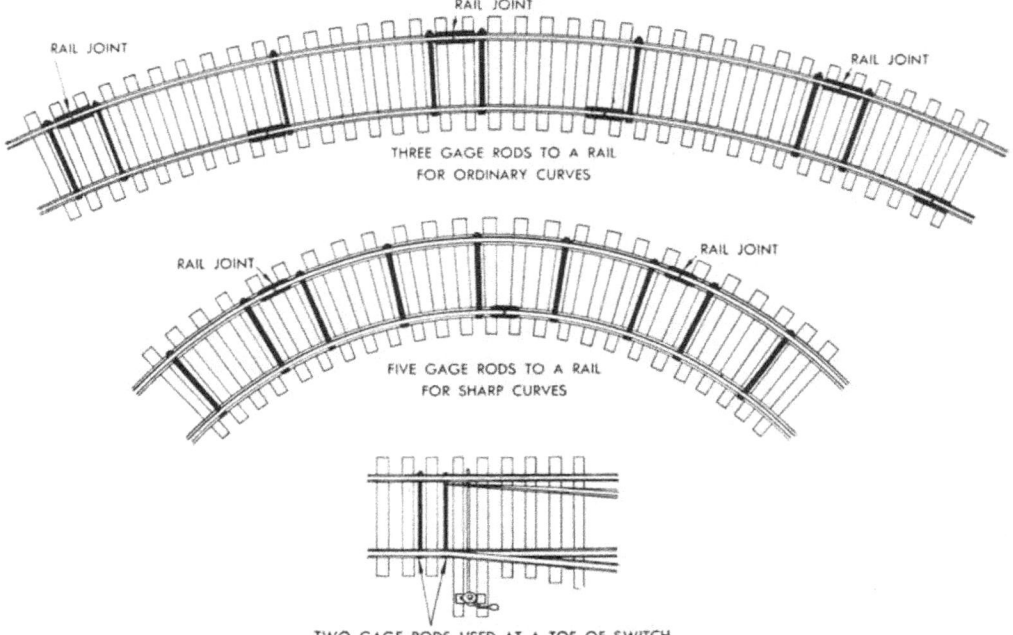

The illustrations, above, show typical arrangements of gage rods at locations where they are most needed.

TIE PLATES

Tie Plate Design 800

Bethlehem Tie Plate Design 800, made of heavy rolled steel, is used for rails over 60 lb per yd, where traffic is heavy. It protects the ties against wear and tends to keep track to proper gage.

This tie plate is ½-in. thick, 9-in. long, and 6-in. wide, and is normally punched with four ¾-in. square spike holes, so that the rail base overlaps $\frac{1}{16}$ in. of the holes. Pairs of holes are spaced on 3½-in. centers longitudinally, and are centrally located. Tie plates of other widths and hole punching can be furnished.

Tie Plate Design 814

Bethlehem Tie Plate Design 814, made of rolled steel, is designed with three ribs on the bottom for assuring a firm grip on the ties and avoiding sliding. Standard size is $\frac{7}{16}$-in. thick, 7½-in. long, and 5-in. wide, and the plate is canted 1 in 40.

Normally punched with four ¾-in. square spike holes, so that the rail base overlaps $\frac{1}{16}$ in. of the holes. Pairs of holes are spaced on 2½-in. centers longitudinally, and are centrally located. Plates of other widths and special punching may be specified. This tie plate is made for any rail section from 20 lb to 60 lb, inclusive.

Tie Plate Design 815 With Welded Brace

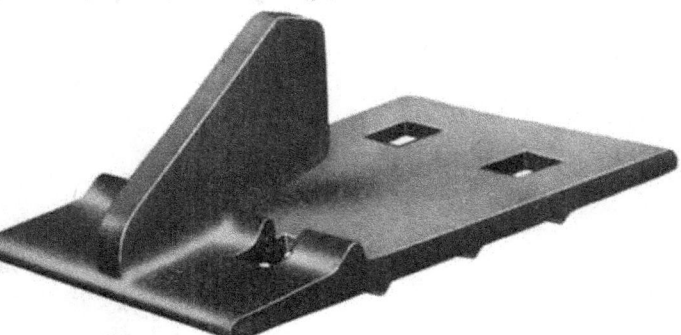

Bethlehem Tie-Plate Design 815 is made by welding a brace to the Design 814 plate. This insures strength and less vibration. This tie plate with welded brace is made for any rail section from 20 lb to 60 lb, inclusive. Plates will be punched to suit the rail section specified. Tie plates of this design are particularly recommended for curves, as they insure strength and aid in holding the track to gage.

HOOK-TWIN TIE PLATES

The Bethlehem Hook-Twin Tie Plate is a rolled-steel plate with spike holes punched to admit track spikes. A forged hook, integral with the tie plate, engages the base of the rail or frog in much the same manner as the offset head of a rail spike.

Bethlehem Hook-Twin Tie Plates are designed to be used in pairs, side by side on the ties. Any pair of Hook Twins can be adapted to almost any position in holding down frogs, closure rails, tee guard rails, graduated riser switches, or tongue switches and mates. Two plates of proper length will fit almost any position on any frog or crossing.

Hook-Twin Tie Plates can normally be furnished from stock in 20-in., 23-in., 27-in., and 31-in. lengths, 3-in. and 4-in. widths, and in thicknesses of ½-in., ⅝-in. and ¾-in. Hooks may be specified "low" for contacting rail bases; "high" for cast-manganese sections. Reverse-hook plates, used at heel-ends of switches and frogs, are available in the above lengths.

Hook-Twin Tie Plates are widely used in mine haulage systems and other track installations, using any weight of rail.

Bethlehem Hook-Twin Tie Plates used under a cast manganese frog. Note the ease of installation.

RAIL BRACE DESIGN 806

Bethlehem Rail Brace Design 806, made of forged steel, is an unusually heavy rail brace, press-forged. This rail brace is also used as a guard-rail brace, or switch brace.

All parts for this layout were furnished by Bethlehem Steel Company. Bethlehem Mine Ties and Mine Cars in the background.

COMPROMISE JOINT DESIGN 976

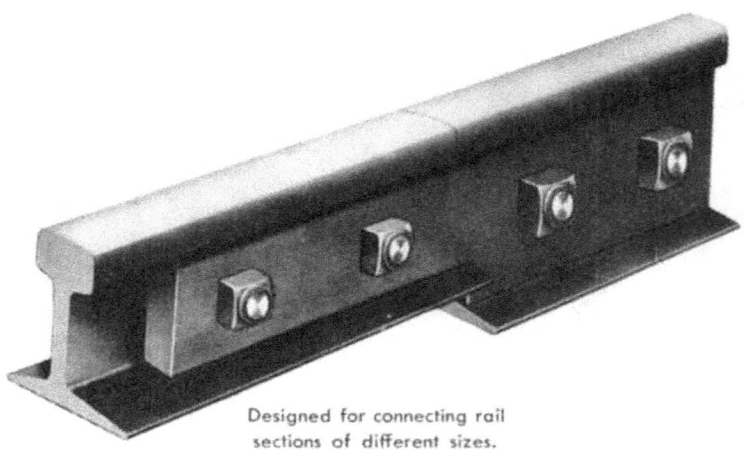

Designed for connecting rail sections of different sizes.

Bethlehem Design 976 is specified as a "compromise joint," but it is also called an "offset splice bar," or a "step joint." It is forged and machined from a heavy flat bar, to connect rails of different section, or rails of the same section but of different joint drillings. Bolts are not furnished unless specified on the order.

Method of Ordering Compromise Joints

Do not refer to joints as "pairs," for this is misleading. Use the word "joint" and describe as outlined, below. A joint consists of two plates, one plate on each side of the rail.

When ordering, give the number of compromise joints required, specifying how many RH (right-hand) and LH (left-hand) joints are needed. Also advise the rail section and rail drilling (if other than standard drilling is desired). Unless otherwise specified, half RH and half LH joints will be furnished. Example:

    24 Bethlehem Design 976 Compromise Joints:
      12 RH and 12 LH for connecting
      85 lb ASCE Rail with 60 lb ASCE Rail.

BETHLEHEM YIELDABLE MINE ARCHES

Bethlehem Yieldable Mine Arches are designed for use in haulage roads, drifts, tunnels, slopes or any type of opening which requires roof support.

The use of Bethlehem Yieldable Arches results in a strong and safe type of mine roof support for conditions brought about by heavy roof, squeezing, swelling ground, or rock pressure. The arches are made of a special rolled U-shaped section of high-strength steel. The shape permits the sections to nest together to form a strong

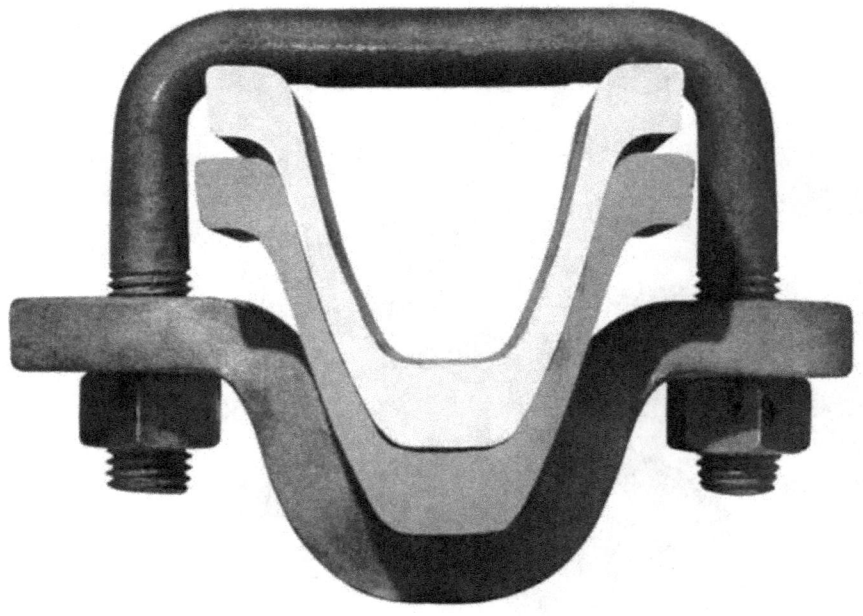

The special U-shaped sections nest together to form a strong, yieldable joint.

yieldable joint. It has bulbous flanges which offer great resistance to torsional stresses.

This type of support is based on the principle of having yieldable joints which permit the set to yield slightly each time roof forces become excessive. In yielding, the structural integrity of the arch is preserved, and a natural pressure arch is formed which will eventually carry the major burden.

Sizes and Shapes. Yieldable arches may be furnished in various sizes and shapes to fit individual conditions. An arch set is usually composed of two legs, a cap piece, two yieldable joints and necessary spacer struts. Complete yieldable ring sets having four yieldable joints are recommended where ground pressures come from all directions.

The standard U-shaped section is 5-in. wide, 4-in. deep, and weighs 15 lb per ft. A heavier section weighing approximately 21 lb per ft can also be furnished for use especially in wide openings. For small mine openings, or in areas where roof conditions are not so severe, Bethlehem can furnish a lighter type of yieldable support. A Bethlehem Steel Company engineer will be glad to discuss your needs.

BETHLEHEM MINE ROOF BOLTS

Old-fashioned supports are no longer good enough to provide safe, adequate roof support. Bethlehem Mine Roof Bolts are a safe, practical and economical method of insuring mine roof support. These bolts reduce the number of accidents from falls of roof, and increase the operating efficiency of the mine.

The U. S. Bureau of Mines recommends roof bolting as a roof-control measure. Their experience has shown that roof bolting definitely reduces roof-fall accidents, and that it is scientifically sound in principle.

Roof Stabilization. The primary effect of roof bolting is to consolidate several strata into a thick beam, holding the layers together as a single unit, to prevent sagging. This is accomplished by anchoring the roof bolt at its upper and lower limits. The tension in the bolt increases the friction between the layers, thereby reducing horizontal movement, and preventing sagging of the strata. In some instances, roof bolts act as "sky hooks," securing loose lower layers to an upper stratum of sandstone or other solid rock mass.

For best results, roof bolts should be installed immediately after loading-out a place, before a new cut is made. They should be placed as close to the face as possible, to prevent sagging of the newly exposed roof.

Anchoring a square-head bolt is accomplished by tightening the bolt head with a wrench. This action anchors the shell and stresses the rod.

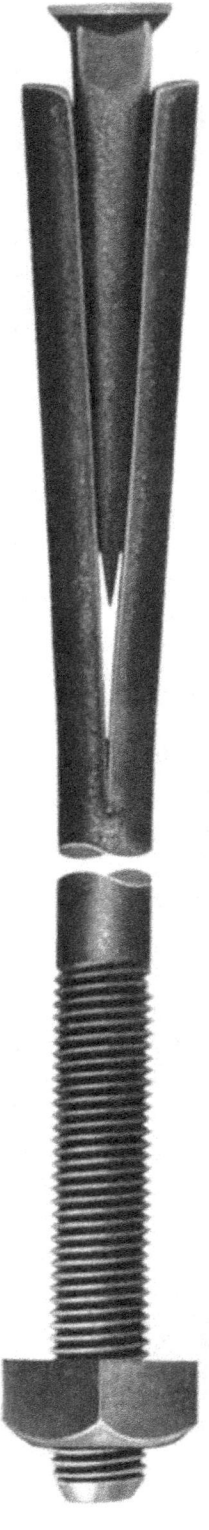

Other Uses. Roof bolting is not only applicable in coal mines, but it can be used to good advantage in gypsum, iron, potash and other ore mines. In addition, roof bolts are used extensively in railroad, vehicular, and water-tunnel projects. They are also ideal for preventing rock slides along highway and railroad rights-of-way. In the latter application they are known as "Rock Bolts."

Two Types of Roof Bolts. Bethlehem Roof Bolts are made in two types—a square head bolt used with an expansion shell, and a slotted bolt used with a wedge. Each type has its proper application, depending upon the roof conditions and equipment available at each individual site. The bolts, together with the accessories with which they are used, meet or exceed the requirements of American Mining Congress standards. Both types of bolts are carried in stock in a variety of lengths.

Write for Catalog 434, "Bethlehem Mine Roof and Rock Bolts," which describes bolts and accessories, and how to install them.

After the wedge is inserted into the slot of a slotted roof bolt, the rod is driven into the rock to the refusal point. Then the nut is tightened to create a tension in the bolt.

BETHLEHEM MINE ROOF TIES

Bethlehem Mine Roof Ties are made of Bethlehem No. 5, No. 6 and No. 9 Steel Tie Sections (see pages 143 and 144). The numbers indicate the weight in pounds per foot. Ties can be furnished in any length required. Spacing of the bolt holes is to be specified on the order.

Use of Ties. The use of Bethlehem Mine Roof Ties takes advantage of the greater beam strength of these sections, giving more holding power. Ties are used with Bethlehem Mine Roof Bolts, which can be inclined into overlying strata at angles of 45 deg, 60 deg, or 90 deg (vertical), depending on the type of washer used.

With some rock formations, operators find it preferable to use roof ties with wire mesh, with the ties spaced intermittently in the roof to hold the mesh in place. Mine roof bolts are run through the holes in the tie, using plate or angle washers.

Ordered in Sets. Materials are usually ordered in sets, each consisting of one roof tie punched with four suitable holes, four slotted bolts, with nuts, wedges, and washers (four angle washers, or two angle washers and two plate washers, or four plate washers). Or you can order one roof tie, and four headed bolts, with expansion shells and washers.

MINE ROOF ACCESSORIES

Plate Washer

This flat steel-plate washer, size 4 in. x 4 in. x ⅜ in., provides a firm base between the roof tie and nut on a mine roof bolt extending upward vertically.

Angle Washer

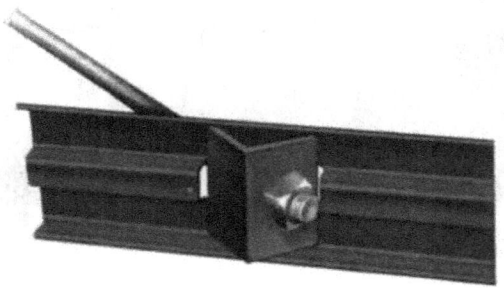

This angle washer is 3 in. x 3 in. x ⅜ in., and is 4¼-in. long. The washer permits the roof bolt to be inclined upward at an angle of 45 deg. The angle washer has a flush bearing against the roof tie and nut. Angle washers 3½ in. x 2½ in. may be specified for installation of bolts at 60 degree angle.

Dished Plate

This dished plate is 6-in. square, and ¼-in. thick. It is used in providing roof support, in the same manner as the square flat plate. Because of the dishing operation, the dished plate although it is only ¼-in. thick, is just as strong as a flat plate of ⅜-in. thickness. Holes in dished plates are the same as in flat plates.

Flat Plate

This square plate, size 6 in. x 6 in. x ⅜ in., bears against the roof top without benefit of roof tie or header. Because of its width, it provides a firm base for the bolt, and an additional means of support for the roof. A hardened washer can be furnished, to reduce friction between the bolt head and the plate.

For ⅝-in. and ¾-in. headed bolts, the round center hole of the flat plate is normally ⅛ in. larger than the nominal bolt size, to accommodate bolts having pressed ears. It can also be furnished with a 1⅜-in. hole, which permits assembly of the shell and plug on the bolt, prior to shipment, and the plate can be slipped over the shell and plug when installed. For ⅞-in. bolts, the hole is ¹⁵⁄₁₆ in.; and for 1-in. bolts, the hole is 1⅛ in. diameter.

Hardened Washer

The Bethlehem Hardened Washer has two purposes: it maintains a more uniform relationship between the torque applied to the bolt head, and the resultant tension in the bolt; and it also prevents the bolt head from pulling through the 1⅜-in. hole in the plate, when bolts are shipped with shells assembled.

HOLLOW DRILL STEEL

Bethlehem Hollow Drill Steel is top-quality steel for all mining and quarrying operations. This steel is ideal for use with either forged-on or detachable bits, and it is a dependable performer whether you use the most modern rock drills, or older machines. It is melted and processed under strict metallurgical control. Each lot is thoroughly tested before shipment.

BETHLEHEM HOLLOW DRILL STEEL. Made from a tough, fatigue-resisting steel, Bethlehem Hollow has a wide quenching range that makes it easy to heat-treat for ideal hardness and wear-resistance. Uniform in physical properties, it makes tough shanks, sharp bits, and long-wearing threads. The center hole is both smooth and true, minimizing fatigue failure.

BETHLEHEM ULTRA-ALLOY HOLLOW DRILL STEEL. This steel has been developed for drill rods with detachable bits only. When carefully fabricated and heat-treated this alloy hollow drill steel gives outstanding performance.

BETHLEHEM SOLID DRILL STEEL. Bethlehem also furnishes Solid Drill Steel for general blacksmithing purposes, such as for pinch bars, moil points, chisels, etc.

A full line of Bethlehem Tool Steels for mine and quarry service is available in stock for immediate shipment. A few of the most-used types in addition to Hollow Drill Steel are: Solid Drill Steel, Auger Steel, Broaching Steel, and steel for plug drills, 4-points, hand points, flatters, etc.

ALL-STEEL MINE
AND INDUSTRIAL CARS

Bethlehem has had long experience in building heavy-duty, all-steel mine and industrial cars to meet every condition encountered in the transportation of materials.

Bethlehem builds all-steel mine and industrial cars in the four-wheel and eight-wheel (double-truck) types, either end-dump or rotary-dump, high sides or low sides, in welded or riveted construction.

When you are ready to plan new mine or industrial cars, let a Bethlehem representative give you additional information about these all-steel units, and discuss with you the types of cars that would best meet your operating conditions.

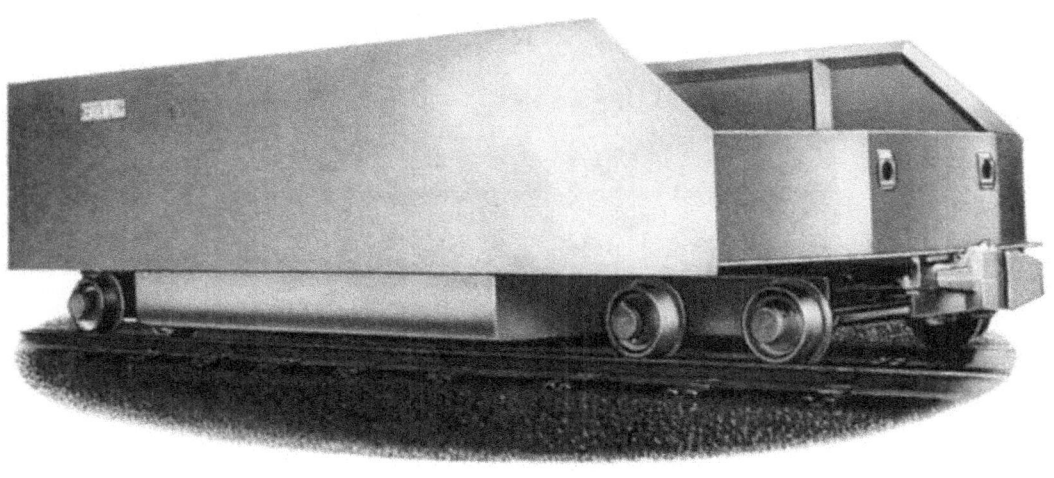

OTHER BETHLEHEM STEEL PRODUCTS FOR MINES AND INDUSTRIAL PLANTS

Rivets

Bolts and Nuts

Special Fasteners

Wire Rope

Fence and Fence Posts

Forgings

Castings

Head Frames for Mine Shafts

Lagging for Tunnels

Nails

Wire

Steel Pipe

Pipe Cradles and Supports

Piles and Piling

Mine Crib Releases

Mayari-R Steel (High-Strength, Corrosion-Resisting Steel)

Structural Shapes

Wheel and Axles

Bars and Special Sections

Tool Steels

Steel Sheets

Plates

Tunnel Ribs

Roofing and Siding

Bethlehem Steel Company will gladly supply catalogs and other information covering these products. Write to the nearest Bethlehem sales office.

USEFUL INFORMATION

The following pages contain general information in regard to mine track. Recommendations for laying track in mines, formulas for curving rail, American Mining Congress wheel contour, and various conversion tables are included. Tables have been selected which contain such data as are most frequently required for rail and track work.

TYPES OF CROSSOVERS AND TURNOUTS

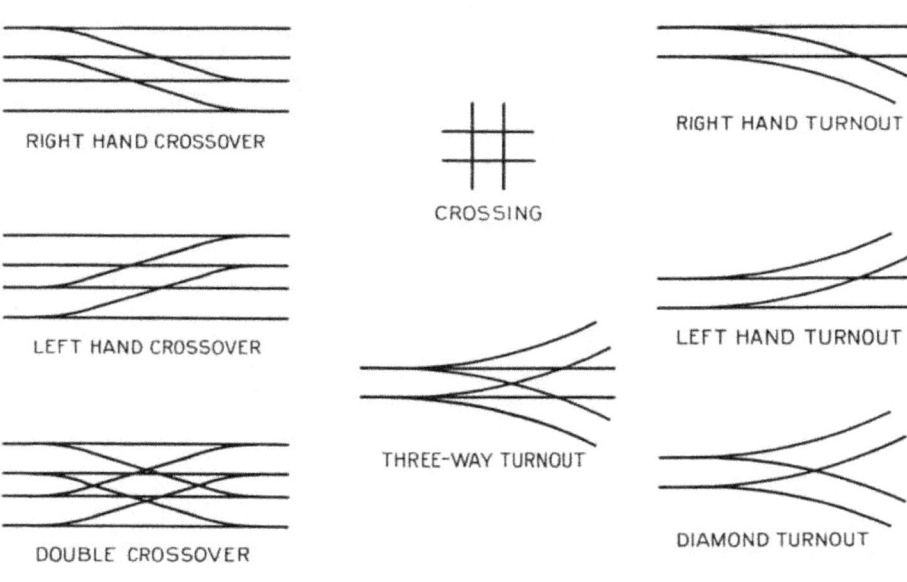

STANDARD WHEEL CONTOUR

American Mining Congress Standard Contour Applies to All Wheels, 12-in. to 18-in. Diameters

Bethlehem Forged-Steel Mine-Car Wheels

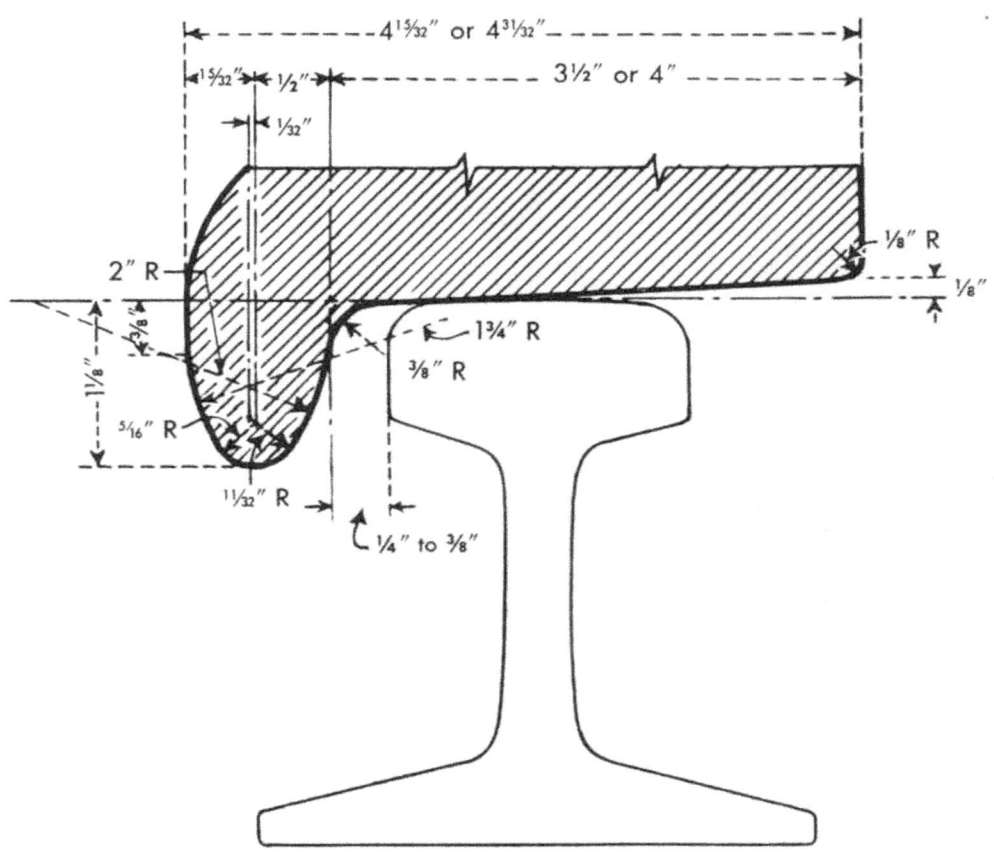

RECOMMENDATIONS FOR LAYING TRACK IN MINES

The general practice in coal mines is to use refuse from the seam for ballast. This is the cheapest ballast, but it is not the best. The best ballast is crushed rock, or slag, because it affords free drainage and does not yield as readily to weight as other materials. Crushed rock is not difficult to obtain, but it is costly. There are conditions, however, that would warrant its use on permanent haulage roads.

STRAIGHT TRACK

For main haulage tracks, treated wood ties with tie plates are recommended. The entry should first of all be cleared of gob material from the sides. In laying the track, one of the best methods is to use wood ties with steel ties interspersed every third or fourth tie. The ties are dropped at proper intervals, after which the rails are fastened to the steel ties and connected with angle bars. The rails, being held in proper track gage, are then spiked to the wood ties. If SC (staggered clip) steel ties are used, they may be removed and moved to another location without disturbing the gage. However, it is good practice to leave the steel ties in the track to act as gage rods and keep track from spreading.

After a sufficient length of track has been put down, ballasting and alignment can begin. The track should be kept as straight as possible. Sometimes the track must be kept near one rib in order to provide necessary clearance on the opposite side. In order to align the track, three or four men equipped with bars should be stationed at intervals along the rails to force the track over at a given signal.

When the track has been aligned, it should be leveled. In doing this work, great care should be given to the ballasting of the track. Every tie should be uniformly tamped throughout its entire length or, at least, should be tamped very tightly under the rails where the tie receives the load.

CURVES

In laying track around curves, the rails should not be forced into position. They should be bent by means of a rail-bender to conform to the radius of the curve. The best procedure is to buy the curved rails direct from the manufacturer. Bethlehem can furnish curved rails in specified lengths for any radius.

All curves should be of sufficient radius to allow the easy movement of cars and locomotives around them. Locomotives having a heavy, rigid wheelbase require curves of long radius.

Since the wheels of cars and locomotive bind on sharp curves, the usual amount of clearance between the rails and the wheel flanges must be increased on sharp curves. The exact amount of additional width of gage required on a curve depends on the radius of the curve, the gage of the track, and the wheelbases of the rolling stock, and no rule can be given which will apply to all cases. The width of the tread of the wheels limits the amount of extra width of gage that is practical.

DATA FOR CURVING RAILS

$$M.O. = +12R - 6\sqrt{4R^2 - C^2} \qquad R = \frac{36C^2 + (M.O.)^2}{24(M.O.)}$$

R = Radius of curvature in feet — M.O. = Middle ordinate in inches

C = Length of chord in feet — Δ = Angle of circular arc

D = Circular arc in feet

To determine angle of circular arc (Δ):

$$\sin\frac{\Delta}{2} = \frac{C}{2R} \qquad 2 \times \frac{\Delta}{2} = \Delta$$

To determine length of circular arc (D) when radius and angle Δ are known:

Multiple radius (R) by figures shown in the table on page 192 (Lengths of Circular Arcs to Radius 1), that equal the total angle of Δ (in radians).

Example: R = 50.00 ft

10 deg =	0.1745329
16 min =	0.0046542
30 sec =	0.0001454
Total =	0.1793325

Δ = 10 deg 16 min 30 sec

R x Δ = 50 x 0.1793325 = 8.9666250 ft

= 8.967 ft = Length of circular arc.

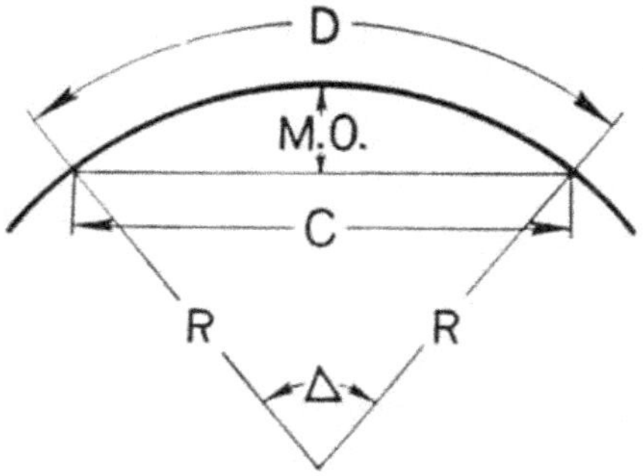

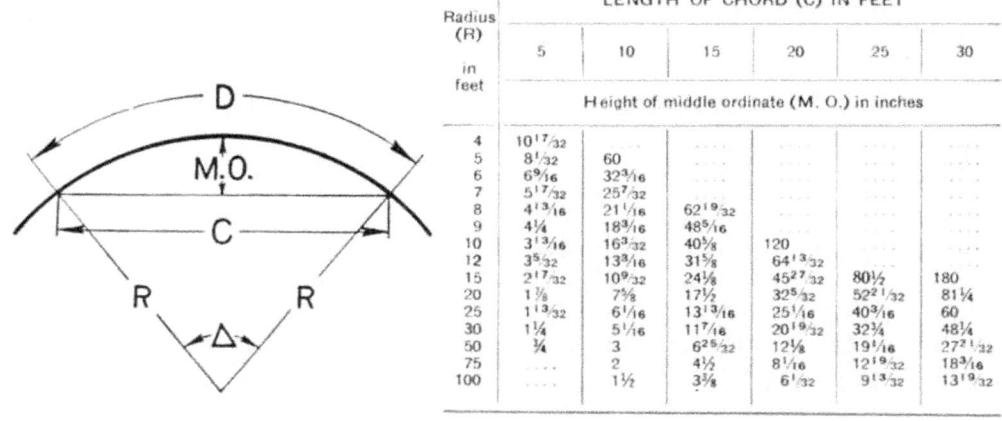

Radius (R) in feet	LENGTH OF CHORD (C) IN FEET: 5	10	15	20	25	30
	Height of middle ordinate (M. O.) in inches					
4	10 17/32	....	....	....	....	....
5	8 1/32	60	....	....	....	....
6	6 9/16	32 3/16	....	....	....	....
7	5 17/32	25 7/32	....	....	....	....
8	4 13/16	21 1/16	62 19/32	....	....	....
9	4 1/4	18 3/16	48 5/16	....	....	....
10	3 13/16	16 3/32	40 5/8	120	....	....
12	3 5/32	13 3/16	31 5/8	64 13/32	....	....
15	2 17/32	10 9/32	24 1/8	45 27/32	80 1/2	180
20	1 7/8	7 5/8	17 1/2	32 5/32	52 21/32	81 1/4
25	1 13/32	6 1/16	13 13/16	25 1/16	40 3/16	60
30	1 1/4	5 1/16	11 7/16	20 19/32	32 3/4	48 1/4
50	3/4	3	6 25/32	12 1/8	19 1/16	27 21/32
75	....	2	4 1/2	8 1/16	12 19/32	18 3/16
100	....	1 1/2	3 3/8	6 1/32	9 13/32	13 19/32

DATA FOR CURVING RAILS—(MIDDLE ORDINATES)

Degree of Curve for 100' Chord	Radius in Feet	LENGTH OF RAIL IN FEET						
		20	22	24	26	28	30	33
		Middle Ordinates in Inches						
0°-30'	11459.2	1/16	1/16	3/32	3/32	3/32	1/8	5/32
1°-00'	5729.6	3/32	1/8	5/32	3/16	7/32	1/4	9/32
1°-30'	3819.8	5/32	3/16	7/32	9/32	5/16	11/32	7/16
2°-00'	2864.9	7/32	1/4	5/16	11/32	13/32	15/32	19/32
2°-30'	2292.0	9/32	11/32	3/8	7/16	17/32	19/32	23/32
3°-00'	1910.0	11/32	3/8	7/16	17/32	5/8	23/32	7/8
3°-30'	1637.3	3/8	7/16	17/32	5/8	23/32	27/32	31/32
4°-00'	1432.7	7/16	1/2	19/32	23/32	27/32	31/32	15/32
4°-30'	1273.6	15/32	9/16	11/16	13/16	15/16	1 1/16	1 9/32
5°-00'	1146.3	17/32	21/32	3/4	29/32	1 1/32	1 3/16	1 7/16
5°-30'	1042.1	19/32	23/32	27/32	31/32	1 1/8	1 5/16	1 9/16
6°-00'	955.4	5/8	25/32	29/32	1 1/16	1 7/32	1 13/32	1 23/32
6°-30'	881.9	11/16	27/32	1	1 5/32	1 11/32	1 17/32	1 7/8
7°-00'	819.0	3/4	29/32	1 1/16	1 1/4	1 7/16	1 21/32	2
7°-30'	764.5	25/32	31/32	1 1/8	1 11/32	1 17/32	1 3/4	2 5/32
8°-00'	716.8	27/32	1 1/32	1 7/32	1 7/16	1 21/32	1 29/32	2 9/32
8°-30'	674.7	29/32	1 3/32	1 9/32	1 1/2	1 3/4	2	2 7/16
9°-00'	637.3	15/16	1 5/32	1 11/32	1 19/32	1 27/32	2 3/32	2 9/16
9°-30'	603.8	1	1 7/32	1 7/16	1 11/16	1 31/32	2 1/4	2 23/32
10°-00'	573.7	1 1/16	1 9/32	1 1/2	1 25/32	2 1/16	2 3/8	2 27/32
11°-00'	521.7	1 5/32	1 13/32	1 11/16	1 31/32	2 1/4	2 19/32	3 5/32
12°-00'	478.3	1 9/32	1 17/32	1 13/16	2 5/32	2 15/32	2 27/32	3 7/16
13°-00'	441.7	1 3/8	1 21/32	1 31/32	2 5/16	2 21/32	3 1/16	3 23/32
14°-00'	410.3	1 15/32	1 25/32	2 3/32	2 1/2	2 7/8	3 5/16	4
15°-00'	383.1	1 19/32	1 29/32	2 1/4	2 11/16	3 3/32	3 9/16	4 9/32
16°-00'	359.3	1 11/16	2 1/16	2 13/32	2 27/32	3 9/32	3 3/4	4 7/16
17°-00'	338.3	1 25/32	2 5/32	2 9/16	3	3 1/2	4	4 27/32
18°-00'	319.6	1 7/8	2 9/32	2 23/32	3 3/16	3 11/16	4 7/32	5 1/8
19°-00'	302.9	2	2 13/32	2 7/8	3 3/8	3 29/32	4 15/32	5 13/32
20°-00'	287.9	2 3/32	2 9/16	3	3 9/16	4 3/32	4 23/32	5 11/16
21°-00'	274.4	2 3/16	2 21/32	3 5/32	3 23/32	4 9/32	4 15/16	5 31/32
22°-00'	262.0	2 5/16	2 13/16	3 5/16	3 29/32	4 1/2	5 5/32	6 1/4
23°-00'	250.8	2 13/32	2 15/16	3 7/16	4 1/16	4 11/16	5 13/32	6 17/32
24°-00'	240.5	2 1/2	3 1/32	3 19/32	4 1/4	4 13/16	5 5/8	6 13/16
25°-00'	231.0	2 19/32	3 5/32	3 3/4	4 13/32	5 3/32	5 27/32	7 3/32
26°-00'	222.3	2 23/32	3 9/32	3 7/8	3 19/32	5 5/16	6 3/32	7 3/8
27°-00'	214.2	2 13/16	3 13/32	4 1/32	4 3/4	5 1/2	6 9/32	7 5/8
28°-00'	206.7	2 29/32	3 17/32	4 3/16	4 15/16	5 23/32	6 9/16	7 15/16
29°-00'	199.7	3	3 21/32	4 11/32	5 3/32	5 29/32	6 25/32	8 7/32
30°-00'	193.2	3 1/2	3 7/16	4 1/2	5 1/4	6 3/32	7	8 15/32
31°-00'	187.1	3 3/16	3 7/8	4 5/8	5 7/16	6 5/16	7 3/16	8 3/4
32°-00'	181.4	3 5/16	4	4 3/4	5 9/16	6 1/2	7 3/8	9 1/8
33°-00'	176.0	3 3/8	4 1/8	4 7/8	5 3/4	6 5/8	7 5/8	9 5/16
34°-00'	171.0	3 1/2	4 1/4	5	5 15/16	6 7/8	7 7/8	9 5/8
35°-00'	166.3	3 5/8	4 3/8	5 3/16	6 1/16	7 1/16	8 3/16	9 11/16
36°-00'	161.8	3 11/16	4 1/2	5 3/8	6 1/4	7 1/4	8 3/8	10 1/16
37°-00'	157.6	3 13/16	4 5/8	5 1/2	6 7/16	7 3/8	8 9/16	10 3/8
38°-00'	153.6	3 7/8	4 3/4	5 5/8	6 5/8	7 5/8	8 13/16	10 11/16
39°-00'	149.8	4	4 7/8	5 3/4	6 3/4	7 7/8	9	10 13/16
40°-00'	146.2	4 5/16	5 1/16	6	7 1/16	8 3/16	9 3/8	11 1/2
45°-00'	130.7	4 3/4	5 11/16	6 13/16	7 7/8	9 1/4	10 1/2	12 13/16
50°-00'	118.3	5 1/4	6 5/16	7 1/2	8 1/8	10 1/2	11 3/4	14 3/16
60°-00'	100.0	6	7 5/16	8 5/8	10 1/16	11 1/8	13 1/2	16 3/8
83°-36'	75.0	7 3/4	9 1/2	11 1/8	13 1/16	15 3/16	17 1/2	21 5/16
180°-00'	50.0	12	14 1/2	17 1/8	20	23 1/2	27	32 1/4

Expansion Table for Laying 30 and 33 Ft Rails on Outside Track

90 Degrees Fahrenheit gives 0" Expansion Space. 30 to 50 Degrees Fahrenheit gives 3/16" Expansion Space.
70 to 90 Degrees Fahrenheit gives 1/16" Expansion Space. 10 to 30 Degrees Fahrenheit gives 1/4" Expansion Space.
50 to 70 Degrees Fahrenheit gives 1/8" Expansion Space. 10 to 1 Degrees Fahrenheit gives 5/16" Expansion Space.

LENGTHS OF CIRCULAR ARCS TO RADIUS 1

Deg.	Length	Deg.	Length	Deg.	Length	Deg.	Length	Deg.	Length
1	.0174533	37	.6457718	73	1.2740904	109	1.9024089	145	2.5307274
2	.0349066	38	.6632251	74	1.2915436	110	1.9198622	146	2.5481807
3	.0523599	39	.6806784	75	1.3089969			147	2.5656340
4	.0698132	40	.6981317	76	1.3264502	111	1.9373155	148	2.5830873
5	.0872665			77	1.3439035	112	1.9547688	149	2.6005406
6	.1047198	41	.7155850	78	1.3613568	113	1.9722221	150	2.6179939
7	.1221730	42	.7330383	79	1.3788101	114	1.9896733		
8	.1396263	43	.7504916	80	1.3962634	115	2.0071286	151	2.6354472
9	.1570796	44	.7679449			116	2.0245819	152	2.6529005
10	.1745329	45	.7853982	81	1.4137167	117	2.0420352	153	2.6703538
		46	.8028515	82	1.4311700	118	2.0594885	154	2.6878070
11	.1919862	47	.8203047	83	1.4486233	119	2.0769418	155	2.7052603
12	.2094395	48	.8377580	84	1.4660766	120	2.0943951	156	2.7227136
13	.2268928	49	.8552113	85	1.4835299			157	2.7401669
14	.2443461	50	.8726646	86	1.5009832	121	2.1118484	158	2.7576202
15	.2617994			87	1.5184364	122	2.1293017	159	2.7750735
16	.2792527	51	.8901179	88	1.5358897	123	2.1467550	160	2.7925268
17	.2967060	52	.9075712	89	1.5533430	124	2.1642083		
18	.3141593	53	.9250245	90	1.5707963	125	2.1816616	161	2.8099801
19	.3316126	54	.9424778			126	2.1991149	162	2.8274334
20	.3490659	55	.9599311	91	1.5882496	127	2.2165682	163	2.8448867
		56	.9773844	92	1.6057029	128	2.2340214	164	2.8623400
21	.3665191	57	.9948377	93	1.6231562	129	2.2514747	165	2.8797933
22	.3839724	58	1.0122910	94	1.6406095	130	2.2689280	166	2.8972466
23	.4014257	59	1.0297443	95	1.6580628			167	2.9146999
24	.4188790	60	1.0471976	96	1.6755161	131	2.2863813	168	2.9321531
25	.4363323			97	1.6929694	132	2.3038346	169	2.9496064
26	.4537856	61	1.0646508	98	1.7104227	133	2.3212879	170	2.9670597
27	.4712389	62	1.0821041	99	1.7278760	134	2.3387412		
28	.4886922	63	1.0995574	100	1.7453293	135	2.3561945	171	2.9845130
29	.5061455	64	1.1170107			136	2.3736478	172	3.0019663
30	.5235988	65	1.1344640	101	1.7627825	137	2.3911011	173	3.0194196
		66	1.1519173	102	1.7802358	138	2.4085544	174	3.0368729
31	.5410521	67	1.1693706	103	1.7976891	139	2.4260077	175	3.0543262
32	.5585054	68	1.1868239	104	1.8151424	140	2.4434610	176	3.0717795
33	.5759587	69	1.2042772	105	1.8325957			177	3.0892328
34	.5934119	70	1.2217305	106	1.8500490	141	2.4609142	178	3.1066861
35	.6108652			107	1.8675023	142	2.4783675	179	3.1241394
36	.6283185	71	1.2391838	108	1.8849556	143	2.4958208	180	3.1415927
		72	1.2566371			144	2.5132741		

Min.	Length	Min.	Length	Sec.	Length	Sec.	Length
1	.0002909	31	.0090175	1	.0000048	31	.0001503
2	.0005818	32	.0093084	2	.0000097	32	.0001551
3	.0008727	33	.0095993	3	.0000145	33	.0001600
4	.0011636	34	.0098902	4	.0000194	34	.0001648
5	.0014544	35	.0101811	5	.0000242	35	.0001697
6	.0017453	36	.0104720	6	.0000291	36	.0001745
7	.0020362	37	.0107629	7	.0000339	37	.0001794
8	.0023271	38	.0110538	8	.0000388	38	.0001842
9	.0026180	39	.0113446	9	.0000436	39	.0001891
10	.0029089	40	.0116355	10	.0000485	40	.0001939
11	.0031998	41	.0119264	11	.0000533	41	.0001988
12	.0034907	42	.0122173	12	.0000582	42	.0002036
13	.0037815	43	.0125082	13	.0000630	43	.0002085
14	.0040724	44	.0127991	14	.0000679	44	.0002133
15	.0043633	45	.0130900	15	.0000727	45	.0002182
16	.0046542	46	.0133809	16	.0000776	46	.0002230
17	.0049451	47	.0136717	17	.0000824	47	.0002279
18	.0052360	48	.0139626	18	.0000873	48	.0002327
19	.0055269	49	.0142535	19	.0000921	49	.0002376
20	.0058178	50	.0145444	20	.0000970	50	.0002424
21	.0061087	51	.0148353	21	.0001018	51	.0002473
22	.0063995	52	.0151262	22	.0001067	52	.0002521
23	.0066904	53	.0154171	23	.0001115	53	.0002570
24	.0069813	54	.0157080	24	.0001164	54	.0002618
25	.0072722	55	.0159989	25	.0001212	55	.0002666
26	.0075631	56	.0162897	26	.0001261	56	.0002715
27	.0078540	57	.0165806	27	.0001309	57	.0002763
28	.0081449	58	.0168715	28	.0001357	58	.0002812
29	.0084358	59	.0171624	29	.0001406	59	.0002860
30	.0087266	60	.0174533	30	.0001454	60	.0002909

Yard tracks like these help to promote mine efficiency.

FRACTIONS OF INCHES AND THEIR DECIMAL EQUIVALENTS IN INCHES AND FEET

DECIMALS OF A FOOT FOR EACH 1/64 OF AN INCH

Fraction of an Inch	Decimal of an Inch For Each 1/64"	0"	1"	2"	3"	4"	5"	6"	7"	8"	9"	10"	11"
0	0	0	.0833	.1667	.2500	.3333	.4167	.5000	.5833	.6667	.7500	.8333	.9167
1/64	.015625	.0013	.0846	.1680	.2513	.3346	.4180	.5013	.5846	.6680	.7513	.8346	.9180
1/32	.03125	.0026	.0859	.1693	.2526	.3359	.4193	.5026	.5859	.6693	.7526	.8359	.9193
3/64	.046875	.0039	.0872	.1706	.2539	.3372	.4206	.5039	.5872	.6706	.7539	.8372	.9206
1/16	.0625	.0052	.0885	.1719	.2552	.3385	.4219	.5052	.5885	.6719	.7552	.8385	.9219
5/64	.078125	.0065	.0898	.1732	.2565	.3398	.4232	.5065	.5898	.6732	.7565	.8398	.9232
3/32	.09375	.0078	.0911	.1745	.2578	.3411	.4245	.5078	.5911	.6745	.7578	.8411	.9245
7/64	.109375	.0091	.0924	.1758	.2591	.3424	.4258	.5091	.5924	.6758	.7591	.8424	.9258
1/8	.125	.0104	.0937	.1771	.2604	.3437	.4271	.5104	.5937	.6771	.7604	.8437	.9271
9/64	.140625	.0117	.0951	.1784	.2617	.3451	.4284	.5117	.5951	.6784	.7617	.8451	.9284
5/32	.15625	.0130	.0964	.1797	.2630	.3464	.4297	.5130	.5964	.6797	.7630	.8464	.9297
11/64	.171875	.0143	.0977	.1810	.2643	.3477	.4310	.5143	.5977	.6810	.7643	.8477	.9310
3/16	.1875	.0156	.0990	.1823	.2656	.3490	.4323	.5156	.5990	.6823	.7656	.8490	.9323
13/64	.203125	.0169	.1003	.1836	.2669	.3503	.4336	.5169	.6003	.6836	.7669	.8503	.9336
7/32	.21875	.0182	.1016	.1849	.2682	.3516	.4349	.5182	.6016	.6849	.7682	.8516	.9349
15/64	.234375	.0195	.1029	.1862	.2695	.3529	.4362	.5195	.6029	.6862	.7695	.8529	.9362
1/4	.25	.0208	.1042	.1875	.2708	.3542	.4375	.5208	.6042	.6875	.7708	.8542	.9375
17/64	.265625	.0221	.1055	.1888	.2721	.3555	.4388	.5221	.6055	.6888	.7721	.8555	.9388
9/32	.28125	.0234	.1068	.1901	.2734	.3568	.4401	.5234	.6068	.6901	.7734	.8568	.9401
19/64	.296875	.0247	.1081	.1914	.2747	.3581	.4414	.5247	.6081	.6914	.7747	.8581	.9414
5/16	.3125	.0260	.1094	.1927	.2760	.3594	.4427	.5260	.6094	.6927	.7760	.8594	.9427
21/64	.328125	.0273	.1107	.1940	.2773	.3607	.4440	.5273	.6107	.6940	.7773	.8607	.9440
11/32	.34375	.0286	.1120	.1953	.2786	.3620	.4453	.5286	.6120	.6953	.7786	.8620	.9453
23/64	.359375	.0299	.1133	.1966	.2799	.3633	.4466	.5299	.6133	.6966	.7799	.8633	.9466
3/8	.375	.0312	.1146	.1979	.2812	.3646	.4479	.5312	.6146	.6979	.7812	.8646	.9479
25/64	.390625	.0326	.1159	.1992	.2826	.3659	.4492	.5326	.6159	.6992	.7826	.8659	.9492
13/32	.40625	.0339	.1172	.2005	.2839	.3672	.4505	.5339	.6172	.7005	.7839	.8672	.9505
27/64	.421875	.0352	.1185	.2018	.2852	.3685	.4518	.5352	.6185	.7018	.7852	.8685	.9518
7/16	.4375	.0365	.1198	.2031	.2865	.3698	.4531	.5365	.6198	.7031	.7865	.8698	.9531
29/64	.453125	.0378	.1211	.2044	.2878	.3711	.4544	.5378	.6211	.7044	.7878	.8711	.9544
15/32	.46875	.0391	.1224	.2057	.2891	.3724	.4557	.5391	.6224	.7057	.7891	.8724	.9557
31/64	.484375	.0404	.1237	.2070	.2904	.3737	.4570	.5404	.6237	.7070	.7904	.8737	.9570
1/2	.5	.0417	.1250	.2083	.2917	.3750	.4583	.5417	.6250	.7083	.7917	.8750	.9583

FRACTIONS OF INCHES AND THEIR DECIMAL EQUIVALENTS IN INCHES AND FEET

DECIMALS OF A FOOT FOR EACH 1/64 OF AN INCH

Fraction of an Inch	Decimal of an Inch For Each 1/64"	0"	1"	2"	3"	4"	5"	6"	7"	8"	9"	10"	11"
33/64	.515625	.0430	.1263	.2096	.2930	.3763	.4596	.5430	.6263	.7096	.7930	.8763	.9596
17/32	.53125	.0443	.1276	.2109	.2943	.3776	.4609	.5443	.6276	.7109	.7943	.8776	.9609
35/64	.546875	.0456	.1289	.2122	.2956	.3789	.4622	.5456	.6289	.7122	.7956	.8789	.9622
9/16	.5625	.0469	.1302	.2135	.2969	.3802	.4635	.5469	.6302	.7135	.7969	.8802	.9635
37/64	.578125	.0482	.1315	.2148	.2982	.3815	.4648	.5482	.6315	.7148	.7982	.8815	.9648
19/32	.59375	.0495	.1328	.2161	.2995	.3828	.4661	.5495	.6328	.7161	.7995	.8828	.9661
39/64	.609375	.0508	.1341	.2174	.3008	.3841	.4674	.5508	.6341	.7174	.8008	.8841	.9674
5/8	.625	.0521	.1354	.2188	.3021	.3854	.4688	.5521	.6354	.7188	.8021	.8854	.9688
41/64	.640625	.0534	.1367	.2201	.3034	.3867	.4701	.5534	.6367	.7201	.8034	.8867	.9701
21/32	.65625	.0547	.1380	.2214	.3047	.3880	.4714	.5547	.6380	.7214	.8047	.8880	.9714
43/64	.671875	.0560	.1393	.2227	.3060	.3893	.4727	.5560	.6393	.7227	.8060	.8893	.9727
11/16	.6875	.0573	.1406	.2240	.3073	.3906	.4740	.5573	.6406	.7240	.8073	.8906	.9740
45/64	.703125	.0586	.1419	.2253	.3086	.3919	.4753	.5586	.6419	.7253	.8086	.8919	.9753
23/32	.71875	.0599	.1432	.2266	.3099	.3932	.4766	.5599	.6432	.7266	.8099	.8932	.9766
47/64	.734375	.0612	.1445	.2279	.3112	.3945	.4779	.5612	.6445	.7279	.8112	.8945	.9779
3/4	.75	.0625	.1458	.2292	.3125	.3958	.4792	.5625	.6458	.7292	.8125	.8958	.9792
49/64	.765625	.0638	.1471	.2305	.3138	.3971	.4805	.5638	.6471	.7305	.8138	.8971	.9805
25/32	.78125	.0651	.1484	.2318	.3151	.3984	.4818	.5651	.6484	.7318	.8151	.8984	.9818
51/64	.796875	.0664	.1497	.2331	.3164	.3997	.4831	.5664	.6497	.7331	.8164	.8997	.9831
13/16	.8125	.0677	.1510	.2344	.3177	.4010	.4844	.5677	.6510	.7344	.8177	.9010	.9844
53/64	.828125	.0690	.1523	.2357	.3190	.4023	.4857	.5690	.6523	.7357	.8190	.9023	.9857
27/32	.84375	.0703	.1536	.2370	.3203	.4036	.4870	.5703	.6536	.7370	.8203	.9036	.9870
55/64	.859375	.0716	.1549	.2383	.3216	.4049	.4883	.5716	.6549	.7383	.8216	.9049	.9883
7/8	.875	.0729	.1562	.2396	.3229	.4062	.4896	.5729	.6562	.7396	.8229	.9062	.9896
57/64	.890625	.0742	.1576	.2409	.3242	.4076	.4909	.5742	.6576	.7409	.8242	.9076	.9909
29/32	.90625	.0755	.1589	.2422	.3255	.4089	.4922	.5755	.6589	.7422	.8255	.9089	.9922
59/64	.921875	.0768	.1602	.2435	.3268	.4102	.4935	.5768	.6602	.7435	.8268	.9102	.9935
15/16	.9375	.0781	.1615	.2448	.3281	.4115	.4948	.5781	.6615	.7448	.8281	.9115	.9948
61/64	.953125	.0794	.1628	.2461	.3294	.4128	.4961	.5794	.6628	.7461	.8294	.9128	.9961
31/32	.96875	.0807	.1641	.2474	.3307	.4141	.4974	.5807	.6641	.7474	.8307	.9141	.9974
63/64	.984375	.0820	.1654	.2487	.3320	.4154	.4987	.5820	.6654	.7487	.8320	.9154	.9987
1	1												1.0000

INDEX

A

Accessories for one mile of track, 136, 137
Accessories for 1,000 net tons of rails, 136, 137
A.R.E.A. practical leads for turnouts,
   standard gage, heavy rail, 108
All-steel mine and industrial cars, 185
Angle bars, 118-126

B

Bars, angle, 118-126
Bars, splice, 116-119, 128
Bolts and spikes, 133-135
Bolts, track, 134, 135
Bolted clips, 164-167
Bolted-plate crossings, 75, 76
Bolted-rigid frogs, 16-19
Brace, rail, 175

C

Cars, Bethlehem all-steel mine and industrial, 185
Clips, bolted, for steel ties, 164-167
   No. 7, 164
     Type L bolt for use with No. 7, 164
   No. 8, 164
     Type H bolt for use with No. 8, 165
   No. 9-S and No. 9-L, 165
   No. 11-S and No. 11-L, 166
Clips, riveted, for steel ties, 162, 163
   movable, 162, 163
   stationary, 162
Clips, rail, 167
   No. 62, 167
Clips, special riveted, for steel ties, 163
   No. 32, 163
   No. 42, 163
Compromise joint, 176
   Design 976, 176
   method of ordering, 176

Crane rails, Bethlehem, 129-131
    Section 104-CR, and joint bar A-104-CR, 130
    Section 135-CR, and joint bar P-135-CR, 130
    Section 171-CR, and joint bar P-171-CR, 131
    Section 175-CR, and joint bar P-175-CR, 131
Crossings, Bethlehem, 73-78
    bolted plate, 40-lb to 100-lb rail, 75, 76
        Design 400, 2-rail, angles 40° to 90°, 75
        Design 229, 3-rail, angles 40° to 90°, 76
    bolted rail, 70-lb and heavier, 77, 78
        A.R.E.A. Plan 702-55, 2-rail, angles 50° to 90°, 77
        A.R.E.A. Plan 701-55, 3-rail, angles 50° to 90°, 78
    riveted-plate, 20-lb to 100-lb rail, 74
        Design 233, angles 30° to 90°, 74
Crossovers and turnouts, types of, 187
Curving rails, data for, 190, 191, 192

D

Drill steel, hollow, 184

F

Features of good track, 6
Frog ties, 88, 89
Frogs, Bethlehem, 8, 9, 13-25
    bolted-rigid, for light and heavy rails, 16-19
        Design 15, 16
        Design 16, 16
        Design 72, 17
        Design 83, 18, 19
    determining the frog number, 8, 9
    frog and switch data, table of, 98, 99
    frog data, table of, 97
    ordering, 13
    rail-bound manganese steel, for heavy rails, 25
        A.R.E.A. Standard Plan 600-55, 25
    riveted-plate, for light rails, 14, 15
        Design 97, 14, 15
    solid manganese steel, for heavy rails, 23, 24
        Design 285, 23, 24
        lengths of Design 285, table of, 24

Frogs, Bethlehem—continued
   solid manganese steel, for light rails, 20-22
     Design 289, 20, 21
      dimensions of Design 289, tables of, 21
     Design 289-A, 22
      dimensions of Design 289-A, table of, 22

G

Gage rods, 172
   light rail Design 858, 172
   heavy rail Design 853-F, 172
Guard rails, Bethlehem, 63-71
   for steel turnout tie sets, 65
     Design 745-M, one-piece rolled-steel, 65
   for wood ties, 64
     Design 745, one-piece rolled-steel, 64
   hook-flange, 68, 69
     Design 750, 68
     ordering, 69
   other Bethlehem guard rails, 66, 67
     Design 731, for 25-lb to 30-lb rail, inclusive, 66
     Design 732, for 30-lb rail, and heavier, 66
     Design 733, for 30-lb rail, and heavier, 66
     Design 734, for 60-lb rail, and heavier, 67
     Design 735, for 80-lb rail, and heavier, 67
   switch point guard rail, 70, 71
     Model 755, heat-treated, 70, 71

H

Hollow drill steel, Bethlehem, 184
Hook-flange guard rails, 68, 69
Hook-twin tie plates, 174

I

Installing steel ties, 168
Introduction, 4-11

L

Laying track in mines, recommendations for, 189, 190
Leads for turnouts for standard-gage
   heavy rail track, A.R.E.A., 108

M

Mine and industrial cars, Bethlehem all-steel, 185
Mine arches, Bethlehem yieldable, 177, 178
Mine roof accessories, 182, 183
   angle washers, 182
   dished plate, 182
   flat plate, 183
   hardened washers, 183
   plate washers, 182
Mine roof bolts, Bethlehem, 179, 180
Mine roof ties, Bethlehem, 181
Mine ties, steel, 139-161

O

Other Bethlehem steel products for mines and
   industrial plants, 186

P

Prefabricated track, Bethlehem, 6, 111-113
   industrial yard layouts, 111
   mine layouts, 111

R

Rails and accessories for one mile of track, table of, 137
Rail brace, 175
   Design 806, 175
Rail clip No. 62, 167
Rails, data for curving, 191, 192
Rails, steel, 20-lb to 100-lb, 115-128
   rail section No. 20-AS, with
     plain splice bar section No. P-20-AS, 116
   rail section No. 25-AS, with splice bar section
     No. P-25-AS, 117
   rail section No. 30-AS, with splice bar section No. J-30,
     and angle bar section No. A-30-AS, 118
   rail section, No. 40-AS, with splice bar section No. J-40,
     and angle bar section No. A-40-AS, 119
   rail section No. 60-AS, with angle bar section
     No. A-60-AS, 120
   rail section No. 70-AS, with angle bar section
     No. A-70-AS, 121

Rails, steel—continued
    rail section No. 75-AS, with angle bar section
        No. A-75-AS, 122
    rail section No. 80-AS, with angle bar section
        No. A-80-AS, 123
    rail section No. 85-AS, with angle bar section
        No. A-85-AS, 124
    rail section No. 90-AS, with angle bar section
        No. A-90-AS, 125
    rail section No. 100-AS, with angle bar section
        No. A-100-AS, 126
    standard drilling for rails and splice-bar punching, 128
    T-rails, properties and principal dimensions, 127
Recommendations for laying track in mines, 189, 190
Riveted clips, for steel ties, 162, 163
    movable, 162, 163
    stationary, 162
Riveted-plate crossing, 74
Riveted-plate frogs, 14, 15
Roof bolts, 179, 180

S

Special riveted clips, 162, 163
Spikes and bolts, 133-135
Steel rails, Bethlehem, 6, 115-137
    suggested rail weights, table of, 7
    rule for determining weight of, 6, 7
Steel ties, Bethlehem, 7, 139-161
    with depressed ends, 161
Suggested rail weights, 7
Switches, Bethlehem, 27-42
    components of, 27
    for use with steel switch tie sets, 36
        Design 388, from 3 ft to 7 ft 6 in., 36
    heavy-duty, for use with wood ties, 30-34
        Design 393, 3 ft 6 in. long, 30
        Design 395, 5 ft long, 31
        Design 397, 7 ft 6 in. long, 32
        Design 399, 10 ft long, 33
        Design 415, 15 ft long, 34
    heavy side-jaw clips for, 28
    heavy slide plates for, 28

Switches, Bethlehem—continued
- heavy switch braces for, 29
- heavy switch rods for, 29
- medium-duty, for use with wood ties, 35
    - Design 365, 10 ft and 15 ft, 35
    - Design 392 (with rail braces), from 3 ft to 7 ft 6 in., 37
    - Design 389 (without rail braces), from 3 ft to 7 ft 6 in., 37
    - Design 390 (with rail braces), from 3 ft to 7 ft 6 in., 38
    - Design 391 (without rail braces), from 3 ft to 7 ft 6 in., 38
- ordering, 27, 28

Switch and frog data, table of, 97-99

Switch data, table of, 98

Switch heaters, Winter King, 42

Switch heel joints, 39, 40
- Design 990, 39
- how to install, 40
- ordering, 40

Switch heel block joint, 41
- Design 992, 41

Switch-point guard rail, 70, 71
- Design 755, 70

Switch stands, Bethlehem, 45-61
- automatic, 45, 59, 60
    - Model 22, 59, 60
- for heavy rails, 54-60
    - Model 1222, 54, 55
    - Model 1222 component parts, 55
    - Model 51-A, New Century, 56-58
    - Model 51-A component parts, 58
- for light rails, 47-53
    - Model 1201, 47-49
    - Model 1201 component parts, 49
    - Model 1217, 50-52
    - Model 1217 component parts, 52
- ordering, 46
- with reflector target, 53
    - Model 1217-T, 53

Switch tie sets, 81-84

T

Target stand, for switches, 61
    Model 1205, 61
Target switch stand, Model 1217-T, 53
Tie plates, Bethlehem, 173, 174
    Design 800, 173
    Design 814, 173
    Design 815 (with welded braces), 173
    hook-twin, 174
Tie sets, switch, 81-84
    ordering, 81, 84
    switch tie set "A," 82
    switch tie set "B," 82
    switch tie set "C," 83
    switch tie set "D," 84
Tie sets, switch and turnout, 81-87
Tie sets, turnout, 85-87
    ordering, 87
    turnout tie set "E," 85
    turnout tie set "F," 85
    turnout tie set "G," 86
    turnout tie set "H," 87
Ties, Bethlehem steel, 139-161
    No. 2 steel ties, 141, 142, 143, 145, 146
        No. 2-OSC, 145
        No. 2-SC, 145
        No. 232, 145
        No. 242, 146
        No. 27, 146
        No. 28, 146
    No. 3 steel ties, 141, 142, 143, 147, 148
        No. 3-OSC, 147
        No. 3-SC, 147
        No. 332, 147
        No. 342, 148
        No. 37, 148
        No. 38, 148
    No. 4 steel ties, 141, 142, 143, 149, 150
        No. 4-OSC, 149
        No. 4-SC, 149
        No. 432, 150
        No. 442, 150

Ties, Bethlehem steel mine—continued
   No. 5 steel ties, 141, 142, 143, 151, 152
     No. 5-OSC, 151
     No. 5-SC, 151
     No. 532, 152
     No. 542, 152
   No. 6 steel ties, 142, 144, 153-156
     No. 6-OSC, 153
     No. 6-SC, 153
     No. 632, 154
     No. 642, 154
     No. 611, 155
     No. 69, 156
   No. 9 steel ties, 142, 144, 157-160
     No. 9-OSC, 157
     No. 9-SC, 157
     No. 932, 158
     No. 942, 158
     No. 911, 159
     No. 99, 160
   ordering, 140
   steel tie sections, 143, 144
     No. 2, No. 3, No. 4 and No. 5, 143
     No. 6 and No. 9, 144
Ties, frog, 88, 89
  bolted, 88
  riveted, 89
Ties, installing, 168
Ties, with depressed ends, 161
Track bolts, 134, 135
Track equipment, miscellaneous, 171-176
Track, prefabricated, 6, 111-113
Track spikes, 133
Turnout data, 91-108
   A.M.C. helpful calculations, 96-107
     18-in. gage, light rail, 100
     24-in. gage, light rail, 100
     30-in. gage, light rail, 100
     30-in. gage, heavy rail, 101
     36-in. gage, light rail, 101
     36-in. gage, heavy rail, 102
     42-in. gage, light rail, 102

Turnout data—continued
    42-in. gage, heavy rail, 103
    44-in. gage, light rail, 103
    44-in. gage, heavy rail, 104
    48-in. gage, light rail, 104
    48-in. gage, heavy rail, 105
    56½-in. gage, light rail, 105
    56½-in. gage, heavy rail, 106
data for turnouts with long switches, light rail, 106
data for turnouts with long switches, heavy rail, 107
formulas, 95, 96
frog, 97
frog and switch, 98, 99
practical leads, table of, 108
switch, 98

Turnouts, Bethlehem, 91-108
  butt-entry, 93
  main-haulage, 92
  room-entry, 94
  typical turnout with names of parts, 91

Turnout tie sets, 85-87

U

Useful information, 187-195

W

Wheel contour, standard A.M.C., 188
Winter King switch heaters, 42

Y

Yieldable mine arches, Bethlehem, 177, 178

BETHLEHEM STEEL COMPANY
General Offices: Bethlehem, Pa.

SALES OFFICES

Albany 7	90 State St.
Atlanta 1	55 Marietta St.
Baltimore 3	300 St. Paul Place
Boston 10	75 Federal St.
Buffalo 2	424 Main St.
Chicago 1	Prudential Plaza
Cincinnati 2	4th and Walnut Sts.
Cleveland 13	50 Public Square
Columbus 15	17 South High St.
Dallas 2	1412 Main St.
Dayton 2	120 West Second St.
Detroit 2	3044 West Grand Blvd.
Greensboro, N. C.	101 North Elm St.
Houston 1	7100 Clinton Drive
Indianapolis 4	5 East Market St.
Jacksonville 3, Fla.	101 Cantee St.
Johnstown, Pa.	119 Walnut St.
Milwaukee 2	735 North Water St.
New Haven 10	205 Church St.
New York 4	25 Broadway
Philadelphia 3	1617 Pennsylvania Blvd.
Pittsburgh 22	Mellon Square
Providence 3	111 Westminster St.
Richmond 19, Va.	219 East Broad St.
St. Louis 3	1221 Locust St.
St. Paul 1	335 Robert St.
Springfield 3, Mass.	44 Vernon St.
Syracuse 2	420 East Genesee St.
Toledo 2	709 Madison Ave.
Tulsa 3	15 East Fifth St.
Washington 5, D. C.	730 Fifteenth St., N. W.
York	25 North Duke St.

On the Pacific Coast Bethlehem products are sold by

Bethlehem Pacific Coast Steel Corporation
General Offices: 20th and Illinois Streets, San Francisco 19

SALES OFFICES

Los Angeles	6000 South Boyle Ave., Vernon
Portland 5	1010 S. W. Fourteenth Ave.
Salt Lake City 11	455 East Fourth South
Seattle 4	3651 East Marginal Way
Spokane 4	West 725 Sprague Ave.
Phoenix	213 North First Ave.

EXPORT DISTRIBUTOR
Bethlehem Steel Export Corporation
25 Broadway, New York 4, N. Y.

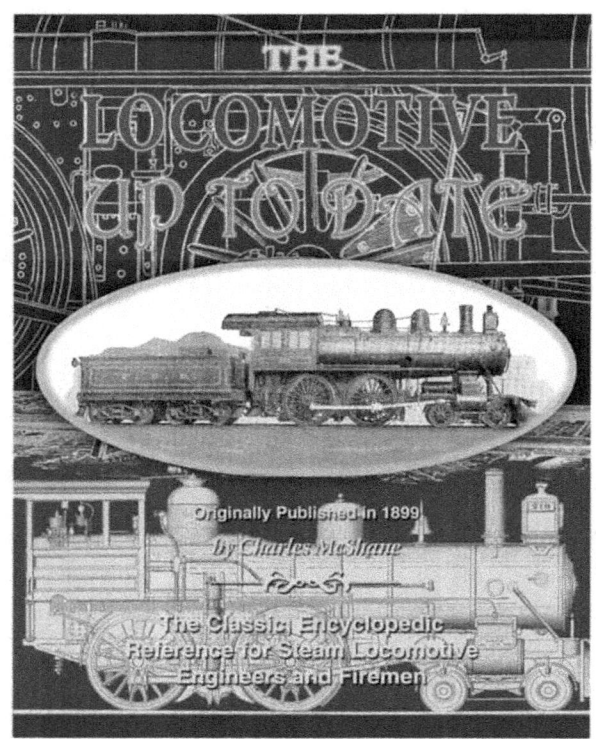

When it was originally published in 1899, **The Locomotive Up to Date** was hailed as "...the most definitive work ever published concerning the mechanism that has transformed the American nation: the steam locomotive." Filled with over 700 pages of text, diagrams and photos, this remains one of the most important railroading books ever written. From steam valves to sanders, trucks to side rods, it's a treasure trove of information, explaining in easy-to-understand language how the most sophisticated machines of the 19th Century were operated and maintained. This new edition is an exact duplicate of the original. Reformatted as an easy-to-read 8.5x11 volume, it's delightful for railroad enthusiasts of all ages.

Originally printed in 1898 and then periodically revised, **The Motorman...and His Duties** served as the definitive training text for a generation of streetcar operators. A must-have for the trolley or train enthusiast, it is also an important source of information for museum staff and docents. Lavishly illustrated with numerous photos and black and white line drawings, this affordable reprint contains all of the original text. Includes chapters on trolley car types and equipment, troubleshooting, brakes, controllers, electricity and principles, electric traction, multi-car control and has a convenient glossary in the back. If you've ever operated a trolley car, or just had an electric train set, this is a terrific book for your shelf!

ALSO NOW AVAILABLE FROM PERISCOPEFILM.COM!

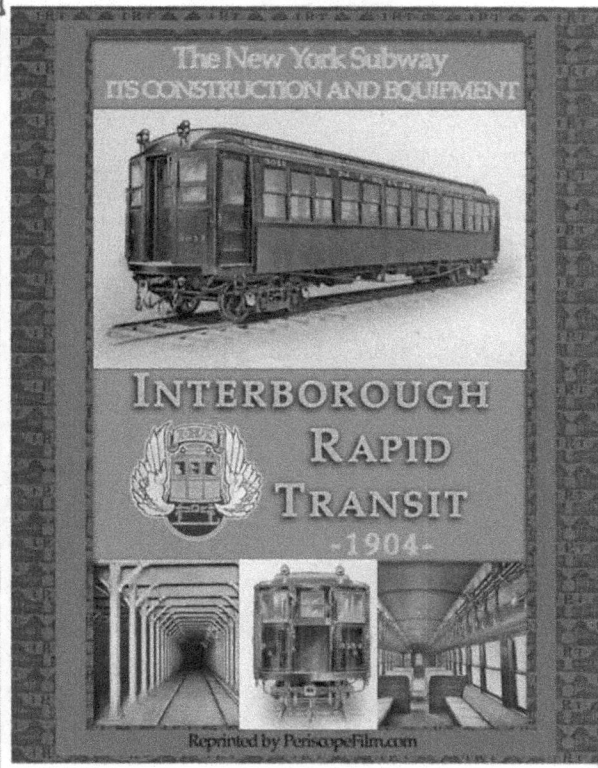

On October 27, 1904, the Interborough Rapid Transit Company opened the first subway in New York City. Running between City Hall and 145th Street at Broadway, the line was greeted with enthusiasm and, in some circles, trepidation. Created under the supervision of Chief Engineer S.L.F. Deyo, the arrival of the IRT foreshadowed the end of the "elevated" transit era on the island of Manhattan. The subway proved such a success that the IRT Co. soon achieved a monopoly on New York public transit. In 1940 the IRT and its rival the BMT were taken over by the City of New York. Today, the IRT subway lines still exist, primarily in Manhattan where they are operated as the "A Division" of the subway. Reprinted here is a special book created by the IRT, recounting the design and construction of the fledgling subway system. Originally created in 1904, it presents the IRT story with a flourish, and with numerous fascinating illustrations and rare photographs.

Originally written in the late 1900's and then periodically revised, A History of the Baldwin Locomotive Works chronicles the origins and growth of one of America's greatest industrial-era corporations. Founded in the early 1830's by Philadelphia jeweler Matthais Baldwin, the company built a huge number of steam locomotives before ceasing production in 1949. These included the 4-4-0 American type, 2-8-2 Mikado and 2-8-0 Consolidation. Hit hard by the loss of the steam engine market, Baldwin soldiered on for a brief while, producing electric and diesel engines. General Electric's dominance of the market proved too much, and Baldwin finally closed its doors in 1956. By that time over 70,500 Baldwin locomotives had been produced. This high quality reprint of the official company history dates from 1920. The book has been slightly reformatted, but care has been taken to preserve the integrity of the text.

NOW AVAILABLE AT
WWW.PERISCOPEFILM.COM

©2008-2010 Periscope Film LLC
All Rights Reserved
ISBN #978-1-935700-19-7
www.PeriscopeFilm.com

www.ingramcontent.com/pod-product-compliance
Lightning Source LLC
Chambersburg PA
CBHW081835170426
43199CB00017B/2740